Cross-Cultural
Management Communication

RICHARD MEAD

Sasin Graduate Institute of Business Administration, Thailand

Visiting Associate Professor, Kellogg School, Northwestern University, USA

JOHN WILEY & SONS
Chichester • New York • Brisbane • Toronto • Singapore

Other Wiley Editorial Offices

John Wiley & Sons, Inc., 605 Third Avenue,
New York, NY 10158-0012, USA

Jacaranda Wiley Ltd, G.P.O. Box 859, Brisbane,
Queensland 4001, Australia.

John Wiley & Sons (Canada) Ltd, 22 Worcester Road,
Rexdale, Ontario M9W 1L1, Canada

John Wiley & Sons (SEA) Pte Ltd, 37 Jalan Pemimpin 05-04,
Block B, Union Industrial Building, Singapore 129809

Library of Congress Cataloging-in-Publication Data

Mead, Richard R. (Richard Ramsay), *1904-*
    Cross-cultural management communication / Richard Mead.
        p. cm.
    Includes bibliographical references.
    ISBN 0 471 92660 4 (cloth)
    ISBN 0 471 93718 5 (paper)
    1. Communication in management— Cross-cultural studies.
    I. Title.
    HD30.3.M45   1990
    658.4'5—dc20   89-70631
                                                              CIP

British Library Cataloguing in Publication Data

Mead, Richard, *1943–*
    Cross-cultural management communication.
    1. Management. Cross-cultural communication
    I. Title
    658.4'5

    ISBN 0 471 92660 4 (cloth)
    ISBN 0 471 93718 5 (paper)

Typeset by Inforum Typesetting, Portsmouth
Printed and bound in Great Britain by
Redwood Books, Trowbridge, Wiltshire

Cross-Cultural
Management Communication

For

K.K.-M. and P.G.M.

Contents

Acknowledgements

This book owes most to the support and encouragement of the Director of Sasin GIBA, Professor Toemsakdi Krishnamara, and the Dean of the Kellogg School, Professor Donald P. Jacobs. The final draft was completed at Ashridge College during a visiting fellowship arranged by the Principal, Philip Sadler, and Dr Laurence Handy. The comments and suggestions made by MBA students of these three institutions, in Thailand, the United States, and the United Kingdom, have had a major influence upon the contents of the text.

Also very useful were two ASEAN seminars (Research Methodology, Bangkok 1986, and International Business, Singapore 1989), organized by Professor Jean-Émile Denis with the financial support of CIDA, under the auspices of the Association of South-East Asian Deans.

I am extremely grateful for the suggestions made by a wide range of scholars (at various professorial ranks): Professors Hervey Juris and Norman McGuinness, both of whom commented upon draft chapters; Julian Cattaneo, Kurt Christensen, Shiv Gupta, Colin Jones, Hiroki Kato, Kullada Kesboonchoo, Ben Mittman, Joe Moag, Mike Rabinovich, Pataya Saihoo. I was greatly assisted by a number of consultants and business people, in particular Dr Chatri Sripaipan, Dr Tony Davison, Cecilia Costa Lopes Davison, Derek Hollweg, John Kelly, Dr Kubet Luchterhand, David Mace, Perran Penrose, Alan Timothy. Finally, I must express my appreciation of the help given me by Wiley's editorial staff and their anonymous readers.

1
Cross-Cultural Management Communication

1.1 INTRODUCTION

George, an American, represented a professional educational agency. The company sent him to negotiate a deal with a Malaysian hospital, which wanted to purchase an advanced training package. The administrator, Dr Ahmad, welcomed him to his office.

George produced his business card and quickly got to the point. He explained the services his company could offer, and produced a file of technical specifications. Dr Ahmad leafed through it without comment. 'Do you think we can do any business, or am I wasting my time?', George asked. Dr Ahmad replied non-committally that he would be delighted to discuss the possibilities. George then proposed returning the next day at the same time, and added 'I hope we can get this settled quickly, I have to be in Korea next week.'

The next day, Dr Ahmad announced his interest but asked for a greatly reduced price. George eventually agreed to augment the services offered, and they arranged to continue the discussions the next day. Again Dr Ahmad asked for concessions and George agreed. This process continued, and George was running up against his deadline. He phoned Bill, his head office manager: 'If this goes on, I'm going to be late at Seoul.' Bill told him: 'Just get the best deal you can in the time that remains. If we do Ahmad a favor now, he'll deal with us again in the future. These people remember favors.'

The deal was signed for a price that reduced the company's profits to the

1

acceptable minimum. But just before the agreed delivery date, George received a message from Dr Ahmad. Unfortunately, conditions at the hospital had changed, and he needed to revise the terms.

'Doesn't he realize that we signed a legal contract and he's stuck with it?', George complained to Bill. They decided to allow the change this one time, but not again. During the life of the contract, Dr Ahmad further complained about the quality and costs of the services provided. Each time, George replied by quoting the relevant sections in the contract, and only conceded once, on legal advice.

A few months before the contract expired, the agency asked to negotiate a further two years. Dr Ahmad courteously replied thanking them for their services, but explained that a deal had already been signed with another company.

The case illustrates several parameters within which cultures differ and which effect how its members communicate. Different cultures give varying importance to:

- RELATIONSHIPS: *How important is a good personal relationship to the communication?*

    In some cultures you can expect to do business on the basis of your company credentials alone. In others, such as Malaysia, you will be more successful if you come introduced; and you should then expect to spend time making casual conversation to create a personal relationship.
- COMMUNICATIVE STYLE: *Is a blunt direct style or an indirect style most effective in communicating your message?*

    In some cultures, blunt speech is respected; elsewhere, it may be interpreted as aggressive and bad-mannered. In different cultures, different communicative styles are appropriate.
- TIME: *How much time should you expect to invest in communicating your message?*

    You cannot always hope to complete a deal as quickly (or slowly) as you might at home. George compounded his error by announcing his time constraint, thus giving Dr Ahmad a weapon with which to pressure him.
- AGREEMENT: *What is communicated by an agreement?*

    In some cultures, a signed agreement is interpreted as a legally binding commitment; elsewhere, it may be regarded as a stage in the implementation process, and always subject to renegotiation.

George applied his American values at each of these points and miscalculated badly. His behavior was inappropriate in the different cultural context. His mistakes cost his company money. This case shows a business failure arising from differences in the communication norms of two cultures.

Good communication helps you develop and maintain good relationships, whether you are negotiating with another organization or managing your own. Good relationships mean increased productivity and profits. Bad communication leads to conflict, inefficiency, and loss. Cultural priorities influence communicative priorities, and differences in the communicative priorities of different cultures can create serious problems for the negotiator and manager.

The communication problems that arise from cultural difference can be overcome, and differences can be turned to advantage. That is the message of this book.

1.2 WHAT IS THE BOOK ABOUT?

This book deals with the cross-cultural communication skills that any manager needs when working with members of another culture.

The manager needs cross-cultural skills in order to avoid and overcome problems arising from differences in management and communication priorities. He or she needs these skills

- when working within the organization, whether as superior, peer, or subordinate;
- when working with some other organization or individual, while negotiating with a customer, supplier, joint venture partner, or government representative;
- at social occasions;
- in an overseas posting or in his or her own country.

The book shows how management priorities are decided and communicated in different cultures. It examines the organizational problems facing managers in cultural contexts other than their own. It shows how to

- recognize cultural differences;
- understand how cultural priorities influence communication styles;
- plan and communicate management messages so that they make most sense to members of the other culture;
- understand the intended meanings of messages sent by members of the other culture;
- overcome communication problems resulting from language difference.

1.3 WHO IS THE BOOK FOR?

The book is written for:

1 Managers in both private and public organizations, based in cultures other than their own.

2   The manager stationed in his or her own country who has to work with members of some other culture.
3   The negotiator who must communicate with members of some other culture.
4   Management trainees.

The corporate world becomes increasingly interrelated. Firms in the USA, Europe, and other Western countries are doing more and more business outside their national boundaries in the search for new suppliers and markets; and newly developing countries are learning that to survive and prosper they must do business with the advanced business nations.

Any newspaper provides the evidence that successful organizations are rapidly internationalizing their operations and attitudes. This process is hastened by wider political and economic ties, the greater ease of transportation, and the development of communications networks.

This growth in multinational operations means that managers increasingly have to communicate with individuals from other national cultures speaking other first languages. Almost every manager in a large company, whether in a developed or developing economy, will come into professional contact with other cultures at some point in his or her career.

Companies are increasingly forced to take part in overseas operations in order to make profits and even survive, and this means that managers able to handle these responsibilities are in growing demand. But there is another side to the coin; the ethnocentric manager who is unable to or does not wish to deal with members of another culture is increasingly at risk of greatly restricted career opportunities.

A failure in an overseas posting costs your organization money and will perhaps cost you your job. A study of 639 Swedish expatriate managers in 26 countries found that 257 returned home before the end of their contracts.[1] In 1979 a failure rate of expatriate Americans since 1965 was estimated at between 25 and 40 percent[2], and Harris and Moran calculate the cost at $55 000 to $150 000 per family, not counting replacement costs.[3]

A major reason for failure in an overseas posting is inadequate cross-cultural training; this includes training in cross-cultural communications and the other language. So the company's policy on communications training takes on economic significance and affects profit and loss figures.

Management schools respond to this new priority by emphasizing various aspects of cross-cultural management, including communication studies. One school alone in the United States grants more than 800 Master of International Business degrees each year, and in 1987 reckoned to have more than 20 000 graduates then working in multinational corporations around the globe.[4] Most schools now devote courses or parts of courses to international studies.

1.4 WHAT CROSS-CULTURAL COMMUNICATION SKILLS DOES THE MANAGER NEED?

Collins' *English Language Dictionary* defines communications as 'the activity or process of giving information to other people or to other living things . . .'. In order to exchange information you need a common language. There can be no proper substitute for knowing the language. Ideally, the cross-cultural manager learns as much of the other language as possible: he or she would like to be fluent.

Being fluent means having a mastery of vocabulary and grammatical systems, and the banks of metaphor which native speakers use naturally. It means being able to speak and write the language easily and smoothly.

But even if the cross-cultural manager were able to find sufficient time to develop a technical mastery of the other language, this would not guarantee that he or she could communicate effectively with native speakers of the language. In order to communicate effectively with another person you need more than a common language.

You can test this for yourself by looking around at people you know who are native speakers of your language. Most are fluent, but some are more effective communicators than others.

1 Who always gets what they want from a negotiation, and why?
2 Who always seems to lose out in a negotiation, and why?
3 Whose advice do you listen to, and why?
4 Whose advice do you always ignore, and why?
5 Whose opinions do you respect most, and why?
6 Who seems incapable of getting cooperation from other people, and why?

Try analyzing your answers to the questions 'Why?' above. Some of your answers may be categorized in terms of official function: for instance, 'I value X's praise most because he's the boss.' Some may be categorized in terms of personal attributes: 'He's got a strong clear voice', or 'She mumbles so I can't hear the words.' Others can be categorized in terms of values, and these should give you most food for thought:

'We share the same educational background.'
'We see things the same way.'
'He goes about things the wrong way. No one knows what he really wants and no one trusts him.'

Just as communication within one culture depends on more than a common language, so does communication across cultures. This is shown by the fact that members of different cultures which share the same language (for instance, Americans, British, Australians, Canadians, many Caribbean

Islanders and Indians, all of whom have English in common) may have problems in communicating.

True, there are differences between the versions of English they use. At the level of grammar, an American might say 'Did you complete the report yet?' and a Briton 'Have you completed the report yet?; of vocabulary, 'specialty' and 'speciality'; of spelling, 'labor' and 'labour'; of pronunciation, 'schedule' pronounced [skedul] and [shedul]; of idiom, 'How did you find X?' which in British English can mean 'Did you like X?'. But these differences are minor, and are usually of no greater significance than dialectical differences within each of these different cultures (for instance, between the English of Glasgow and Bristol, or New York and Louisiana). Members of these cultures are separated not by language but by *values*.

A common first language does not mean that members of different cultures share the same attitudes towards their roles and responsibilities and is no guarantee of communicative effectiveness. If these individuals take for granted that a literal understanding of the words used is sufficient to bridge the differences between them, a common language may hinder rather than enhance understanding.

In summary:

- The more you know of the other language, the better.
- Fluency does not guarantee effective communication.
- Effective communication also depends upon understanding the other person's cultural priorities.

1.5   HOW EXPERIENCE AFFECTS PERCEPTIONS

We communicate and interpret each other's messages in terms of our *perceptions* of the environment. These perceptions are *selective* of what seems important. So what decides importance?

The well-known example shown in Figure 1.1 answers the question effectively. Tell a group that you are going to show them a drawing (do *not* say what of), refer to the problems of age and ask them to think of old women they have known. Then ask them what the drawing represents. Most likely they will see an old woman. This perception is determined by their experience of memory.

Now ask a different group to think of young women they have known, and then ask them to identify the same drawing. Probably they will see a young woman.

Figure 1.1

Now suggest to the first group that the drawing in fact shows a young woman and to the second that it shows an old woman. You may be surprised by their difficulty in seeing the other 'hidden' drawing.

Both answers are right. The drawing includes features that support both interpretations; for instance, the lines making up the old woman's nose also make the young woman's jaw. By directing each group's attention differently you set the conditions for them to expect a certain type of image. The point is that people tend to perceive what they expect to find, to focus on those features of the environment that support their expectations and screen out those that are not supportive.

Your perceptions of the world are based on the experience against which you measure it. This is largely determined by your experience of your culture.

All of your early life is devoted to learning culture. By the age of five you have internalized the rules of your language, and you use it to communicate your cultural values. You are skilled at performing communicative functions of

- requesting information or permission, or asking to be given what you want;
- negotiating;
- expressing pleasure and irritation;

- expressing willingness and agreement, unwillingness and disagreement;
- addressing individuals in different age and sex groups, family members, friends, strangers.

Over time this process becomes more focused, as you begin to watch television, listen to and read stories, attend school, and so on.

You have become a skilled communicator within your culture group. But this does not mean that you are equally adept when communicating with someone who does not share your cultural experience. Members of different culture groups interpret information differently because they apply different sets of values.

An Arab and a Chinese were shown the same pictures and specifications of a Western factory farm, which included a slaughter farm for pigs. Because of his cultural and religious values (Muslims are not permitted to eat pork) the Arab found the subject of pigs distasteful and reacted against the entire project which he condemned as unhygienic and unsatisfactory — even if the slaughter house were modified. But the Chinese, belonging to a culture which prizes pork on the table, was immediately interested in the slaughtering procedures and expressed his full satisfaction with the health precautions. Thus the same information communicated two very different messages because the two individuals applied different cultural values when evaluating it.

YOU CANNOT FORCE MEMBERS OF ANOTHER CULTURE GROUP TO ACCEPT YOUR PERCEPTIONS OF REALITY AS THE ONLY RIGHT PERCEPTIONS AND SUPERIOR TO THEIR OWN. This is not a moral point; this is a practical point. The history of colonialism shows repeated attempts made by great powers to enforce their value systems upon other peoples, and in general these have failed. The cross-cultural manager who attempts to impose his or her perceptions upon employees, colleagues, and negotiating partners from another culture faces similar odds against success.

1.6 HOW CULTURAL PERCEPTIONS INFLUENCE COMMUNICATION

Cultural priorities influence communication on both general and specific levels. On the GENERAL level they determine:

- perceptions of what should be communicated because it is important, being new, extraordinary, and/or relevant;

- perceptions of what need not be communicated because it is unimportant, being old, insignificant and obvious, and/or irrelevant.

If you do not share the other person's priorities of importance and relevance, you are in danger of sending ambiguous messages and of misinterpreting the messages that he or she sends to you. Cultural differences increase the likelihood of misinterpretation. The book shows how misinterpretations can arise, and how they can be avoided.

We shall also see how culture influences communication on a SPECIFIC level. For instance, culture may determine that one grammatical form or vocabulary item is used in preference to another when both alternatives exist in the language, and there are no language rules specifying which one has to be used. That is, culture determines *how* content is expressed. In different cultural contexts a direct order ('Please close the door') may be more or less effective than an indirect form ('It's getting cold in here') as a way of exerting control. So cultural priorities determine how the message is interpreted, whether the direct order is interpreted as legitimate or as unnecessarily aggressive, and a request as polite or a signal of indecision and evasiveness.

So you always have a range of forms from which to choose when you have information and ideas to communicate. The effective cross-cultural manager knows enough about the other person's cultural perceptions to guess which form is most likely to communicate the desired message and achieve the desired purpose.

Developing communicative competence means developing a sensitivity to those factors within the context, including culture, that the speaker (writer/listener/reader) needs to know in order to communicate effectively in social settings. It means developing the confidence to reveal your own priorities to others in order that they can relate to you. And because effective communication is always a two-way process, it means making it easy for the other person to reveal their priorities.

By studying problems of cross-cultural communication the manager becomes more aware of what other cultures may not understand about his or her own culture and behavior. By becoming conscious of his or her own cultural traits and by being able to reveal them, the manager becomes better understood and is better able to understand others.

Communicating across cultures is often difficult. Cross-cultural relationships do impose stresses and strains; but they also present opportunities to gain insights from the other culture and to develop one's own experience. They can be intensely creative.

A successful cross-cultural relationship benefits the individuals concerned by developing understanding and tolerance. If the cross-cultural relationship fails, the reverse happens: stereotypes are reinforced, attitudes narrow, misunderstandings proliferate; and instead of gaining from the cultural variety, the organization is in danger of flying apart as members seek to protect their own interests.

The purpose of this book is to help managers develop their cross-cultural management and communication skills so that the problems can be overcome and the opportunities exploited to everyone's advantage.

In summary:

The cross-cultural manager communicates effectively with members of the other culture when he or she understands:

- how its members perceive reality;
- why they perceive it this way;
- how they express their perceptions;
- how these perceptions and their expressions differ from his or her own.

1.7 HOW THE BOOK IS ORGANIZED

This chapter has introduced a number of issues to be discussed in detail throughout the book.

Chapter 2 summarizes what the manager needs to know about culture and shows the implications of cultural analysis for management communication.

Chapter 3 looks at how decisions are communicated, and Chapter 4 at why a message may be appropriate or inappropriate depending upon the cultural and situational context.

Chapter 5 looks at the medium by which a message is transmitted, and sees how culture determines the choice of medium. Chapters 6 and 7 then concentrate on *spoken communication*: the first deals with communicative style, and shows why a style appropriate within one culture may be inappropriate within another; and the second examines why spoken messages are so often ambiguous and how ambiguity can be resolved. Chapter 8 discusses *non-verbal communication*.

Chapters 9 and 10 both deal with cross-cultural negotiations, the first with preparation and the second with the negotiation process.

Chapters 11 and 12 confront the problems of communicating with members of the other culture when you do not share the same language. Chapter 11 discusses the advantages and disadvantages of learning and using the other language as against alternative means of communicating (their using your language, or using interpreters). Chapter 12 discusses language training and the implications that this has for the management training officer.

Chapters 2–12 each has a section discussing the practical IMPLICATIONS FOR THE MANAGER. Chapter 13 summarizes these in the form of a cross-cultural management communications *audit*, which concludes the book.

EXERCISES

These exercises are designed to examine how messages communicated by members of a culture reflect their values.

1 In your daily newspaper, find examples of stories that discuss the topics below. Then answer the questions.
   • Business and finance
   • National and local politics
   • Ethical and moral issues
   • Fashion and social news
   • Arts and high culture
   • Foreign news
   • Legal issues
   • Sports news
   • Crime

   (a) How much emphasis is given to each? What do these emphases tell you about the values of the readership?
   (b) What issues are *not* reported or discussed? Why not?
   (c) What topics amuse the readership? What problems worry them? (What political issues are debated? What types of crime are discussed?)
   (d) How much focus is given to individual achievement and how much to group achievement? (Look at the sports news.)
   (e) What issues unite social groups? What issues separate them? How effective are political leaders in asserting their authority, and how do they achieve and maintain authority? (Look at the political news.) How do business and social leaders maintain their authority?
   (f) What issues separate individuals? How far can individuals exploit family and social ties in resolving conflicts?
   (g) What does the foreign and business news tell you about your country's relations with other countries?

2 What social groups read this newspaper? Examine newspapers read by other social groups, and see how they deal with the same issues. How far do the values of these different social groups coincide? What values distinguish them?

3 Examine newspapers from another country, using the topics in (1) and (2) above. What differences in cultural values can you find? What issues are emphasized in the newspapers serving one culture but are absent in newspapers of the other?

4 What does this comparison tell you about the two cultures?

NOTES

1 Torbiörn, I. (1982) *Living Abroad*. John Wiley, New York.
2. Mendenhall, M. and Oddou, G. (1985) The dimensions of expatriate acculturation: a review. *Academy of Management Review*, **10**, 39–47.
3 Harris, P.R. and Moran, R.T. (1979) *Managing Cultural Differences*. Gulf, Houston,
   p. 9.
4 Prospectus for the Thunderbird Management Center, American Graduate School
   of International Management, Glendale, Arizona.

2

Culture and Management

2.1 INTRODUCTION

An Israeli making a first visit to the United States visited an international fair in New York. The crowds leaving the fair were massive, and a policeman was stationed to signal that pedestrians could only make a right turn into the neighboring streets. The crowds followed his instructions. The Israeli followed suit but afterwards confessed his astonishment: 'In Israel there would always be a wise guy who would figure out that if a policeman told you to go right it's better to go left. America is much more disciplined.'

But while the Israeli sees evidence of discipline in the Americans' relationship with authority, a German or Frenchman might think pedestrian behavior to be far more chaotic in the United States than at home. This chapter considers why behavior seen as normal in one culture is unusual in another.

Your cultural priorities determine your behavior with other people and influence your attitudes towards other people in the organizations to which you belong. Specifically, they influence how you manage and expect to be managed, and how you communicate within the organization.

We see here how the culture of a community affects the work priorities of its members. We focus on the relationship between culture and management communication priorities. When you have to exchange management messages with members of another culture who have other cultural values, you can expect difficulties in getting your point across and in understanding what is communicated to you. The chapter explains why cultural difference cause these difficulties.

2.2   DEFINING CULTURE

The anthropological, sociological, and management literature define 'culture' in hundreds of different ways. A definition used by Geert Hofstede[1] suits our purposes best:

> '[Culture is] the collective programming of the mind which distinguishes the members of one human group from another. Culture, in this sense, includes systems of values; and values are among the building blocks of culture.'

This identifies a culture as a *set of values* which are shared by a group. Cultural values shared by one group may be rejected by another. The values are learned by members of the group, and hence taught by other members. A culture is passed down from one generation to the next. It is acquired, and is not innate.

A number of problems arise in applying this definition, and these are discussed below.

2.2.1   How Large is the Group?

How far can we talk of a single culture in Switzerland, for instance, where the French Swiss, German Swiss, Italian Swiss and Romansch Swiss retain their own identities and speak their own first languages? Similarly, the United States includes White, Black, Latino and Asian American groups, each of which has distinct values and may be further categorized in terms of culture of origin and region within the United States. But how useful is it to distinguish the cultures of, for instance, Boston Irish Americans and Chicago Irish Americans?

These questions are of practical importance to the manager. In some countries the differences between sub-cultural groups are greater than in the examples above, and have profound political and economic effects; the individual may be deeply insulted if you mistake him or her for a member of some other sub-culture. Other countries, such as Japan and Saudi Arabia, are far more homogeneous.

This book adopts a rough and ready solution; culture groups are assumed to correspond to national groups (American culture shared by all, and only, Americans; French culture shared by all, and only, French men and women). Where it is necessary to differentiate sub-cultures, these are explicitly identified.

2.2.2   How Does a Culture Change?

As a member of a group you are taught the appropriate culture at an early age, and the lessons you learn at this age stay with you for the rest of your life. Language learning provides an example. Few individuals forget the primary language they are taught in the first five years, and few acquire the bilingual skills to master a second language as fluently, when this is taught at a later stage. Hence cultural values are highly resistant to change. One anthropological study of Mexican Americans showed that even second- and third-generation Americans held Mexican values that significantly differed from mainstream American values.[2]

This newspaper story[3] on Japanese 'yuppies' or *shinjinrui* (new human beings) also suggests that fundamental change is slow:

'. . . Japan's new human breed are engaging in an orgy of conspicuous consumption. . . . [But] In their attempt to be "individualistic", Japan's shinjinrui are as clannish as other Japanese, say sociologists.
"What we have evolving in Japan is a new middle mass," said [sociologist Valerie Wee] Chan. "Not a middle class, but a middle mass within the middle class who, despite their pretensions of individuality, still want to belong to the group."
That will not change, say anthropologists such as Oxford University professor Joy Hendry, unless the current generation of shinjinrui departs radically from child-rearing methods that have become the norm in Japan.
Unlike in the US or Europe, where children are encouraged to be independent, Japanese mothers still rear their children to be totally dependent on home and family by continually warning them of the dangers that lurk without. . . . Ultimately, this is expanded to include the "group" and eventually the "country", both of which offer protection from the "dangers" that exist "out there" and which may explain why Japanese travellers are almost always part of a tour group.'

So cravings to own a foreign car and dress in chic Western clothes perhaps demonstrate only superficial changes in Japanese culture. They do not necessarily indicate any real shift in fundamental Japanese values.

But this does not mean that *no* change is occurring, or that the superficial changes are insignificant. The significance of change in the other culture is determined by the precise nature of your relations with its members rather than by any intrinsic quality.

The French marketing director responsible for selling fashion to the Japanese youth market may be little concerned with the implications of apparent change for Japanese social structures. But if you have the job of organizing a long-term joint venture with a Japanese company, then you may be vitally interested in estimating how far traditional control and communication structures will be applied by a younger generation of Japanese managers in your joint project.

The question has practical importance. For instance, you may not be able to assume that members of a culture group are motivated by the same needs that motivated a previous generation. In South Korea, employees at all levels felt a strong need for loyalty to the organization and strikes were rare. But economic development has now brought the promise of increased material rewards, and this sense of company unity has fractured. Workers more frequently push their individual interests even when these are antagonistic to those of the company, and strikes are increasingly common.

In general, culture change seems to be generated by economic change. Hofstede's research data (discussed in section 2.3 below) led him to the conclusion that, in all the 53 countries and regions under investigation except Pakistan, an increase in wealth led to an increase in individualist tendencies, and a decrease in collectivism.[4]

2.2.3   What Does this Definition of Culture Exclude?

We are defining culture in terms of taught/learned values and are not centrally concerned with expressions of the values. These expressions include material expressions, such as art and craft forms, clothing and fashion design, food and cuisine, and technology.

Second, we exclude behavior that can be explained adequately in terms of the perpetrator's individual psychological make-up. What psychology is to the individual, culture is to the group, and the two should not be confused. In any one culture, certain personality types may be more typical than others. For instance, in an individualist culture risk-taking loners are given greater opportunities to express themselves than in a collectivist culture. In general, though, all cultures offer examples of a full range of types; and although the individual's psychology is heavily influenced by the culture within which he or she is raised, it does not provide a reliable guide to that culture.

Third, we are not immediately concerned with political and economic systems. The group's choice of these systems may reflect its cultural values, but economic and political changes can be very rapid and determined by external events which lie outside the control of the group members.

We are interested in social and organizational expressions of cultural values when these affect the role of the manager. We now go on to see how culture determines the selection and use of management structures, including structures for planning, motivating, resolving conflicts, and in particular communicating within the organization.

2.3   COMPARING MANAGEMENT CULTURES

The work of Geert Hofstede shows that managers in different cultures apply very different values to their organizational responsibilities and preferences.[5] It clearly demonstrates how culture determines the variations.

Hofstede's research compares work-related attitudes across a range of cultures. He investigated the attitudes held in 53 countries or regions, using 116 000 employees of a multinational corporation as informants. Comparisons between the different cultures were plotted across four dimensions, largely independent of each other. These are:

- POWER DISTANCE: the distance between individuals at different levels of a hierarchy
- UNCERTAINTY AVOIDANCE: more or less need to avoid uncertainty about the future
- INDIVIDUALISM *versus* COLLECTIVISM: the relations between the individual and his or her fellows
- MASCULINITY *versus* FEMININITY: the division of roles and values in society.

These dimensions are discussed below. Figures 2.2–2.4 show where Hofstede plots the attitudes expressed by managers of the countries researched. Figure 2.1 keys the countries.

ARA	Arab countries	JAM	Jamaica
	(Egypt, Lebanon, Lybia, Kuwait,	JPN	Japan
	Iraq, Saudi-Arabia, UAE)	KOR	South Korea
ARG	Argentina	MAL	Malaysia
AUL	Australia	MEX	Mexico
AUT	Austria	NET	Netherlands
BEL	Belgium	NOR	Norway
BRA	Brazil	NZL	New Zealand
CAN	Canada	PAK	Pakistan
CHL	Chile	PAN	Panama
COL	Colombia	PER	Peru
COS	Costa Rica	PHI	Philippines
DEN	Denmark	POR	Portugal
EAF	East Africa	SAF	South Africa
	(Kenya, Ethiopia, Zambia)	SAL	Salvador
EQA	Equador	SIN	Singapore
FIN	Finland	SPA	Spain
FRA	France	SWE	Sweden
GBR	Great Britain	SWI	Switzerland
GER	Germany	TAI	Taiwan
GRE	Greece	THA	Thailand
GUA	Guatemala	TUR	Turkey
HOK	Hong Kong	URU	Uruguay
IDO	Indonesia	USA	United States
IND	India	VEN	Venezuela
IRA	Iran	WAF	West Africa
IRE	Ireland		(Nigeria, Ghana,
ISR	Israel		Sierra Leone)
ITA	Italy	YUG	Yugoslavia

Figure 2.1   *Key to the countries and regions plotted in Figures 2.2, 2.3 and 2.4* (Reproduced with permission from Hofstede, G. (1983) The cultural relativity of organizational practices and theories, *Journal of International Business Studies*, Fall, 75–89)

2.3.1   Power Distance

This dimension indicates how a culture adapts to inequalities among its members. In some cultures, natural physical and intellectual inequalities generate wide economic, political, and social inequalities which may eventually be perpetuated on a hereditary basis. Other cultures try to narrow power distances between their members. The dimension shows how far the culture tolerates and fosters pecking orders, and how actively members try to reduce them. In high power distance cultures, employees manage their work according to what the manager wants. They are more cooperative in dealings with superiors and more frightened of disagreeing with them, but reluctant to cooperate with peers. Authoritarian attitudes are readily accepted. In low power distance cultures, the reverse applies, and the individual is freer to implement his or her own structure.

In Figure 2.2 the Philippines, Mexico and India exemplify cultures with wide power distances, and Austria, Israel and the Scandinavian countries are among the lowest. A journalist[6] describes the

> 'all-pervasive Scandinavian social imperative that no one must dare excel, no one must be allowed to fall behind, all should seek the middle ground. . . . In Norwegian schools, grades no longer exist for pre-teen students, and the message in classrooms throughout the region — nurtured as much by the absence of reward and the example of life around them as by any overt policy — is that to be average is to be safe.'

These non-elitist values and the lack of a will to compete are expressed in an all-embracing welfare state system which protects the individual from cradle to grave. In industry the traditional barriers between management and workforce have broken down to a far greater extent than elsewhere. Workers' rights to participation and codetermination in Norway date back to the last years of the last century, and employees in companies with at least 50 employees now have the right to elect one-third of the members of the board. Norway, Denmark and Sweden have gone furthest in establishing industrial democracy.

2.3.2   Uncertainty Avoidance

This dimension measures how far different cultures socialize their members into accepting ambiguous situations and tolerating uncertainty about the future. Members of high uncertainty avoidance cultures appear anxiety-prone and feel the uncertainties inherent in life as continuous threats that must be fought. They devote considerable energy to 'beating the future'.

In the organization, they fear failure, take fewer risks, resist change, and place a premium on job security, career patterning, retirement benefits,

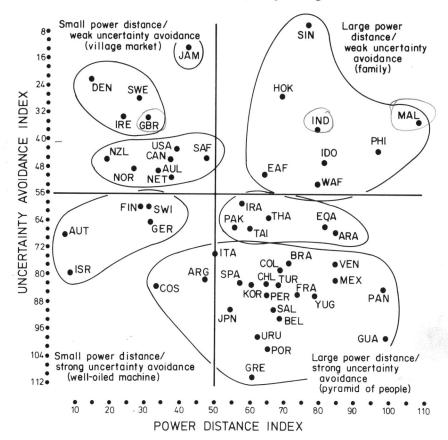

Figure 2.2   *Power distance plotted against uncertainty avoidance* (Reproduced with permission from Hofstede, 1983)

health insurance. The manager is expected to issue clear instructions, and subordinates' initiatives are more tightly controlled. Loyalty to the employer is seen as a virtue and employees tend not to job-hop. They prefer to work for a larger organization. Few wish to live abroad and foreigners are not easily accepted as managers.

Strong uncertainty avoidance cultures include Greece, Portugal and Japan — where the occupational elite can hope for lifetime employment. Until very recently, Japanese workers consistently saved an average of 20 percent of their income as against 5 percent in the United States, where needs to avoid uncertainty about the future are much less.

In Belgium, an American multinational discovered that it was expected to give employees six months' notice before firing them, and severance pay for between six months and two years depending on length of service. This contrasts with the situation in the United States, where managers are relatively unconstrained in hiring and firing. Unwilling to tolerate the costs, the American company closed its local operation.

Members of weak uncertainty avoidance cultures are more likely to accept the uncertainty inherent in life and to take each day as it comes. Hard work is not perceived as a virtue per se. Conflict and competitiveness can be contained and used constructively, and dissent is tolerated. Needs for written rules and regulations are relatively few, and if rules cannot be kept, they are easily changed. These cultures include Singapore and Hong Kong, both of which are highly entrepreneurial.

2.3.3   Individualism Versus Collectivism

This describes the relationship between the individual and the group to which he or she belongs. *Individualist cultures* stress individuals' achievements and rights and expect individuals to focus on satisfying their own needs. The individual values personal time away from work and autonomy, is emotionally independent of the company, and may prefer to work for a small organization. He or she aspires to leadership positions. Social order is associated with the needs of society rather than with the needs of a particular community.

Collectivist cultures are characterized by tight social networks in which members identify closely with their organization. The needs of the organization heavily influence the individual's private life and choice of friends, and membership serves as an ideal. The organization or community to which the individual belongs determines his or her notions of social order. A high premium is placed on group loyalty, and loyalty may be valued above efficiency.

Individualist cultures control and motivate their members by internal pressures, by inducing guilt and developing opportunities for self-achievement. Collectivistic cultures exert control through shame at stepping outside group norms and motivate by pride in the group's achievement.[7]

The Anglo countries rank among the most individualist, whereas Pakistan and Central and South American countries including Guatemala, Equador and Panama rank among the most collectivist (see Figure 2.3).

An example from Taiwan demonstrates collectivist industrial values. (It also shows how these values are being modified under the pressure of radical economic growth.) In May 1988 the train drivers staged a one-day strike for higher wages, significantly the first time in the 101-year history of Taiwanese railways that service had been halted. The strike was called for May Day, a holiday falling on a Sunday, in order that the least possible number of commuters should be affected. This suggests that it was intended to achieve its purposes through symbolic action rather than actual disruption.

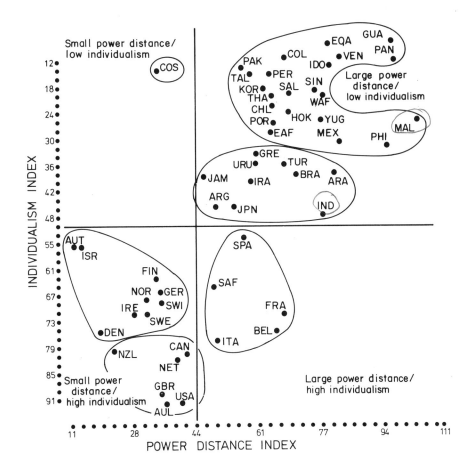

Figure 2.3 *Power distance plotted against individualism* (Reproduced with permission from Hofstede, 1983)

2.3.4 Masculinity Versus Femininity

In masculine cultures sex roles are sharply differentiated, and traditional masculine values such as achievement (defined in terms of recognition and wealth) and the effective exercise of power determine cultural ideals. Men are expected to be assertive and competitive. Members accept greater job stress and the company's interference in private life, and prefer a higher salary to shorter hours. Managers have leadership independence. In feminine cultures sex roles are less sharply distinguished, and the dominant values are those usually identified with the feminine role. Members prefer to relate to others rather than compete with them. Individual brilliance is suspect and the outsider and anti-hero are regarded sympathetically.

Hofstede identifies Japan as by far the most masculine culture and the Scandinavian cultures of Sweden, Norway and Denmark as the least (see Figure 2.4). A newspaper story[8] demonstrates this femininity: 'We don't admire big stars or heroes very much', said Jacob Vedel-Petersen, Director of the Institute for Social Science Research in Copenhagen, 'the man in the street is our hero.' Even for those with power, that seems to be the role model. Prime Minister Ingvar Carlsson of Sweden carries his own bags, lives in a rented apartment, and, by law, opens his mail to any citizen interested enough to drop by and read it.

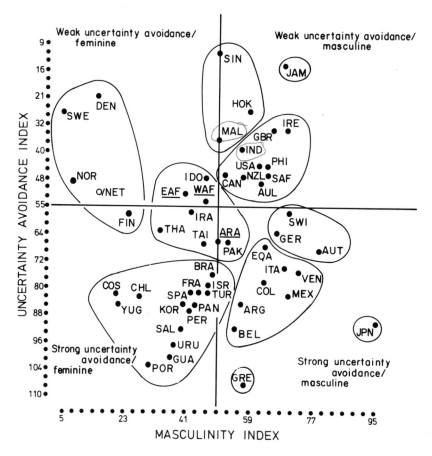

Figure 2.4 *Masculinity plotted against uncertainty avoidance* (Reproduced with permission from Hofstede, 1983)

2.3.5 Evaluating Hofstede's Model

It must be admitted that Hofstede's model has weak points.[9]

1. It assumes a correspondence between national territory and the limits of the culture. We have already noted the problems of sustaining this position, but also the problems of applying a system which distinguishes culture groups more discretely.
2. As Hofstede recognizes,[10] the questionnaire respondents represent 'an extremely narrow and specific sample of their countries' populations. They belong to the middle class of their society rather than to the upper, working, or peasant class.'
3. In addition, the questionnaire respondents are all members of single multinational, and a single industry.
4. The masculinity/femininity category may be misnomered (and should not be interpreted as measuring 'male chauvinism', although some of the more masculine cultures may also be those commonly labeled chauvinistic). It perhaps constitutes a residual category accounting for a range of features associated with role preferences and not explained by the other categories.

But these objections are dwarfed by the importance of Hofstede's work in relating different cultures and applying cultural analysis to practical management problems. As two other writers[11] have said:

> '[It is] useful heuristically as a starting point for further investigation of culture and cultural variation, particularly for more qualitative research and analysis.'

It promises to be the major influence for a long time to come.

2.4 APPLYING THE MODEL TO MANAGEMENT

Hofstede's research demonstrates that management values are *not* the same across the world. Your headquarters may be making an expensive mistake if they suppose that a single policy can dictate the details of organizational culture and values across a range of local branches. Local cultural values will always influence how headquarters policy is interpreted at the local level. A policy appropriate to one culture may be quite inappropriate if applied to another.

Hofstede's research indicates which orientation *most* members of a culture group are likely to take when faced with the need to make a choice. The fact that the Hong Kong Chinese have low needs to avoid uncertainty does not mean that they actively court disaster. We can expect that in general they would welcome lifetime employment, full social security, an absence of anxiety about working conditions, *all other things being equal.*

But in the real world all other things are not equal, and avoidance of uncertainty has to be traded off against the possibilities to make entrepreneurial fortunes which necessarily entail risk. The Hong Kong Chinese are willing to gamble a degree of security in return for these possibilities; but the majority of Greeks forgo these opportunities because the level of risk is perceived as unacceptable. Of course, they would also prefer to be rich than poor, but are less willing to take the same risks given the odds against achieving wealth.

Hofstede's analysis leads us to perceive cultures in terms not only of shared values, but of shared *choices between values.* Over time, a culture has opted for the advantages offered by one orientation as against those offered by another. The cross-cultural manager makes a serious mistake when assuming that his or her cultural and organizational values are obviously the best possible and should be adopted by the other culture. On the contrary, its members are entirely justified in preferring to organize their relationships in their own way.

If the manager comes from an individualist culture, the advantages of systems which encourage self-expression and achievement seem to outweigh the dangers of social alienation and competition within the group. But a member of a collectivist culture values social harmony and his identity as a member of the group; he has no good reason to exert his personality if it means surrendering these advantages.

2.4.1   Culture and Bureaucracy

Although the terms 'bureaucracy' and 'bureaucratization' have come to have negative connotations, Weber and other early sociologists used them in a neutral sense to describe how modern organizations operate. And no company can work efficiently without some bureaucratic division of labor and responsibilities.

The 'ideal' bureaucracy sets rules that organize its members' relationships, their job specifications, what tasks they should perform and how to perform them. It sets criteria for rewards and punishment. Bureaucratic organization is impersonal to the extent that the rules apply to all members, whatever their identity (social status, family relationships, etc.) outside the organization. The individual is appointed and promoted on the basis of his knowledge and professional expertise. He is employed to serve the organization's interests rather than his own. He fills a particular specialized function which complements functions performed by other members.

The term 'bureaucracy' is sometimes thought to refer only to government and state organizations. Used correctly, it describes any organization that sets impersonal rules to regulate its members' functions and roles.

In practice, or course, bureaucracies very seldom (perhaps never) fit this 'ideal' model at all points. In different cultures, cultural priorities determine how the bureaucratic 'ideal' is interpreted.

Hofstede shows how bureaucratic types vary across cultures; his analysis focuses on variations in power difference and the need to avoid uncertainty.[12]

2.4.2   The Full Bureaucracy

An organization adopts bureaucratic rules in order to make members' behavior predictable and to reduce uncertainties. So a culture that has most need for these rules creates bureaucracies that most nearly approach the ideal type. Hofstede names these 'full' bureaucracies (see Figure 2.5). Relationships between members, and the procedures required to perform tasks correctly, are highly regulated. Typically, members respect the unequal distribution of power and the right of superiors to enforce rules, and they have a strong need to avoid ambiguous procedures. France, Japan, and Mediterranean and Latin countries belong in this wide-power-distance/strong-uncertainty-avoidance category.

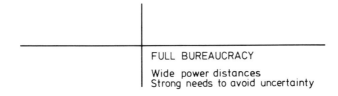

FULL BUREAUCRACY

Wide power distances
Strong needs to avoid uncertainty

Figure 2.5

Functions are tightly distinguished; the accountant does not make marketing decisions, and the marketing manager does not propose policy for the warehousing department. Members attach most importance to maintaining line authority, and communication is mainly downward. This means that in each department (accounting, marketing, warehousing, etc.) power flows down and individuals report up. Departments communicate between each other at the highest levels. Any criticism of higher levels is likely to be communicated upward only through informal channels and third parties.

2.4.3   The Market Bureaucracy

In the opposite way, bureaucratic structures tend to be weakest in cultures marked by small power distances and weak needs for uncertainty avoidance. Members put more reliance on personal relationships and depend less on their place in the bureaucratic hierarchy (see Figure 2.6). They have relatively greater control over how they perform their tasks. Hofstede describes this form of implicit structure in terms of a market, where power is less centralized and emanates from a number of sources. The Anglo and Scandinavian countries and The Netherlands most closely fit this pattern.

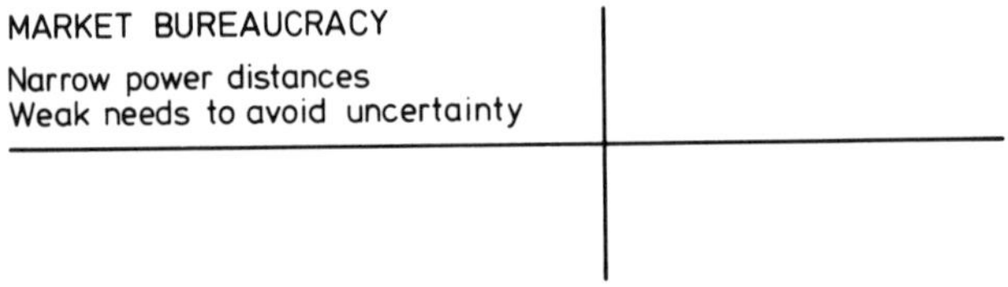

MARKET BUREAUCRACY

Narrow power distances
Weak needs to avoid uncertainty

Figure 2.6

In these market bureaucracies members negotiate for power and influence, creating alliances by trading support and the threats of reprisals if support is not forthcoming: 'you scratch my back and I'll scratch yours, but if you give me trouble you can expect trouble in return.' These informal alliances may cross departmental lines.

2.4.4   The Workflow Bureaucracy

Between these two extremes lie the workflow bureaucracies typified by the German-speaking countries, Finland and Israel, and the personnel bureaucracies, typified by the South East Asian countries. The organizational structures of workflow bureaucracies place more emphasis on regulating activities than relationships. Hofstede compares them to well-oiled machines.

The need to avoid uncertainty is relatively much stronger and requirements for job performance are tightly specified, but power distances are narrow (see Figure 2.7). Note, for instance, that in large German companies

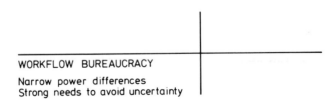

WORKFLOW BUREAUCRACY

Narrow power differences
Strong needs to avoid uncertainty

Figure 2.7

executives and workforce may share common canteen facilities, whereas in the Soviet Union, different facilities may be provided for up to six different grades.

2.4.5   The Personnel Bureaucracy

Personnel bureaucracies occur in collectivist cultures where power distances are wide, and Hofstede likens them to the oriental family (see Figure 2.8). The organization is typically built around a strong leader who controls by direct supervision, and authority is associated with this individual rather than with the organization or his or her rank (as in the full bureaucracy).

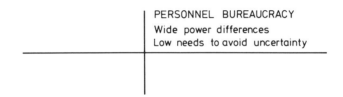

```
                              │ PERSONNEL  BUREAUCRACY
                              │ Wide  power  differences
                              │ Low  needs  to avoid  uncertainty
──────────────────────────────┼──────────────────────────────────
                              │
                              │
```

Figure 2.8

In a United Nations report, Ross and Bouwmeesters[13] describe patterns of authority in tropical African companies:

'Where delegation of authority does occur, it is usually confined to relatives (in private enterprises) or persons with whom top managers have political ties (in public enterprises). . . . mistrust of those not related by ties of kinship or ethnicity limits the possibilities of delegation and teamwork.'

Subordinates may be unwilling to take responsibility. This is because the culture teaches them to avoid stepping outside their social roles, not because they lack technical competence.

Personnel bureaucracies are typified by Chinese family companies in South East Asia. The individual starts a company, and staffs senior levels with family members. Family and company responsibilities are paralleled; the owner deserves respect both as family and company head. Non-family members (whose loyalty is always suspect) are employed at lower levels only.

The communication and implementation of decisions is rapid and efficient for as long as there is harmony within the family. Responsibilities can be explained and delegated over the family dinner table. But this close identification of family and company interests also carries a weakness. A family conflict is echoed within the business; for instance, a disagreement between two brothers who refuse to speak with each other may have disastrous consequences within the company when they are responsible for the production and marketing functions.

Even in a publicly owned or public sector personnel bureaucracy, ranks are tightly differentiated and promotion is restricted. But roles are specified less precisely, and workflow is less restricted. One study found that Indian organizations tended to have many more hierarchical layers than did American subsidiaries in India, but fewer control systems on production.[14]

Status is attached to the number of subordinates that one controls. Where labor is cheap, a trusted manager may be rewarded with additional staff. Hence the number of staff in his or her unit has symbolic importance, indicating the manager's value.

When personal loyalties to superiors are strong, and job specifications are loose, the subordinate interprets his or her role implicitly from careful observation of the superior's needs. This relationship between superior and subordinate has cross-cultural implications; for instance:[15] 'Americans, a Japanese boss [managing a US branch] often feels, need more supervision than their Japanese counterparts, who try to intuit their superior's desire.' This sense of a personal relationship with the superior is mirrored by a similar loyalty down to subordinates. A Taiwanese manager said that, in his culture, the effective manager worked actively to create this sense of obligation in subordinates: 'Make friends with them, show you are concerned, make them think of their obligations to return the good things back.'

The case of a pathologist employed by South Korea's National Institute of Scientific Investigation can be used to illustrate the concept of collective loyalty and obligation. Dr Hwang felt impelled to resign because he had inadvertently upset the status quo. He had submitted a routine report concluding that a student who died while undergoing police questioning about his political connections had been tortured.

The report was taken up by a journalist friend, and to Dr Hwang's astonishment was published.[16] The atmosphere at the institute grew instantly hostile:

'I had to resign', he said. 'Under the circumstances that exist in Korea, I would not have been able to work any longer in that place. I caused my superiors to lose face, and, according to the ethics of our society, one cannot stay in the job after that. . . . It disturbs me that I disrupted the normal processes of that organization and I feel guilty about it,' he said. 'I would assume now that every intellectual Korean would criticize me because I didn't do the right thing as an organization man. . . . I didn't think it would turn out like this. I'm not interested in being a hero. Frankly, I think I may be a fool.'

2.5   APPLYING THE MODEL TO MANAGEMENT COMMUNICATION

In all bureaucratic types, the individual is placed in relationships with superiors, peers and subordinates. These relationships enable control to be exerted and messages communicated. We consider here how the bureaucratic type determines the relative strength and weakness of these relationships.

Figure 2.9 shows a simple relationship between a superior (A) and a subordinate (B). What degree of control does A exert, and what types of messages get communicated down, and up?

A

B

Figure 2.9

The wider the power distance between A and B, the more restricted are the opportunities for communication. The control that A imposes, and the distance between A and B, is determined by:

1   THE TASK. When the task is complex and B needs assistance, or B is new to the task, A imposes greater control and may need to invest heavily in giving instructions and checking B's understanding.
2   THE CULTURE, AND HOW THIS INFLUENCES RULES GOVERNING STRUCTURAL RELATIONSHIPS. When relationships between superior and subordinate are governed by wide power differences, and A expects to exert heavy control and B to be controlled, the distance between A and B is wide. Even when the task is routine, A imposes heavy control in a wide power difference culture.
3   RELATIONSHIPS WITH OTHER MEMBERS OF THE ORGANIZATION.

The relationship becomes more complex when a third worker (C) joins B. Figure 2.10 shows A directly supervising both B and C when hierarchical relationships (between A and B, A and C) are more significant than the horizontal relationship between B and C. They both report directly to A. They are more likely to check their understanding of how the task should be accomplished and resources allocated by communicating with their boss than by negotiating between themselves. When B and C represent different functions (marketing, production) they communicate up and down through the superior level rather than directly.

This structure is effective when the task requires strict supervision and B and C do not need to negotiate their sharing of resources. All other things

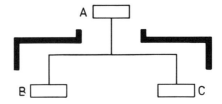

Figure 2.10

being equal, it is more likely to occur within the full bureaucracy (e.g. France) and personnel bureaucracy (e.g. Indonesia) where members of the culture readily accept wide power differences and control by superiors.

Figure 2.11, on the other hand, shows the relationship between superior A and subordinates B and C when power differences are narrow, and B and C are concerned to check their activities with a higher authority. A exerts only light control on B and C, who have greater autonomy in interpreting their job specifications and in deciding between themselves how the task can best be performed. This structure is effective when a complex task needs collaboration; for instance, when the production and marketing departments work together on launching a new product.

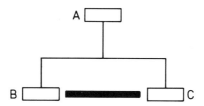

Figure 2.11

It is effective when cultural values foster collaboration between peer individuals and functional groups. They prefer to communicate, secure resources, negotiate power and resolve conflicts without routing messages through a superior level, and superiors do not feel impelled to control every detail. All other things being equal, it is more likely to typify the market bureaucracy (e.g. the United States, United Kingdom) and the workflow bureaucracy (e.g. Germany).

Figure 2.12 shows a relationship in which C feels free to communicate directly with B, and C with B, even though this means bypassing C's direct superior. For instance, B may have expertise which is essential to C in order to complete a task, and direct communication is more likely to result in efficient work than routing their messages through A.

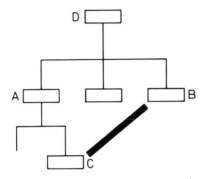

Figure 2.12

In cultures where a premium is placed on efficiently achieving work targets, even when this appears to challenge the integrity of the organizational structure, members of the organization may feel relatively unconstrained about communicating outside the hierarchy. This is most likely to occur in the market bureaucracies. Laurent found that only 22 percent of his Swedish respondents disagreed with the statement 'In order to have efficient work relationships, it is often necessary to bypass the hierarchical line', as against 75 percent of his Italians.[17]

Figure 2.13 shows another case in which C bypasses a superior in order to communicate with their common superior. Of course, in all cultures C's superior might resist this practice; but, as in Figure 2.12, this resistance is likely to be weakest in lower power distance cultures. It is strongest in the

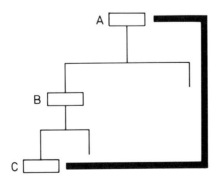

Figure 2.13

full and personnel bureaucracies where a premium is placed on maintaining the hierarchical integrity of the organization even though this may cost in terms of efficiency.

Figure 2.14 represents a *matrix structure*, in which C reports to two superiors, A and B. Some companies have established formal matrix structures, which work successfully when their members are prepared to work together, share information in a relationship of interdependence and collaboration, and trust each other. For instance, C may be the warehousing manager reporting to both the production manager and the marketing manager.

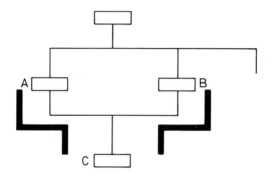

Figure 2.14

Because they depend so heavily on mutual trust and a willingness to share resources, including information, matrix structures are difficult to operate effectively even in the market bureaucracies, and pose extremely grave problems in cultures that have a high need to avoid uncertainty.

2.6   IMPLICATIONS FOR THE MANAGER

- Examine Figures 2.2–2.5, and see where Hofstede plots *your own* culture and *another culture* in which you are interested. If your own culture or the other culture is not plotted, identify some alternatives which are similar.

- From your own experience and understanding, what evidence can you find for arguing each of the following about management and organizations in *your own culture*?

   (a)   Power distances are as wide/narrow as they are plotted.
   (b)   Power distances are significantly wider/narrower than as plotted.
   (c)   Needs to avoid uncertainty are as high/low as they are plotted.

(d) Needs to avoid uncertainty are significantly higher/lower than as plotted.
(e) Social values are as collectivist/individualist as they are plotted.
(f) Social values are significantly more collectivist/individualist than as plotted.
(g) Perceptions of role are as masculine/feminine as they are plotted.
(h) Perceptions of role are significantly more masculine/feminine than as plotted.

- From your own experience and understanding, what evidence can you find for arguing each of (a)–(h) above about management and organizations in *the other culture*?

- How do you expect differences between your own culture and the other culture along each of Hofstede's four dimensions to affect each of the following?

  (a) Motivators. (Motivators effective in your own culture are ineffective in the other culture, and vice versa.)
  (b) Causes of conflict.
  (c) Techniques for resolving conflict.
  (d) Criteria and techniques for planning.
  (e) Criteria and techniques for communicating plans for persons likely to be affected.
  (f) Patterns of communication.

Where the differences are significant, how do you expect them to affect your management style when you deal with members of the other culture?

- Within the other-culture organization, which of the following (a) is likely to be rewarded? (b) is likely to be punished? (c) receives neither reward nor punishment?

1 The individual follows his or her job specification to the letter, whatever the task.
2 The individual departs from his or her job specification when this seems more likely to accomplish the task.
3 The individual follows authorized reporting procedures, whatever the task.

- Examine the organizational chart shown in Figure 2.15. Describe the circumstances under which each of the following five communicative events typically occurs in *your own culture*:

1 D has a work-related problem and asks E for assistance before asking B.

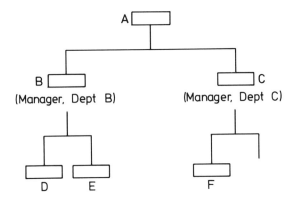

Figure 2.15

2   D asks B for assistance before asking E.
3   D directly asks F for assistance.
4   D directly asks A for assistance.
5   D directly asks C for assistance.

Assume equal access to all the persons involved and take into account the following:

(a)   Needs for efficiency.
(b)   Needs to respect organizational integrity.
(c)   Urgency.
(d)   The message to be communicated.

Describe the circumstances under which each of the five communication events typically occurs in *the other culture*.
    Where the differences between your own and the other culture are significant, how do you expect them to affect your management style when you communicate with members of the other culture?

2.7   SUMMARY

The culture of the group determines how its members perceive the world and solve their problems, both individual and shared. These choices of perception and action may seem irrational to a member of some other group, but in terms of their own culture are logical and coherent.
    This chapter has seen how cultural priorities influence organizational priorities. Section 2.2 defined culture in terms of values. It examined the managerial implications of changes in the culture, which are necessarily very slow, and indicated what aspects of group behavior and expression are

excluded by the definition. Section 2.3 shows how Hofstede's model compares cultures along dimensions of power distance, uncertainty avoidance, collectivism/individualism, and masculinity/femininity. These are used to explain differences in work-related attitudes and behavior.

Section 2.4 discussed Hofstede's application of his model to distinguishing culture-based styles of bureaucratic organization: full, market, workflow and personnel bureaucracies. Section 2.5 applied the model to management communication, and demonstrated how cultural factors influence preferred relationships for control and communication.

EXERCISES

Exercise 1

This exercise examines how cultural priorities influence communication. Consider the following extract from an invented office encounter:

| Assistant Manager X: | 'Have you got any ideas how I can deal with the Amex report?' |
| Assistant Manager Y: | 'Sorry. But the boss has just gone into his office.' |

Which of the two paraphrases below makes sense of this dialogue when (i) the two assistant managers are French? and (ii) the two assistant managers are Danish? Explain your answers.

| Assistant Manager X: | 'How do you suggest I deal with the Amex report? I'm asking you because you might be able to give me some useful input and I'll use good ideas wherever they come from.' |
| Assistant Manager Y: | 'Unfortunately I don't think I should comment. You should go and ask the boss, who's just gone into his office. He's the person most qualified to help you.' |

OR

| Assistant Manager X: | 'How do you suggest I deal with the Amex report? I'm asking you because you might be able to give me some useful input and I'll use good ideas wherever they come from.' |
| Assistant Manager Y: | 'I'm quite willing to help you but unfortunately I have to go see the boss and he's just gone into his office. But we can talk about it after that.' |

Exercise 2

This exercise shows how cultural priorities influence the conditions for organizational change.

In the Kingdom of Darana, the Daranese Paint Company (DPC) has a 90 percent share of the local market. Three local competitors account for the remaining 10 percent. There are no exports; Darana's neighbor, the Republic of Godali, operates strong tarriff barriers in order to protect its own industry.

DPC employs 300 people. Many have been with the company all their working lives, and grew up with the President, Mr B. Aaba. Some long-term employees even remember the President's father, Mr A. Aaba, the founder. In Daranese culture, needs to avoid uncertainty are high, and power distances are wide. The company chart is shown in Figure 2.16.

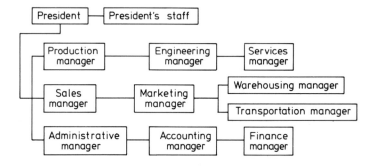

Figure 2.16

Then Mr Aaba retires. He is succeeded by his only son, Mr C. Aaba, who recently received his MBA from the London Business School and is anxious to apply his new expertise. Then a few weeks later, the Godalese government lifts all tariff barriers. DPC's three local competitors announce that they are making massive investments in order to take advantage of the new export opportunities and to win much larger shares of the local market.

The new President decides to reorganize DPC along more efficient lines, in order

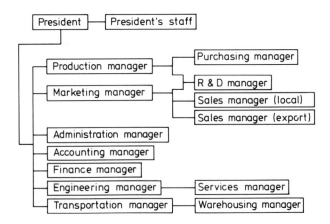

Figure 2.17

to grab a share of the Godalese market and beat off the local competition. Figure 2.17 shows the new chart, which incorporates the same number of employees.

Now answer these questions:

(a)   How might this reorganization lead to an improvement in efficiency and help the company achieve Mr Aaba's objectives?
(b)   How might this reorganization retard efficiency?
(c)   Now suppose that Darana's culture is *not* as described above (strong needs to avoid uncertainty, wide power differences), but instead members have only low needs to avoid uncertainty and power distances are narrow; and the company is not old but was established only recently. How does this effect your answers to (a) and (b)?

NOTES

1   Hofstede, G. (1984) *Culture's Consequences*. Sage, Beverly Hills, p. 21.
2   Chilcott, J.G. (1968) Some perspectives for teaching first generation Mexican Americans. In *Readings in the Socio-Cultural Foundations of Education* (eds. J. G. Chilcott et al.) Belmost, Mass: Wadsworth, 1968, pp. 358–68.
3   Yates, R.E. (1988) Yuppies. *Chicago Tribune*, 24 April.
4   Hofstede, G. (1983) National cultures in four dimensions. *International Studies of Management and Organization*, **XIII**(1–2), 46–74.
5   See Hofstede, G. (1980) Motivation, leadership, and organization: do American theories apply abroad? *Organizational Dynamics*, Summer, 42–63; (same author) (1983) The cultural relativity of organizational practices and theories. *Journal of International Business Studies*, Fall, 75–89. And see also the more detailed discussion in (same author) (1984) *Culture's Consequences*. Sage, Beverly Hills.
6   Marshall, T. (1988) The Scandinavian good life: would a few hurdles hurt? *International Herald Tribune*, 15 December.
7   The significance of social shame in Japan is discussed by Benedict, R. (1946, 1974) *The Chrysanthemum and the Sword: Patterns of Japanese Culture*. New American Library, New York.
8   Marshall, T. (1988), *op. cit.*
9   See comments and references in Jaeger, A. (1986) Organizational development and national culture: Where's the fit? *Academy of Management Review*, **11**(1), 178–90.
10   Hofstede, G. (1983), *op. cit.*, pp. 55–6.
11   Westwood, R.G. and Everett, J.E. (1987) Culture's consequences: a methodology for comparative management studies in Southeast Asia. *Asia Pacific Journal of Management* (Singapore), **4**(3), 187–202.
12   Hofstede, G. (1984), *op. cit.*, in particular pp. 215–18.
13   Ross, H., Bouwmeesters, J. and other Institute staff (1972) *Management in the Developing Countries*. UN Research Institute for Social Development, Geneva.
14   Neghandi, A.R. and Prasad, S.B. (1971) *Comparative Management*. Appleton Century Crofts, New York.
15   The 'Salaryman' Blues. *Newsweek*, 9 May 1988.
16   Haberman, C. (1988) How a pathologist reshaped Seoul's politics. *New York Times*, 4 May.
17   Laurent, A. (1983) The cultural diversity of western conceptions of management. *International Studies of Management and Organization*, **XIII**(1–2), 75–96.

3
Communicating Decisions

3.1 INTRODUCTION

Top management in an Indonesian company decided not to renew their training officer, a locally contracted American, and to replace him with his Canadian assistant. They were unwilling to risk a confrontation by giving Paul the news directly, and instead depended on him to recognize a hint that his resignation would not come amiss. They moved the Canadian into an office on a more prestigious corridor, despite there being an empty office next to Paul's. This meant shifting a middle-ranking Indonesian out of the prestigious office to elsewhere in the building.

The Indonesian staff understood immediately why the switch in offices had been made, but were shy of explaining its significance to Paul and could not understand why he failed to take the hint. He was not accustomed by his culture to look for symbolic meaning in an office shake-up which apparently did not directly affect himself. His relations with top management continued superficially good, and he only realized what was being communicated two weeks later.

When he announced that he had no intention of seeking a further contract and senior management was thus spared the embarrassment of dismissing him, the strategy had eventually achieved its objective. However, this was at the cost of his resentment that local staff had been given the information before him, their embarrassment, and the annoyance of the Indonesian manager who had been obliged to move offices in order to facilitate this indirect communication.

This case shows an Oriental organization communicating bad news. The use of a covert message prevents overt conflict. This strategy does not immediately succeed because it is used within a cross-cultural context in which the message receiver applies different values to recognizing and assessing information.

It illustrates the problems of selecting the appropriate message to communicate a management decision. In different contexts, different message forms are more or less appropriate, depending on the needs of both sender and receiver. Here we focus on the form of messages designed to communicate decisions.

3.2   COMMUNICATION AND THE STRUCTURE OF THE ORGANIZATION

The organization only communicates effectively when its messages are clear, and the reasons for sending them convincing. Achieving these goals of clarity and conviction is particularly difficult, and important, in a cross-cultural context where individuals apply different perceptions when communicating.

Individuals and groups communicate in order to reach common understanding, and this is often a necessary first stage to achieving some purpose. A group reaches common understanding when it shares perceptions, beliefs, attitudes, knowledge about someone or something. This sharing enables the group to act as a single unit rather than as an assembly of individuals, each trying to achieve his or her own ends which may not match. By communicating, members

- exchange experiences;
- recognize common interests;
- agree on immediate aims;
- negotiate strategies aimed at achieving these aims;
- implement and monitor these strategies.

In a group where all members are equal, all have equal rights to share their views and suggest solutions to common problems — for instance, when you and your friends decide how to spend a holiday, by going to a picnic or to a football game, by car or by bus.

In a bureaucratic organization, where members have different responsibilities, perform different functions and occupy different ranks within the organization, and so are not equal, rights to decide on group activities are restricted. The organization is structured so that:

1 Members who need to take part in the decision making process are given the necessary information on which to base their decisions.
2 Members who need to implement and monitor decisions made by others understand these decisions.

3　Non-implementing members understand as much as they need to know of the decision and its implementation in order that they have a sense of 'what's going on' and so their loyalty to the organization is strengthened.

These functions can only be performed efficiently if the communication systems are efficient, and match the decision making processes. The structure by which the organization takes decisions and the system by which it communicates them are very closely linked. A decision intended to control other people's behavior is effective only if it is communicated to them in an appropriate style. And so the manager is effective to the extent that he or she communicates effectively.

Whether the organizational structure determines the form of the communication system or vice versa is a moot point. But scholars increasingly argue the latter position, that the organization is best described in terms of how its communication systems are structured and that 'interacting individuals are the organization'; if they cease to interact, it disintegrates.[1] How the organization structure and communication system influence and reflect each other is modeled by Figure 3.1.

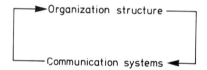

Figure 3.1

We can go one stage further. The previous chapters have shown the influence of culture on organization structure, and this can be built into the model as in Figure 3.2. In practice, this means that if all decisions are made by top management in a high power distance organization, they will be communicated in such a way that lower ranks are given little opportunity to suggest alternatives or to disagree; and in a more 'democratic' narrow power distance organization, decision making is achieved by a correspondingly more open process of trading opinions, and discussion is expected.

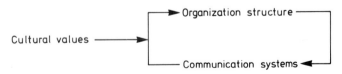

Figure 3.2

3.2.1   One- and Two-way Communication

The term 'one-way communication' describes a process by which one group or person, in practice the superior, contributes messages which are intended to control and direct activity and the subordinates do not participate meaningfully, although they may be responsible for implementation. (At this point we are not concerned with how the superior most effectively asks questions for information.)

One-way communication may be modeled by a five-stage model as shown in Figure 3.3.

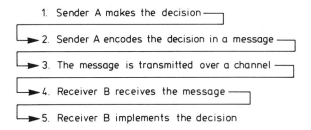

1. Sender A makes the decision
2. Sender A encodes the decision in a message
3. The message is transmitted over a channel
4. Receiver B receives the message
5. Receiver B implements the decision

Figure 3.3

For example, a manager wants his marketing assistants to start directing the product towards a new market. He chooses what message to communicate and decides to address them in a meeting:

Manager: 'You marketing people should start looking at the kids market.'

and the assistants nod their heads and make notes.

The receiver (in this example, the assistants) receives the message but does not make any overt response. Hence one-way communication assumes understanding by the receiver whether or not this exists. But if the receiver misunderstands, or does not know how to implement the decision, or actively disagrees, the one-way process not only falls short of promoting full understanding but may detract from it.

In the example, the assistants might misunderstand what is meant by the 'kids market' and go off to plan a campaign marketing the product to pre-teenagers when the manager intends a market of teenagers. The sender (the manager) does not know whether his message has achieved its intended purpose. He may not recognize that a misunderstanding has occurred until too late, when money has already been invested in a pre-teen marketing campaign.

If the receivers are unable to attach meaning to the message, nothing has been communicated. If they attach the wrong meaning, the message has been miscommunicated. Communication is efficient only if the receiver derives the meaning intended by the sender.

Miscommunication wastes resources of time, labor, and so on; but it has an even more destructive effect on future events. The frustrations felt by both sides create resentment and conflict and so dampen their motivation to communicate and work together further in the future. Over time these effects of bad communication multiply, and cannot be easily reversed.

Two-way communication gives some protection against misunderstanding. A two-way communication process incorporates the receiver as the new sender, transmitting feedback to the original message. That is, the communication becomes an interactive process. The term 'feedback' is used here to mean any propositional response to an opening utterance. This new communication process may be modeled by a ten-stage model as shown in Figure 3.4.

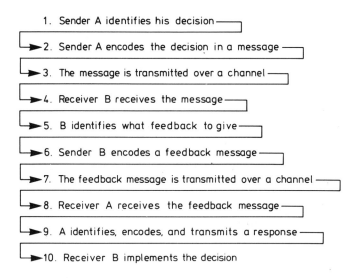

1. Sender A identifies his decision
2. Sender A encodes the decision in a message
3. The message is transmitted over a channel
4. Receiver B receives the message
5. B identifies what feedback to give
6. Sender B encodes a feedback message
7. The feedback message is transmitted over a channel
8. Receiver A receives the feedback message
9. A identifies, encodes, and transmits a response
10. Receiver B implements the decision

Figure 3.4

Between stages 9 and 10 each of A and B may send each other a number of messages (which may lead to a radical modification in the original decision) until stage 10 is reached. For instance, in the following the assistants' utterances (1)–(4) all contribute feedback:

Manager: 'You marketing people should start looking at the kids market.'
Assistant: (1)   'Which precise age group do you mean?'

(2) 'Yes, we could see if the kids have a different use for our product.'
(3) 'Okay, I'll get you a draft report by Monday.'
(4) 'But the kids don't have that much money to buy our product.'

These feedback utterances have different functions:

Utterance
(1) asks for clarification
(2) makes a statement that adds a new idea
(3) interprets the original utterance as a directive and indicates how it will be performed
(4) argues with the original utterance.

Many other functions could be added: for instance, asking a question for further information, commenting, redefining the message in terms of personal experience, criticizing and offering alternatives, and so on. All have in common that they carry the interaction forward and ask for a further contribution from the manager. Thus the extended interaction more closely defines, amplifies, and modifies the manager's original message.

Note that minimal feedback consisting only of a marker to show that the audience is attending does not contribute propositional content; for instance:

Manager: 'You marketing people should start looking more at the kids market.'
Assistant: (5) 'Hm.'

'Hm' has the function of encouraging the manager to continue speaking, and perhaps develop the original message; but it is not propositional, and does not contribute any new ideas or information to the interaction. This fragment of the communication is one-way only, and minimal utterances like (5) do not make this a two-way communication.

3.3 COMPLEX AND SIMPLE MESSAGES

When the manager needs to communicate a highly complex decision, he or she sends a complex message. When the decision is simple, the message is simple.

Suppose that the company decides to set up a subsidiary in Hong Kong. A large number of staff will be involved, and so when the chief executive officer explains the board's decision to the departmental managers he may need to go into considerable detail about whom they should delegate to oversee various stages of the operation, including the actual management of the subsidiary. This complex decision engenders a complex two-way communication process.

Second, suppose that the manager of a packaging company is approached by a potential customer who wants a quantity of high-grade packaging material produced to his own specifications. The manager has to instruct his marketing assistant to negotiate the deal when the following conditions apply:

1   The company has not dealt with this customer before.
2   The company has not produced this item to these specifications before.
3   This is a new market.
4   The marketing assistant is new to the job.

The marketing assistant requires a range of information relating to customer needs, production and materials costs, production and shipment dates, price ranges, the competition, and so on. In this instance, the message is bound to be complex and the manager needs to spell out the assistant's responsibilities clearly in order that there is no misunderstanding. The chosen mode may be a long face-to-face meeting.

On the other hand, when the original message is simple and routine, the participants have fewer needs to give and react to feedback, and it is less important that their communication should be two-way. This happens when the receiver does not need to be told how to implement the decision. And now suppose that in the same situation:

1   The company has dealt with this customer many times before.
2   The order is routine, and the same customer makes the same purchase on a routine basis.
3   The market is unchanged.
4   The marketing assistant is highly experienced in selling this product to this customer.

Now relatively little information is required by the assistant and the message is reduced. The manager can communicate his decision to make the deal by the channel of a short memo: 'Delta want their usual order of CX-123. The usual pricing and shipment rates apply. Please complete by Friday.' The experienced assistant limits his response to merely making acknowledgement in a return memo, and no face-to-face meeting is necessary.

If the manager cuts his message any further he omits essential information; if he adds unnecessary details, he wastes his time and is in danger of confusing the assistant. The message is optimally efficient when it contains no more and no less information than the receiver needs in order to implement it efficiently.

3.3.1   Essential and Redundant Information

What *sort* of information needs to be communicated in order that a decision can be implemented? A highly complex message may need to answer all these questions:[2]

- WHO has to implement the decision?
- WHAT action has to be taken in order to implement the decision?
- WHAT action has to be taken in order to monitor implementation?
- HOW should this action be performed and with what resources?
- HOW will this action satisfy the requirements of the decision?
- HOW will successful implementation meet the needs of the organization and/or the implementor?
- WHEN should this decision be implemented?
- WHERE should this decision be implemented?
- WHY has this decision been taken?
- WHY does the chosen implementation strategy best fit the decision?

Obviously not every message needs to answer all these questions. The principles of 'need for feedback' and 'need to know' apply. To go back to our Hong Kong subsidiary example, the CEO explains in detail why this decision has been taken (opportunities to exploit the China market, declining home sales, the world economic environment) because he decides:

1 He needs their feedback. What opportunities and problems do they foresee? What alternative suggestions do they have?
2 They have to decide how to cooperate in order to best implement the decision, and so they need to know the scope of the issues involved.

But the individual departmental manager may decide that her subordinates do not need all this background information in order to implement her directives. Assume that she is responsible for finance; she selects the data on sales projections, but her subordinates do not need to know the production estimates, and cannot give useful feedback. Her decisions partly reflect the structure of the organization, and patterns of communication between her department, marketing, and production.

When the manager tells the experienced marketing assistant in the second example above that 'Delta want their usual order of CX-123', he does not need to add information explaining that it is in the interests of the company to fill the order and suggesting what actions to take. Within the context of their shared experience and the routine situation, this is obvious.

When they do not share experience of the situation (this is the marketing assistant's first day in the job), nothing can be taken for granted. More information is needed, and the message becomes correspondingly complex. A parallel situation occurs where the sender and receiver view the situation from different cultural vantage points, and process it in terms of their different perceptions and priorities.

3.3.2 Cross-Cultural Complexity

When sending *any* message, we make decisions about how much information the other person already has (and is thus old information, and perhaps redundant) and how much new information is needed. Most of the time, we make these decisions unconsciously, and take for granted the other person's data-bank of information, opinions, and perceptions.

In a cross-cultural situation, we cannot make the same assumptions, and we have consciously to process these basic communication decisions:

(a)   what information to provide (and how this should be ordered and presented);

(b)   what information to omit.

These decisions are made with reference to the shared and different cultural perceptions of sender and receiver. This means understanding how the other culture interprets the context, and recognizing that what is obvious to you may not be obvious to them, and vice versa.

The next two sections show how the power distance between sender and receiver is reflected by the communication system.

3.4 COMMUNICATING WHERE POWER DISTANCES ARE WIDE

We know that when power distances are wide, communication tends to be one-way, from the top down. Only the superior may decide what experiences, interests, aims and strategies are appropriate, and how strategies should be implemented and monitored. His or her messages tend to take the form of directives rather than suggestions. Even when a message begins 'I suggest that . . .' the wise subordinate first tries to interpret it as a directive.

The superior is the only person who contributes substantively to the communication, and the subordinates' rights to communicate with the superior are restricted. They cannot lightly challenge the superior, offer alternative interpretations of data or make proposals that would modify the superior's decision. Their opportunities to initiate messages are constrained to the narrow range of 'appropriate' topics associated with their functions, and they are similarly inhibited from giving feedback.

When the culture is collectivist and members place a priority on preserving social harmony, they avoid making any negative or unwelcome contributions to the communication. In practice, this can mean keeping as silent as is (politely) possible; there may be reasons unknown to the subordinates why an apparently innocuous contribution may be offensive to the superior.

For instance, the British general manager of an international hotel chain with branches throughout South East Asia comments on the tendency of his local managers to give positive answers to all their guests' questions and comments:

Western guest:	'The refrigerator in my room is broken.'
Local manager:	'Yes sir.'
Guest:	'Can you get it fixed today?'
Manager:	'Yes sir.'

When the manager understands what the guest has said, and knows that the refrigerator cannot be fixed until the day after, this is not a simple question of language proficiency that can be resolved by language instruction. It reflects attitudes towards superior–subordinate relations and problem-solving. In this specific context, the long-term effect of these 'polite' answers is to lose the hotel its Western business.

Why does the local manager avoid explaining that the refrigerator cannot be fixed for 24 hours? His cultural priorities tell him to give a pleasing answer and to satisfy immediate needs; the long-term problem can be re-solved at a later date or may disappear. The guest may decide that he doesn't need to use the refrigerator; or will change his travel plans and move out that day; or can be accommodated in some other room. Why does he not immediately suggest this change of accommodation? Because the guest may have his own unsuspected reasons for preferring to stay where he is. His deference to a superior is reinforced by his shyness and respect for a West-ern foreigner.

The Western guest expects that the second 'Yes sir' promises the desired service that the refrigerator will be promptly fixed. If he is told immediately that this service cannot be delivered he may very well argue — a situation which the manager wants to avoid. But the guest would prefer to confront the issue now than experience greater frustration tomorrow when the re-frigerator is still broken.

3.4.1   Feedback Perceived as a Challenge

In traditional agricultural societies, economic activity is geared to perform-ing routine tasks, and communication to organizing these routines and en-suring proper use of resources and equipment. It is not necessary that superior and subordinate should develop a relationship of psychological closeness. To members of traditional organizations, the concept that em-ployee feedback should be encouraged is startlingly novel.

The right to delegate tasks is associated with social and political authority;

and the discussion, even criticism, of management decisions seems to invite criticism of the manager's right to delegate, and of the social status quo. It is welcomed neither by manager nor by the workforce, who share his needs for social harmony and mutual dependence.

Negative feedback expressing disagreement is particularly avoided. It endangers the superior's face and provokes conflict. When hierarchical ranks are valued as a means of signifying place and function within the organization, all its members stand to lose from this challenge to the structure, and hence resent it. If the subordinate needs to communicate a negative topic to higher levels, he overcomes this problem by resorting to informal channels — for instance by sending a message through an intermediary to whom the superior will listen.

This hierarchical communication system facilitates the implementation of routine decisions between clear-cut levels on the hierarchy when the superior's rights to decide on matters of opinion are unchallenged. But it does not favor decision-taking processes when the decision is complex and there is no general agreement on the right of the decision maker to the opinions that the decision reflects.

Japanese and American students in an American business school showed striking differences in their feedback behavior during class lectures. The Japanese initially assumed that only 'experts' should contribute comments, experiences and questions, were unwilling to assume expert status, and so said very little. But the Americans placed a premium on participation, even when their contributions added little to the topic.

3.4.2   Feedback Problems for the Cross-Cultural Manager

The power distance values associated with communicating one way down the hierarchy rather than two ways creates problems in cross-cultural situations when the cross-cultural manager comes from a narrow power distance and individualist culture. The manager is in danger of assuming from a minimal response ('Yes sir') or silence that a decision has been understood and will be implemented. The interaction between the local manager and Western guest in the foregoing example shows why this assumption may be false. But insisting on a prolonged response and discussion may merely result in confusion, embarrassment, and further silence.

The manager does not receive the feedback expected, or receives only positive feedback, and may be seriously misled.

The Anglo manager may be used to giving subordinates a minimum of background information, expecting that they will ask for whatever additional information they need. This strategy is likely to cause confusion if the manager applies it in a cross-cultural situation with members of a wide power distance culture. They are inhibited from asking: asking implies that

A British manager in Columbia was astonished by evidence of low morale in his plant, and claimed that he never received a complaint:

'I have an open-door policy. Anyone can see me at any time. And I do management by walking around. Every hour on the hour I'm out on the shop floor asking questions. But "Yes sir, no sir" is all I get.'

He should have listened to the silence and learned when it indicated assent and when a lack of understanding and dissent. Simply announcing an open-door policy does not dispel inhibitions about complaining to a foreign superior. Unfortunately, as an outsider he did not have access to the informal networks in this culture by which negative feedback is normally routed.

his or her instructions were not given sufficiently clearly the first time, and thus imply criticism; and if they do not know his or her work routines sufficiently and lack common cultural values, they have no basis from which to intuit an elaboration to the message.

When addressing a group of employees in a highly collectivist culture, do not expect critical feedback from one individual within the group; and do not ask an individual to explain back to a group of fellow workers what you have just told them. If he fails to do the job adequately, or implies criticism of yourself, he is likely to lose face. The individual's public loss of face causes general embarrassment, and lowers morale. It also reflects his lack of manners in causing you to lose face.

Time might be usefully invested in a procedure that restricts the dangers of cross-cultural breakdown:

1 Explain to the group, taking care not to demand feedback.
2 Then explain to each local-culture supervisor *in private* precisely what is wanted.
3 Then have him or her perform the operation with you to show how he or she thinks it should be handled, and along the way invite comments on how it might be improved to meet local conditions.
4 Then have him or her explain the operation to the sub-group, negotiating any modifications with them.
5 Then have him or her report back to you and discuss proposed modifications.

3.5 COMMUNICATING WHERE POWER DIFFERENCES ARE NARROW

We have seen how narrow power differences affect organizational structure. In the Anglo and Scandinavian cultures, for instance, this fact favors the development of two-way communication systems. Restrictions on who may address whom and on what topic are likely to be fewer than elsewhere, and the subordinate is correspondingly less inhibited about giving feedback.

When influence and informal power is widely traded across the organization, this leads to a disparity between supposed and actual lines of communication. One study[3] comparing English, Scottish and French factories says of the English:

> 'The patterns of communication that emerged bore no relation to the "official" communication chart. In fact there was no "official" chart, although three people showed the researcher copies of a "secret" chart. . . . [Each employee in the factory was] obliged to maintain his own network of communication for, as the most senior English interviewee put it, "One can do an enormous amount of things unofficially." '

The employee who is adept at using his unofficial networks garners a rich supply of information and may be highly productive. But in all systems determined by cultural values, a price has to be paid for the advantages offered — and in the market bureaucracies, the price paid for the heavy use made of informal two-way communication networks is a perception of confusion. It seems that official communication systems, and hence official structures, are not working efficiently.

When information is consistently transmitted down through a hierarchy, the amount of information relayed can be regulated and the significance of each message is relatively clear. But when information is coming from a range of official and unofficial networks, each member of the organization is liable to suffer from communication overload, and the significance of the information becomes ambiguous — particularly when messages contradict each other.

3.5.1 Task Urgency

In these cultures, problems arise in implementing decisions when the task is urgent and speed is essential. For instance, a fire-fighting team cannot afford to indulge in extended two-way communication on ideal fire prevention measures when the fire rages (although they may do so when back at the fire station).

A culture that resists hierarchical organization is less willing to adapt to the demands of this type of task and to the constraints that it imposes on hierarchical organization is relatively better equipped.

A supplier to racing teams in California explains the dominance of British teams (in this context more collectivist than their American equivalents):

'They run like an army . . . [there is] no time to express our opinions. We have to be very fast, people just have to listen to what they have to do and get cn with the job. American teams have more problems in these conditions. Everyone wants to offer an opinion and this makes them unstable. The British teams stick together for a longer time, they get very close. American teams are more transient. . . . [A racing team] doesn't have room for flexibility or even democracy. I don't know if that's stretching it . . . but it's more like a military operation.'

The British team works efficiently because the limitations on two-way communication are accepted, and the team refrains from giving feedback to the leader's instructions unless absolutely necessary. They have worked together for some time, and so although each task may consist of a number of stages (and appear complex to a newcomer) it has become routine.

In a military organization, the nature of the tasks and the hierarchical structure needed to perform them determine that communication is largely one-way. But even here, when urgency and accuracy in sending and receiving messages is at a premium, the underlying cultural norms may be an important influence on the communication process. A magazine article[4] describes a unit of the United States army trained to model Soviet battle strategy and provide combat training for regular US forces. The 'Russians' replicate Soviet behavior as closely as possible:

'Talk on the radio, for example, flows in only one direction — down from the commander. American units, on the other hand, have many more people talking, which can add to confusion during a battle.'

3.5.2 Feedback Problems for the Cross-Cultural Manager

The cross-cultural manager from a wide power distance culture working in a narrow power distance culture faces problems of dealing with more feedback than he or she is used to. Feedback comes when the manager does not expect it, does not invite it, and does not want it. Even routine instructions may generate lengthy communications. Informal communication networks have to be employed. Attempts to restrict the communication process to only one-way and to formal lines of control create resentment and endanger morale and efficiency.

3.6   CONDITIONS FOR SUCCESSFUL COMMUNICATION

We have seen that communication is more likely to be successful when the sender and receiver agree on the needs for one- or two-way communication and the degree of message complexity suits their needs. A range of other conditions are necessary:

1   The sender and receiver must be appropriate; the message must be transmitted at the right time in the right place and circumstances; by an appropriate channel and mode; for an appropriate reason. These sociolinguistic conditions for successful communication are dealt with in the next chapter.
2   Sender and receiver must share a common language. The range of strategies available to the manager when he or she and the other person(s) do not share a common language are dealt with in Chapters 11 and 12.
3   The message must be of common interest to the sender and those expected to implement it.
4   Access between sender and receiver must be appropriate.

The last two factors are dealt with here.

3.6.1   Common Interest

If the decision transmitted in the message is perceived by both sender and audience as a common threat or opportunity, or as a legitimate interest of the organization, they share the need to solve their problems and maximize their benefits. When there is obvious common interest in implementing a decision, the audience is motivated to participate in the communication.

Perceptions of threat and opportunity are influenced by cultural priorities. In a mixed culture group, members perceive their environment differently. They are motivated by different needs. Hence the cross-cultural manager has the job of understanding the other group's perceptions, communicating his or her own, and identifying the common interest that makes the message effective.

In order to create a sense of common interest, as a manager you may have to invest time in explaining the reasons for making a decision and why it is important, and in eliciting participation in deciding how best to implement it. (But this strategy is not effective in all situations, as we see in the next chapter.)

3.6.2   Proper Access

When the message is spoken, direct access between sender and receiver opens up opportunities for two-way communication and is almost always more efficient than indirect access. The following examples show the circumstances under which direct access works best. In each of Figures 3.5–3.9, assume that manager A wishes to communicate with subordinates B, C and D.

The double-headed arrows in Figure 3.5 indicate that A takes part in two-way communication with B, C and D, all of whom are present at the same time and who communicate among themselves. When the decision is complex and requires feedback among all persons concerned, this situation is ideal. There is a cost, which can be measured in terms of the time spent in holding the meeting at the expense of other activities.

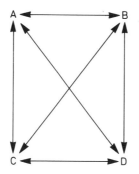

Figure 3.5

Figure 3.6 shows a pattern of restricted access. Manager A communicates directly with each of B, C and D, who give feedback but have only indirect

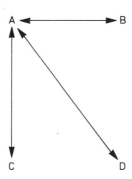

Figure 3.6

links with each other. Each communicates with the others, only through A. This pattern occurs:

- in a presentation or formal meeting, when B, C and D feel free to ask A questions but not to respond to each other;
- when A meets with B, C and D individually.

The second situation obviously saves the cost involved in bringing B, C and D together at one time; it enforces the cost of A giving the message three times.

With restricted access, each of B, C and D have less awareness of how the other two interpret the message. If they need to reach a joint understanding of A's message in order to perform a task for which they are jointly responsible, they have to reconstruct a meaning by negotiating it between themselves. Figure 3.7 models this reconstruction process, from which A is excluded.

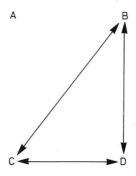

Figure 3.7

Figure 3.8 models the communication process when B, C and D do not have either the opportunity or the willingness to give feedback; one-way communication is indicated by the single-headed arrows from A. Again, B, C and D are forced to reconstruct the meaning between themselves (as in Figure 3.7); but because they have not been able to check their individual understandings with A, the likelihood of their correctly interpreting the original message is even more distant. The errors that arise from an incorrect understanding can easily cost more than the time and effort involved in developing the extensive two-way communication process shown in Figure 3.5.

In a cross-cultural situation, when manager A is from culture Y and subordinates B, C and D from culture Z, the importance of good access is fundamental. When B, C and D need to cooperate closely, A is usually best served by the two-way model in Figure 3.5. Exceptions may occur when each of B,

Figure 3.8

C and D feels inhibited from giving feedback to A in the presence of the compatriots, but not when alone with A. In these situations, A may need to communicate alone with B, make sure that the message is properly understood, and then depend upon B relaying it accurately to C and D. After communicating with C and D, B checks back with A, relaying their feedback (see Figure 3.9). B is chosen as the crucial link on the basis of his or her formal or informal leadership of C and D, and communicative competence.

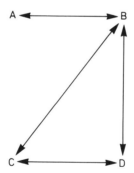

Figure 3.9

3.7 IMPLICATIONS FOR THE MANAGER

- Find out how communications systems work in the local organization and culture, and answer these questions.

  (a) Do superiors typically communicate simple and routine decisions in one-way or two-way communication?

  (b) Do superiors typically communicate complex decisions and new information in one-way or two-way communication?

(c)   How far are subordinates willing to give feedback to their superiors' decisions, (i) to comment, and (ii) to make suggestions which may have the affect of modifying the decisions?

(d)   How easily do superiors accept negative feedback? How is negative feedback sanctioned?

(e)   How easily does the organization adapt communications systems when the task is urgent?

(f)   How much attention do superiors give to making sure that subordinates understand the wording of a decision?

(g)   How much attention do superiors give to creating common interest in the implementation of a decision?

(h)   Does the superior typically communicate directly (in speech) or indirectly (via another person or in writing) when communicating (i) a simple decision, and (ii) a complex decision?

(i)   How easily do individuals with different functional specialisms communicate?

- Now answer these questions for your home culture. Where are the differences most pronounced? How do you have to adapt your usual communication priorities in order to fit with the local culture?

Developing a Diary: 1

In a cross-cultural situation, how successfully are your decisions implemented by members of the other culture? How far can the degree of success be explained by your communication techniques?

One way of checking on your techniques for communicating decisions is by writing and applying a diary.[5] This records a non-quantitative note-form analysis of your communications, as abbreviated as is practicable.

In the first place, try keeping the diary for a single week. For each single interaction in which you communicate a decision to be implemented, try to record information under the following categories:

- WITH WHOM did you communicate (how many people present, for each their rank, function and culture)?
- WHO initiated the interaction?
- WHAT channel was used (face-to-face, telephone, writing, etc.)?
- WHAT degree of simplicity/complexity was expressed in the decision, and how was this reflected in the message?
- HOW did you interact: one-way/mostly one-way/mostly two-way/two-way?
- WHEN and for HOW LONG did the interaction take place?
- WHERE did the interaction take place?
- WHY did you interact (the purpose of the interaction)?

And finally:

- HOW SUCCESSFUL was the interaction in terms of how the decision was implemented, on a scale of 1 to 10?

Apply the diary first by trying to isolate the factors that determine your success or failure in communicating decisions (as measured by the last question). For instance, you might discover that the number of people present is crucial, or that face-to-face communication is generally more effective than written communication (this would conform with much of the theory).

Remember that you need this information to meet your own needs and that you are not preparing a research report, so tailor your data gathering and analysis to these needs. That is, qualitative data may be quite adequate and you do not need to make a statistical analysis.

Second, compare your success with that of your local colleagues in the local situation. Try to persuade them to keep their own diaries, or observe and keep notes of their practice. What factors were present in their communication of decisions that differ from yours and seem to contribute to their success? What modifications do you need to make in your practice (and what modifications might you suggest that they make to theirs?)

You might also decide to investigate how much time your receivers invest outside your formal meetings in negotiating their understanding of your directions. How does this affect your communication practices?

The diary is developed in the corresponding section in Chapters 4, 6, 7 and 10.

3.8 SUMMARY

This chapter has focused on the problems of communicating a decision in cross-cultural contexts. The efficiency of the communication can be measured by the efficiency with which the decision is implemented.

Section 3.2 showed how communication systems reflect and modify the organizational structure, and how this relationship is affected by cultural priorities. Section 3.3 dealt with simple and complex messages, explained the notion of content complexity, and showed how this influences the need for feedback and two-way communication. Sections 3.4 and 3.5 discussed aspects of communicating where power distances are wide and narrow, and showed how cultural values favor the communication of different degrees of complexity in different situations. Section 3.6 introduced discussion of the conditions for successful communication, focused on common interest and appropriate access, and showed the importance of these factors to the cross-cultural manager.

Section 3.7 discussed the implications for the manager and showed the practical value of keeping a diary.

EXERCISES

Exercise 1

This exercise shows the effects of one-way communication when the task is new and complex.

The expatriate director of a small research company gave his assistant instructions for the production of a report on a campaign. He told him the wording required on the front cover. When his local assistant showed him a draft this interaction took place:

Director: 'That's a good typeface but it isn't easy to read so much information quickly.'
Assistant: 'Yes sir.'

Without further discussion the assistant took the draft away and with his secretary spent a further three days experimenting on a new layout, using the same wording. Finally, they had to admit defeat: there seemed no way they could present this same information in a format that was easier to read.

He went back to report his failure to the director. The director commented that he had not expected any further work to be done:

Director: 'That's the information and the typeface that I want. They can't read it quickly, but that can't be helped.'

Now answer these questions:

(a)   Did the director intend his first utterance ('That's a good typeface but . . .') as a comment, a question, or a direction?
(b)   How did the assistant interpret this first utterance?
(c)   Is this interaction most likely to have taken place in a local company in (i) Australia, (ii) Thailand, or (iii) Denmark? Explain your answer.

Exercise 2

This exercise practices analyzing corporate communications.

All organizations these days claim to be in favor of close communications with their employees. (Did you ever hear a top manager boast of being *against* management–employee communications?) But, asks Hari Bedi:[6]

'. . . what do they actually communicate — and to what purpose? Is it to share business problems and prospects with employees as partners, instil pride and promote enthusiasm? Is it an honest attempt to build bridges or repair one that may have snapped due to corporate "rationalization"? Or is it communication for its own sake: pulpit preaching, self-satisfied piffle?'

(a)   Take a company report or newsletter written for its employees.
(b)   How far does it meet Hari Bedi's criteria of effective corporate communication?

Does it share problems, instil pride, promote enthusiasm, build or repair bridges? Or is it merely an exercise in communication for its own sake?

(c) In particular, analyze it from the point of view of those foreign employees who do not belong to the culture represented by headquarters.

(d) How might it be improved?

NOTES

1 Weick, K.E. and Browning, L.D. (1986) Argument and narration in organizational communication. In *Yearly Review of Management* of the *Journal of Management* (eds. J.G. Hunt and J.D. Blair), **12**(2), 243–59.

2 This model is adapted from the decision model given in Micheli, L.McJ., Cespedes, F.V., Byker, D. and Raymond, T.J.C. (1984) *Managerial Communication*. Scott, Foresman and Co., Glenview, Ill., pp. 19–25.

3 Graves, D. (1979) The impact of culture upon managerial attitudes, beliefs and behaviour in England and France. In *Managerial Communication* (ed. T.D. Weinshall). Academic Press, London, pp. 250–53.

4 Robbins, J. (1988) America's Red Army, *The New York Times Magazine*, 17 April.

5 For a discussion of diaries (although not in cross-cultural situations), see Stewart, R. (1979) Diary keeping. In *Managerial Communication* (ed. T.D. Weinshall). Academic Press, London, pp. 33–54.

6 Bedi, H. (1989) Management: medium minus a message, *Asiaweek*, 24 February. Hari Bedi's weekly column is essential reading for all managers working in Asia.

4
Communicating Purpose

4.1 INTRODUCTION

A professor in an American management school made extensive use of cases for classroom discussion. He noticed that students with first-degree majors in the humanities valued the opportunity to exchange ideas and experiences, but those who had graduated from science and engineering programs said little and appeared bored. When asked why he showed so little inclination to participate, a science major commented: 'The professor knows the answer and we don't. Whatever we say is less valuable than his ideas. So why can't he just lecture us and give us the answers? That's his job.'

The professor intended the discussion as a significant teaching process, but the science student perceived it as 'time out' from 'real' teaching. People value and interpret messages differently, according to their needs and experience. In this instance, the humanities and science students had different sets of sub-cultural values which led them to different perceptions of the classroom activity.

In this chapter we focus on communicative functions. We see how situational and cultural factors influence the manager's choice of message, and the interpretation that the receiver makes of it. When the message is appropriate to the situation, its purpose is clear, and it is more likely to be persuasive.

4.2 THE MANAGER AS PERSUADER

Chapter 3 discussed the conditions necessary to successfully communicate a managerial decision. Giving directions is, however, a small part of the manager's job, so we deal here more generally with his or her functions as a communicator.

Mintzberg suggests[1] that the manager derives ten essential roles from formal authority, and classifies these under three categories:

1   INTERPERSONAL ROLES: The manager as figurehead, leader, liaison.
2   INFORMATIONAL ROLES: The manager as monitor, disseminator, spokesman.
3   DECISIONAL ROLES: the manager as entrepreneur, disturbance handler, resource allocator, negotiator.

We can associate with these roles a list of communicative skills that the manager needs in order to perform them. These skills include the following:

- transmitting instructions;
- giving directions;
- reporting;
- eliciting information and opinions;
- generating enthusiasm;
- resolving conflicts;
- motivating;
- negotiating;
- selling.

Very generally, those at the top of the list are more closely associated with the manager's interpersonal roles, those in the middle also with interpersonal roles, and those at the bottom with decisional roles.

In order to perform all of Mintzberg's roles, the manager needs to be *persuasive*. This is obvious when we consider the decisional roles of entrepreneur, negotiator, etc., when the manager is most overtly trying to persuade the other person; but he or she has as strong, though perhaps covert, needs for suasive functions when acting as figurehead and leader. In these roles the leader has the key task of selling himself as someone worth following, whose decisions are worth implementing.

In order to be persuasive the manager needs to

(a)   collect and select information appropriate to the contexts of the tasks to be performed, the situation, the needs of the persons who have to be persuaded;
(b)   use this information appropriately.

The effective communicator is skilled in *both* these functions of collecting and using information. We see below that these are interdependent.

4.2.1 Why Give Information?

In all cultures, people (almost) never give each other information for its own sake. Information is used and communicated for a purpose. The most general purpose in giving information is to persuade, and all Mintzberg's roles and our list of communicative skills associated with these roles demand suasive abilities.

If a stranger approaches me in the street and says 'I am unemployed and hungry and I have a sick wife and children', I deduce that the purpose of this information is to persuade me to give him money. If instead he says 'I am happily employed and comfortably off and my wife and children are also happy and well', I find it less easy to deduce a purpose. Unless he goes on to make his purpose explicit: 'Follow my creed and you can enjoy the same success'. I cannot reach a rational interpretation; because giving away purposeless information is a symptom of irrational behavior, I conclude that he is deranged.

Similarly, an announcement at a railway station, 'The train standing at platform four is the ten five to Brighton and leaves in five minutes', has the purpose of alerting passengers for Brighton that they should go to platform four and board the train standing there. An announcement such as 'The train that left yesterday for Brighton from platform four was driven by Tony. His wife's name is Sharlene' is grammatical and credible, but the information given has no obvious function, and so in this *particular* situation the message is irrational.

This principle applies even in casual greetings. Gossip about the family or the weather might not seem to convey useful information, but it serves the function first of maintaining a relationship. Second, it persuades the receiver that the communicator should be given attention, liked, and trusted. Your immediate priority in all management communication in all cultures, whether writing or speaking, is to build this trust.

In Mintzberg's terms, this means developing your interpersonal roles as figurehead, leader, and liaison. When you have won trust as superior (figurehead and leader), peer, or subordinate, you can go on to achieve more specific purposes in communicating associated with your informational and decisional roles.

The cross-cultural manager needs to ensure that members of the other culture understand why he or she sends a particular message, why certain information has been included and other information excluded, and why the message has been sent in the chosen mode. If they do not understand they are less likely to be persuaded. The example which opened this chapter shows members of a sub-culture (science majors) not understanding the value of information conveyed in the mode of classroom discussion.

When your priorities are obscure, your message may lose persuasiveness. This problem is illustrated by the experience of a Western agency which organized educational fairs in Hong Kong and Bangkok.

The fairs were conducted by university representatives marketing their degree courses. It became apparent that, although applicants required similar information in both situations, they were asking for very different degrees of specificity. A typical interaction at the Hong Kong fair went something like this: 'I want to study medicine. Does your university teach medicine?' Then, after being given details of available medical courses, the enquirer asked 'And what about engineering?' But at Bangkok, focused information was requested about such specialized courses as land surveying, inventory control, and aquaculture.

At first sight it seems the Chinese were requesting information when they had little intention of using it and relatively limited understanding of their own capabilities and needs. But in terms of their different contexts, each group of applicants demonstrated a real grasp of economic and educational realities.

The Chinese were looking for opportunities to study in fields that would enable them to emigrate permanently with their families before the colony was returned to the People's Republic of China in 1997. The precise field was of secondary importance. The Thais were confident of the long-term stability of their society, had every intention of returning home after study, had a sophisticated understanding of their labor market needs, and wanted training that would meet these needs. The Chinese were no less serious than the Thais, but had different priorities.

4.2.2   When is a Message Persuasive?

A message is persuasive when:

1   It takes as given (and therefore not needing lengthy repetition) the same information that the receiver takes as given.
2   It fits the receiver's values, perceptions and experiences of the world.
3   It gives appropriate detail and is perceived as relevant.
4   The style is appropriate.

We deal below with the first three points. The problem of selecting a style appropriate to the other cultural context is examined in the next chapter.

4.3   SELECTING INFORMATION

The manager selects and communicates those items of information that most effectively persuade the receiver to accept his or her point of view. When planning a message, the manager decides:

(a)   what topics to include;
(b)   what information is withheld;
(c)   how these topics are prioritized and ordered.

Criteria for selecting and withholding information, and for prioritizing topics within the message, are determined by:

- organizational norms;
- the market context;
- other environmental (economic, political) contexts;
- the cultural context; the cultural meaning of the situation.

We are concerned here with the last of these factors, the cultural context. This section gives general examples to show how culture influences the encoding and interpretation of messages, and the next section demonstrates more systematically why this influence should be so pervasive.

4.3.1   The Cultural Context

The management literature produced for the Anglo cultures places a premium on both the quantity and quality of information communicated to the subordinate.

In this cultural context, the manager is generally most effective when sharing extensive background information with the subordinate. This information

1   guides the subordinate in taking any further decisions needed in implementation;
2   increases his or her knowledge and reduces uncertainty;
3   implicitly reaffirms his or her self-worth as a human being;[2]
4   justifies the decision and the directions for implementing it: it explains why the decision has been taken and why this implementation strategy is likely to be effective.
5   satisfies the needs for open and equal access to information.
6   encourages participation and counter-proposals, which can be applied in modifications to the decision.[3]

These reasons for sharing information reflect Anglo values associated with the individual's sense of identity, narrow power distances, and the premium given to instrumental efficiency. But even in the Anglo cultures, the manager should not be over-optimistic about the motivational effects of open communication. In a crisis, open communication and participation creates confusion and may actually harm the organization.

Even within one culture, different groups with different needs and experiences respond differently to the free exchange of information. An American manufacturer tried to motivate his manual workforce by giving them background information on a proposed contract; did they think he should sign the deal? They responded with indifference, and one worker told him: 'If you want me to participate in taking your decisions, then you have to pay me more.' The introductory case makes the same point.

These two examples demonstrate variances between sub-groups (management/labor, professor/different student groups) and the variances between cultures can be even wider. For instance, the fifth and sixth of the factors listed above (needs for access, participation) are more likely to be significant in narrow power distance and individualist market bureaucracies than in wide power distance and collectivist cultures, where the decisions made by a superior are far less likely to be questioned.

In Japan the manager is expected to show concern for the personal welfare of his subordinates and may devote considerable energy to discussing all aspects of the decision with them. Pascale's data show far more face-to-face contacts between Japanese managers and subordinates than between their American subordinates and more lower-to-higher initiated communications.[3] But the total volume of communication does not significantly differ, and contrary to much written about Japanese management styles, he does not find evidence that Japanese managers consult with their subordinates more when making decisions.

Elsewhere, where collectivist values are greater, the manager may feel little cause to explain his decisions to subordinates. Motivated by their sense of obligation to the company, they have less need to question the rationale for his decisions.

In some cultural contexts, sharing information may be counter-productive. One study[4] explains why an attempt by American consultants to introduce participative management styles to a Puerto Rican factory resulted in an exodus of hourly-paid workers:

> 'Queried by researchers as to their reasons for exiting, the employees said it was apparent that their supervisors did not know what they were doing anymore, for they kept enquiring what their employees thought. Therefore the obvious conclusion was that the company must be in trouble and would soon fold.'

This shows the problems that occur when the receivers cannot understand the purpose of the information communicated. The communication process fails when it presupposes that sender and receiver share values which in fact they do not share.

4.3.2   The Focus of Detail

We now take up the need for a message to be perceived as relevant in order to persuade. A relevant message is focused at the level of detail that the receiver needs to understand it.

For instance, a financial report on last year's figures that presents a bare set of figures without explanations is inadequate for most readers, who cannot understand its significance. Similarly a report that traces the history of the company and industry back to their early history is providing unnecessary detail. Too much irrelevance compounds the problems involved in processing the message and its purpose, and this affects the receiver's attitude towards the entire report.

Needs for more or less specific or general information vary in terms of what is already known or assumed, the nature of the task, and the needs of the person involved; that is, on how much new information and repetition of old information is needed in order to achieve the function of the message.

If you want a regular business trip booked, an experienced secretary who has made just this booking for you before may need only the barest details. A new secretary on his or her first day needs much more information, even including the name of your regular travel agent. The problems of matching your perceptions of how much and what information is appropriate are particularly acute in cross-cultural situations, where the participants share fewer common reference points and less background information.

4.3.3   Withholding Information for a Purpose

Important information may be withheld because the sender mistakenly interprets the information needs of the other person. It may also be withheld through choice, and here we are concerned with this optional withholding.

The sender protects his information and restricts communication in order to protect his status and control.

In all cultures, information creates and reflects power, depending on who has it, how it is used, and to whom it is transmitted or not transmitted. The possession of confidential information has symbolic value. It distinguishes the 'ins' from the 'outs', and so whether or not you share the secret reflects your social standing. And vice versa, any information restricted to an elite is perceived to be important, perhaps even when it has little instrumental value.

When information is restricted by the elite to themselves, possession of this information gives elite status and distinguishes the 'haves'/'ins' from

A young Thai executive working in a Bangkok finance company is explaining her need to go to the United Kingdom for advanced training:

'In my company there is no in-house training. My director is an expert but he will not tell anybody what he is doing, even me. He is frightened that we are going to take his job. He's old, he has to retire in four years. Everyone respects him because he's old and he's the only one who has the information. He just likes to give orders and nobody can say anything because we don't properly understand. Even he won't help me although our managing director has asked him to. . . . When he goes the company can easily go bankrupt because we don't have his knowledge. So I have to go abroad for training and then come back and train other people.'

This story reflects the high power distances typical of Thai culture, here reinforced by the Oriental respect for age and learning. The possession of expertise is valued both for itself, its instrumental uses and its symbolic value; the expert is perceived as a 'person apart'. By refusing to divulge his professional skills, the director secures both his job and his status. He also ensures that all professional communications are predominantly one-way, since no other members of the organization have either the status or the skills to challenge him. Hence he ensures his control.

the 'have-nots'/'outs'. The Bangkok example above shows that this can be a liability within a commercial organization. It has the additional disadvantage that when subordinates have to act upon this information, they may not be given it until the last moment.

For instance, a Malaysian university department was expecting a visit from a senior American academic. The arrangements were fixed between himself and the three senior faculty members several months in advance. Within the department it was known only that a visit would occur, but all other details acquired the aura of a secret possessed only by the superiors. Clerical staff were only advised to make hotel bookings and arrange the work and entertainment program two days before the visitor arrived. This notice was too short to arrange meetings with all those in the faculty who might have benefited from talking to him. In Anglo terms, this made inefficient use of organizational resources; but in the cultural context, it signified a privileged use of significant information to reflect and enhance legitimate status, and thus to maintain social harmony. That is, an essential resource (authority) had been enhanced.

A further question arises. If the information is communicated to subordinates or outsiders so late that they cannot act upon it, the planned event may not take place and then the elite lose face. So timing the release of information for optimal effect requires fine judgement.

4.3.4   Professional Constraints on Information Flow

Bodies of knowledge develop in such a way that, by design or accident, uninitiated persons are unable to participate. The professions of law and medicine have been frequently attacked for using arcane language that in effect protects these specialized bodies of knowledge from outside understanding, and hence makes it difficult for unqualified persons to criticize or practice them. Thus their career structures are protected.

In the market bureaucracy cultures, a professional association serves to control how information is traded. It provides its members (who have passed the necessary examinations, subscribed to codes of practice, paid their dues, and otherwise proved themselves worthy to belong to this particular elite) with a closed market for trading and exploiting expert information. At the same time it prevents non-members from taking part in the trade. Hence it controls the supply and value of information, and the economic and organizational power of its members.

Similar restrictions on information flow and usage occur within the company. By using different jargons, the marketing manager, production manager, and accountant each protects his or her particular expertise (intentionally or unintentionally). Thus each protects the organizational structure through which he or she applies this expertise. The jargons used by the electronics engineer, computer programmer, and systems expert are even less likely to be comprehensible to outsiders.

4.4   THE CULTURAL MEANING OF A SITUATION

Information is formulated and interpreted in terms of its situational and cultural contexts. You need to read the situation correctly in order to establish appropriate goals and objectives, collect and apply an appropriate information bank, and argue logically on the basis of this data. Information is only communicated persuasively when it reflects these contexts in a way that the receivers perceive to be appropriate.

A verbal message is appropriate when it reflects each of these variables appropriately:

- WHO communicates the message, and TO WHOM.
- WHAT message is communicated.
- HOW the message is communicated.
- WHERE the message is communicated.

- WHEN the message is communicated.
- WHY the message is communicated.

A message is less likely to persuade when it does not reflect these variables appropriately; for instance, it is communicated to the wrong person, and/or at the wrong time, and/or in the wrong place. The appropriate context for one type of message may be entirely inappropriate for another. The importance of matching the message to the context is illustrated below, wherein the management situation is contrasted with a criminal trial. We assume a broadly Anglo cultural context, and the management situation and the trial represent sub-cultural variations.

4.4.1   WHO Communicates the Message, and TO WHOM

In all cultures, people are not equally free to communicate with each other. It is often harder for the social or professional junior to initiate a communication with the senior. In spoken communication, the person who has most freedom in initiating an interaction usually has most freedom in deciding when to end it.

In the (Anglo) *management situation*, subordinates are less restricted in initiating an interaction on a relevant topic. Even in relatively democratic offices, though, access to the manager may be controlled by the secretary, who controls the appointments book and hence the communication system. The manager delegates him or her authority to decide whether the proposed topic is work-related and merits a meeting, for how long and when.

By contrast, in the *criminal trial* hierarchical rules of who communicates with whom are strictly observed. For instance, the judge, the senior person, has wide freedom to interrupt the attorney and the witness and may address whom he or she pleases. The attorney addresses questions to the witness/accused and interrupts irrelevant answers, but seldom interrupts the judge. The witness answers questions and can only ask questions to clarify procedural matters and the questions put.

4.4.2   WHAT Message is Communicated

In the *management situation*, relevance is determined both by the function of the office and the organization, and by needs to manage personal relationships (which have almost no influence on the courtroom communication).

By contrast, rules of relevance are stricter in the *criminal trial*. The attorney is restricted in the topics that may be introduced by the facts of the case and the witness's actual or likely experience of the facts.

4.4.3   HOW the Message is Communicated

Deciding how to communicate the message means choosing the channel (spoken or written) and mode (for instance, when the selected channel is spoken, a face-to-face meeting, formal meeting, telephone conversation, etc.). Channels and modes are discussed in Chapter 5.

In the *management situation*, the organization may have rules governing choice of channel and mode, but even so these are likely to be far less rigid than in the courtroom. The manager can make use of a far wider range of modes and faces a challenge in deciding when, for instance, to make a phone call and when to invest time in relaying the same message in a face-to-face meeting. The criteria for deciding between channels and modes include non-cultural factors such as the topic, distance, numbers of addressees; and cultural factors such as the importance accorded to speed, formality, legality, ranks of seniority.

By contrast, the channel in the *criminal trial* is almost always spoken and face-to-face. Strict rules determine how the channel is used. Often, for instance, the attorney cannot ask leading questions (which presuppose the answer) and asks non-leading questions as if ignorant of the true circumstances. The witness must give precise answers to questions.

4.4.4   WHERE the Message is Communicated

In the *management situation*, Anglo cultures impose relatively few restrictions and the manager communicates business wherever the occasion permits — if not in his or her office, in someone else's office, on the shop floor, in the boardroom, the canteen, a hotel lobby, etc., or at a distance by telecommunication media. The situation of the interaction is determined by the whereabouts of the participants and the means by which they communicate as much as by the topic and activity. In the manager's office, different furniture arrangements facilitate interactions of varying formality with different numbers of other persons.

By contrast, communication in the *criminal trial* is usually restricted to the courtroom itself. The chief participants have to be present for a trial to have validity. The formality of the communicative event is represented by the physical organization of the room and the furniture.

4.4.5   WHEN the Message is Communicated

In the *management situation*, the use of telexes, telephones, etc., means that some messages may be communicated without warning at any time. Other interactions are timetabled; for instance, weekly departmental meetings, monthly board meetings, annual shareholders' meetings. These may be nearly as procedural as the courtroom case and follow precise agendas, starting with a reading and then signing of the minutes of the last meeting and finishing with discussion of any other business. Other meetings may be entirely unplanned; for instance, you discover yourself sitting in a plane next to an acquaintance who offers you a deal.

By contrast, hearings of a *criminal trial* are timetabled, sometimes months ahead. All cases follow the same basic agenda which determines when the charge is heard, evidence is given, pleas in mitigation heard, etc.

4.4.6 WHY the Message is Communicated

In the *management situation*, the superordinate purpose of an organization in the private sector is to make profits and in the public sector to provide services. We have seen that the manager communicates in order to perform the roles listed by Mintzberg and to persuade other people to a wide range of activities.

By contrast, the participants in the *criminal trial* have various responsibilities for discovering and evaluating the facts of the case. The attorney elicits information in order to persuade the court (*not* the accused or the witness, although his questions are directed at them) that his interpretation is most appropriate. The purposes of all utterances are closely tied to the superordinate purpose and rules of relevance are tightly applied.

4.4.7 What Makes Management Communication Different

In any situation you may be punished for communicating inappropriately. If the witness refuses to answer questions or persists in answering irrelevantly, he or she may be held in contempt of court and incur a fine or imprisonment. The manager who employs the wrong level of formality with a superior may lose his or her job, and inappropriate messages that fail to persuade a negotiating partner lose business.

You are punished when you break the cultural norms that constrain the communication. These examples show that different norms apply in different sub-cultures. In the management situation:

1 Formal rules are far fewer; hence the manager has fewer absolute guidelines as to what constitutes appropriate behavior.
2 The manager has to make use of varying formal and informal communication styles and to decide when each is appropriate. (The trial is always formal.)
3 Power distances vary within a single meeting or series of meetings and these variances must be interpreted accurately. (In the trial they remain constant.)

4 The manager continually juggles old and new information and new interpretations of old information. (Almost all information brought to the trial is treated as new.)

We now go on to see that the variances between cultures are even more radical. Different cultures interpret the situational variables differently, and the cross-cultural manager cannot assume that a communication appropriate within a home-culture situation is equally appropriate in some other culture.

4.5   INTERPRETING SITUATIONS IN DIFFERENT CULTURES

The situational variables (who, what, how, where, when, why) are interlinked, and a change in any one affects all others. This means, for instance, that I communicate about topic A only with Mr X, and if I want to know about topic B, I contact Ms Y. With Mr X, I talk on the telephone or face-to-face. He is not interested in my lengthy written reports on topic A, which go to Mr Z, who has very different reasons for needing the information. If I want an immediate answer then I know that I can call Mr X at home as long as it is before ten o'clock. If the matter is not so urgent then I would not bother him outside the office, and he knows by the place and time I contact him how to rate the priority of my message.

Three of the possible permutations make the point:

(a)   WHO communicates WHAT information with WHOM.
(b)   WHAT and WHY information is communicated.
(c)   WHERE and WHEN information is communicated.

Questions of *how* messages are communicated and why different channels and modes may be more appropriate in one culture than another are discussed in the next chapter.

4.5.1   Linking WHO Communicates WHAT with WHOM, in Context

In individualist and low power distance cultures, your specialization determines your professional status. The janitor minds the boiler, while the CEO takes strategy decisions and signs papers. They do not switch jobs, and because signing papers is thought to be a more significant activity than minding boilers the CEO enjoys greater social status than the janitor. This interaction between specialization and social status constrains who communicates what information to whom.

Your specialization determines your right to introduce a topic. The Anglo manager expects his communications to be delimited by the specifications of his job and the other person's and their matching areas of expertise. The marketing manager does not want to be bothered with warehousing problems and is resented if he offers the warehouse department his advice.

In collectivist and high power distance cultures, the status of the person sending the message is particularly significant in determining whether the message is considered important. Age and social position command respect and disarm criticism. This means that a senior person enjoys relative freedom in initiating a topic and that a contribution that might be perceived as 'none of his business' or 'hot air' in the West is accepted.

A South East Asian business school invited expatriate business people to address their students without specifying what topics were suitable. One British businessman was asked a number of times to give a talk. Every time he asked about the needs of his audience, he was told: 'Our students don't mind. They will be interested in anything you have to say.' It was proposed to advertise the talk as 'An interesting topic in business'.

In local terms this licence to introduce whatever topic he wished implied that his importance was such that any words he chose to utter would be appreciated, and thus expressed the height of courtesy. But to the Briton it indicated vagueness and a lack of commitment bordering on bad manners. The freedom given him complicated rather than simplified his task. Frustrated, he finally declined. The talk was never given.

Laurent shows that British and Danish managers do not expect their authority to give them authority and responsibilities outside the organization to the extent that their French and Italian colleagues do.[5] And the British manager is only responsible for activities outside the organization when he or she chooses to make the commitment (as director of a charity, chairperson of a PTA).

Differing notions of his or her social responsibility may create unforeseen problems for the cross-cultural manager. A Pakistan-based Canadian manager was approached during office hours by a cousin of one of his employees, complaining that a neighbor had cheated him over a land deal. By virtue of his status as a manager he was expected to fill a vital social function of social leadership which was not restricted to the company. He was asked to find a solution and arrange compensation.

Finally, different cultures follow different conventions in deciding what information is personal and should not be asked about. Koreans have no difficulties in asking strangers about their salaries as a means of establishing their social status. In the United Kingdom this topic is not normally appropriate unless the other person introduces it first. In the United States, job interviewees are protected from giving information related to marital status and sexual preference, and if discriminated against in the selection process for choosing not to advance these details, can sue in court.

In the Anglo countries you may ask very general questions about a business acquaintance's private life as a means of *maintaining* an ongoing relationship: 'How's the family?', 'Do you still get much gardening done?' But a collectivist West African might enquire in detail about the other person's family when *creating* the relationship. A British manager would not be thought to be speaking appropriately if within five minutes of meeting a business partner he followed this example from Sierra Leone: 'Are you married? Is your wife beautiful? How many children do you have? How many boys?' (And when informed that there was only one child the speaker expressed surprise and suggested that they should have more.)

Arabs place great importance on the privacy of their family lives, and in particular of their women folk. As a general rule, *never* ask an Arab man about his wife and other female family members.

4.5.2 Linking WHAT and WHY, in Context

Because perceptions of what is important in the environment differ between cultures, perceptions of what information constitutes 'business' and is relevant to business also differ.

For instance, job applicants in Thailand may include on their resumés details not only of college education but also of high schools and even primary schools. To the Western manager this elaboration may seem irrelevant and naive, and indicate an inability to sort out essentials — not a good qualification for the job. Primary school education is unlikely to add anything of instrumental value, and an American applying to join a New York bank might disqualify him/herself by providing this information.

But in terms of Thailand's collectivist culture and social structures in which mobility is still relatively restricted, this information serves a function. Schooling is a good indicator of social and economic position, and hence of business connections. Many Thais maintain the friendships made early at school throughout their lives, and an employer might be well advised to hire the applicant graduated from a prestigious primary school (for instance, one used by members of the royal family).

This shows how notions of relevance are determined by cultural priorities, and the manager should beware of applying his or her own standards of relevance when evaluating information.

To take a further example, creating a business relationship means giving and asking for information. In different cultures, different information serves this function. In a collectivist culture, relationship-creation may entirely ignore business topics and instead revolve around factors which in the eyes of the individualist cross-cultural manager appear irrelevant. In Latin America be prepared to discuss the local literature. Latins are proud of their literary traditions, and your interest shows courtesy. It demonstrates that you are *simpatico*, a person of refinement with whom your partner can empathize.

This apparently desultory conversation about your interests, your business experiences and contacts should not be dismissed as a Latin lack of seriousness and cannot be omitted. Your rushing too quickly into detailed discussion of the proposed deal would show bad manners and naivety of how business is done. The discussion serves the vital purpose of establishing your social credentials, business connections, and personal reliability.

Collectivist cultures maintain their cohesiveness by building and using social networks. In India, a marriage links not only two individuals but more importantly, their families. When the idea of a marriage is first mooted, each family invests energy and time in finding out about and meeting members of the other in order to decide whether their interests fit. This imposes considerable pressure on the couple and the families to make the marriage work.

If I know your social ties and your professional and business connections, then I have some idea of how far I can trust you. And if you were to cheat me, and I report your behavior around these networks, your loss of reputation effectively constrains your future activities. Where legal processes work

Similar priorities operate in Arab cultures. A British regional manager in Jordan was preparing feverishly for a visit from his London directors. His Jordanian assistant came in and announced that Mr Ibrahim Aguila, the elder brother of an assistant in the sales department, had come to visit him. His first reaction was to tell the assistant to take care of the matter himself. But the assistant showed obvious embarrassment and it became clear that the family owned considerable properties throughout the Middle East, and this would be taken as a serious insult.

So he relented and spent an agreeable but apparently purposeless hour with Mr Aguila, discussing the crops, the latter's education in the United Kingdom, and how much his younger brother appreciated working in a respected company. Business was not even mentioned, but everyone (including the assistant) felt his sense of honour satisfied. Mr Aguila was happy to have been so courteously received at such a difficult moment, and the company made a useful connection which, at a much later date, led to a very profitable deal with the Syrian government.

slowly to protect the individual's interests and where the culture avoids adversarial confrontations, a few words in the right ears more effectively secure redress for wrongs than do the courts.

4.5.3   Linking WHERE and WHEN, in Context

We know that in the more feminine cultures (as in Scandinavia) the manager gives top priority to family concerns and home life, and may be most unwilling to discuss business outside office hours. This includes taking telephone calls. Scandinavians typically start work early, by 8.0 a.m. (like the Swiss and Germans, and unlike the British who generally do not begin until 9.0 a.m.). They also expect to finish early, and at 5.0 p.m. the Norwegian may already have sat down for dinner.

Spaniards, on the other hand, often do not eat lunch much before 3.0 p.m., and dinner after 10.0 p.m.

In the highly masculine and collectivist culture of Japan there are no such restrictions on time spent with colleagues. After the normal working hours (typically 9.0 a.m. until 6.0 p.m.) colleagues regularly go out for an evening eating, drinking and singing songs in a *kara-oke* bar. This collective activity celebrates and reinforces the spirit that makes their working together successful. Subtle information and comments, which would be inappropriate within the formal confines of the office, can be freely exchanged.

American culture imposes few constraints on where and when a management message is communicated; in airport lounges, on the golf course at weekends, over dinner at home, etc. The priority is not to lose an opportunity to do a deal.

In other cultures, introducing business at any time and place normally considered inappropriate is counter-productive and may lose the deal. A British manager was taken to dinner at a New York restaurant by an American couple with whom he was considering doing business. They were joined by a second couple. It transpired that one of the wives and one of the husbands represented companies negotiating a consultancy. They discussed this throughout the meal and conversation between the other persons was impossible. In the Briton's eyes this showed a lack of consideration and he shelved his business plans.

In American terms the British distaste for talking business outside the appropriate time and place is seen as a lack of earnestness. An American remarked: 'The British aren't interested in making money. They only want to talk about their gardens.'

The British, however, expect business topics to take precedence in the workplace, and they share this perception with other Anglos. This can lead to misunderstandings in Saudi Arabia. The Westerner can easily become frustrated by being kept waiting outside the office of his Saudi client while other people shuttle in and out apparently at will. When he eventually gains access he is continually interrupted by visitors coming to pay respects and discuss family business, clerks with papers to sign, and so on. Obviously these people have nothing important to communicate and he concludes that his business is not considered worth taking seriously, or that the Saudi is so badly organized that any business conducted with him is doomed to failure. This is a serious mistake. The Saudi may be very anxious to do business, but his cultural context imposes other obligations — if he should lose the good-will and respect of his family, social and business contacts and staff, he would very quickly find his organization crumbling beneath him and his business network falling apart. In this case, however readily he agreed to a million dollar contract, it could not be enforced, to his detriment and his clients'.

A Brazilian manager may arrange to meet a prospective business partner in his office only for the purpose of making introductions, from where they immediately adjourn to a neighborhood restaurant. This is a more con-ducive setting in which to build rapport, and has the further advantage that you cannot be overheard by colleagues.

4.6   IMPLICATIONS FOR THE MANAGER

Your management communications are persuasive when they take account of the cultural context. This check-list helps you adapt your information gathering and communication techniques in order to meet the needs of the other culture.

- List and prioritize your sources of information in (1) your home culture, and (2) the other culture.

(a)   What sources of information available to you in the home culture are not available in the other culture?
(b)   How can you make up for this shortfall in sources?
(c)   What new sources are available to you in the other culture?
(d)   How do you rate the difficulties of collecting good-quality information in the other culture, in terms of convenience and time invested?
(e)   By manipulating the situational variables, how can you overcome these difficulties?

- List and prioritize areas of information that you communicate in (1) your home culture and (2) the other culture.

(a)   Who communicates this information to you in (i) the home culture, and (ii) in the other culture?

(b) To whom do you communicate this information in (i) the home culture, and (ii) in the other culture?

(c) Are there persons in the other culture to whom you are not at present communicating information and who could usefully benefit from it? If so, who, and in what topic areas?

(d) Are there persons in the other culture to whom you are at present needlessly communicating information? If so, who, and in what topic areas?

• Compare where and when you gather and communicate information in the home culture and the other culture.

(a) Are there restrictions on where you communicate in the other culture that do not apply in the home culture? If so, how can you overcome these?

(b) Does the other culture offer new opportunities for where you communicate? How can these best be exploited?

(c) Are there restrictions on when you communicate in the other culture that do not apply in the home culture? If so, how can you overcome these?

(d) Does the other culture offer new opportunities for when you can communicate? How can these best be exploited?

Developing a Diary: 2

Revise the diary started in Chapter 3 in order to take account of the new content presented in this chapter.

Chapter 3 dealt only with communicative functions needed to implement decisions and directions. Now list a range of other functions you perform using Mintzberg's roles and skills. Use the Chapter 3 categories in order to describe the context of each example. Finally, HOW PERSUASIVE was the interaction, in terms of how far did it motivate the other person to change his or her behavior and perception of the situation, on a scale of 1 to 10?

Apply the diary as in Chapter 3.

4.7 SUMMARY

Section 4.2 dealt with the importance of using information persuasively, and showed that to be persuasive it must be appropriate. Section 4.3 suggested that the Anglo norms of using information as a motivator may not be appropriate across different sub-cultures and cultures. Selected information must be focused at an appropriate level of detail, and needs for detail are partly determined by cultural perceptions of what is significant in the context. Cultural priorities may determine that some information be withheld.

Section 4.4 showed how the situational variables of WHO, WHAT, HOW, WHERE, WHEN, and WHY, have cultural meaning and how this influences the appropriacy of a management message. Section 4.5 showed how these variables assume different significances when permuted differently in different cultures.

EXERCISES

Exercise 1

This exercise shows how the factors that constrain management communication differ in your home culture and the local culture.

Choose a range of communication partners, topics, channels and models, places and settings, times, and purposes for communicating in the management situation. Answer these questions first for your home culture, then for the other culture.

It is often easiest to discover how cultural norms work by identifying the circumstances under which they do *not* apply. So try to find situations where an appropriate example (say, a topic) in one culture is inappropriate in the other.

(a)   WHEN YOU NEED TO COMMUNICATE WITH (superior/peer/subordinate/ negotiating partner/etc.)
 • What topics are appropriate?
 • What channels and modes are appropriate?
 • Where are appropriate places and settings to communicate?
 • When are appropriate times to communicate?
 • What are appropriate purposes?

(b)   WHEN YOU NEED TO COMMUNICATE ABOUT (topics)
 • Who are appropriate persons to communicate with?
 • What channels and modes are appropriate?
 • Where are appropriate places and settings to communicate?
 • When are appropriate times to communicate?
 • What are appropriate purposes?

(c)   WHEN YOU NEED TO COMMUNICATE IN A PARTICULAR WAY (channels and modes)
 • Who are appropriate persons to communicate with?
 • What topics are appropriate?
 • Where are appropriate places and settings to communicate?
 • When are appropriate times to communicate?
 • What are appropriate purposes?

(d)   WHEN YOU NEED TO COMMUNICATE IN PARTICULAR PLACES AND SETTINGS
 • Who are appropriate persons to communicate with?
 • What topics are appropriate?
 • What channels and modes are appropriate?
 • When are appropriate times to communicate?
 • What are appropriate purposes?

(e)   WHEN YOU NEED TO COMMUNICATE AT PARTICULAR TIMES
- Who are appropriate persons to communicate with?
- What topics are appropriate?
- What channels and modes are appropriate?
- Where are appropriate places and settings to communicate?
- What are appropriate purposes?

(f)   WHEN YOU HAVE PARTICULAR PURPOSES FOR COMMUNICATING
- Who are appropriate persons to communicate with?
- What topics are appropriate?
- What channels and modes are appropriate?
- Where are appropriate places and settings to communicate?
- When are appropriate times to communicate?

If you apply this comparatively to your home culture and the other culture, you have a basis for identifying how the cultural norms vary and how they affect communication style differently. How do you need to change your communication style in order to communicate appropriately and persuasively in the other culture?

Exercise 2

This exercise shows how communicative processes (in this case, reading) are differently constrained across cultures.

A Japanese letter-writer observes Japanese behavior in public transport:[6]

'Has it ever struck you as odd that adults — mostly men — read comic books on trains? Even men in suits read comics. I think comics are crude. I don't know why [these] men read them so intently.'

(a)   Use the variables WHO, WHAT, WHERE, WHEN, and WHY to explain why this phenomenon in Japan is less likely to occur in the Anglo cultures. What does the Anglo manager read on the train, and why?

(b)   What does this tell you about relative perceptions of privacy?

NOTES

1   Mintzberg, H. (1975) The manager's job: folklore and fact. *Harvard Business Review*, July–August, 4–16.
2   See Eisenberg, E.M. and Witten, M.G. (1987) Reconsidering openness in organizational communication. *Academy of Management Review*, **12**(3), 418–26.
3   Pascale, R.T. (1978) Communication and decision making across cultures: Japanese and American comparisons. *Administrative Science Quarterly*, **23**, 91–110.
4   Woodworth, W. and Nelson, R. (1980) Information in Latin American organizations: some cautions. *Management International Review*, **20**(2), 61–9 (see 63).
5   Laurent, A. (1983) The cultural diversity of Western conceptions of management. *International Studies of Management and Organization*. **XIII**(1–2), 75–96.
6   Reprinted in *Asiaweek*, 13 September 1987.

5
Channels and Modes

5.1 INTRODUCTION

A Thai civil servant was told of an inter-office memo announcing his posting to a regional office. He had not been consulted, had not seen the memo, and had strong personal reasons for not making the move. He tracked the progress of the memo to its final recipient, the director general of his department. He explained his objections and was given permission to destroy the memo and thus cancel the posting.

His British wife had previously been a civil servant in London. She pointed out three ways in which British practice differed. First, the individual would have been consulted and his or her agreement secured before the memo was released. Second, once the memo was released, it could not be canceled simply on the word of the superior. Third, the process of canceling the memo would be complicated and would require at least a second memo sent to the same recipients countermanding the first; simply destroying the piece of paper would not negate its message.

In the British government department, the norms of behavior, including communication, are more rule-governed and impersonal, regardless of the persons involved. The official memo both reflects and creates decisions and has semi-legal status. The Thai incident reflects the greater power differences. The bureaucratic superior feels free to make decisions and interpret rules very much as he or she wishes and without consulting subordinates. The Thai memo has correspondingly less legality and may be renegotiated after issue.

Here we deal with this relationship between message medium and cultural values. In different cultures, different criteria influence the choice of a channel and mode, and the choice of a particular channel and mode is interpreted. A MODE ANALYSIS MODEL is developed to assist the manager in

- selecting between modes to communicate a given message;
- planning an application of a mode;
- evaluating alternative applications of a mode.

5.2   SELECTING THE CHANNEL AND THE MODE

When encoding a message, the manager selects from three channels, each of which offers a wide range of modes. The list of modes is not comprehensive and illustrates the width of range.

CHANNELS		
Spoken	**Written**	**Pictorial**
MODES		
One-to-one	Letter	Slides
(face-to-face)	Telex/cable	Film
Small-group	Memo	TV/video
meetings	Large-circulation	Overhead projection
Presentations	publication	Photographs, graphs,
Film	Small-circulation	charts, drawings,
TV/video	report	etc., other print
Telephone	FAX	Media used in
(one-to-one/	Advertising	conjunction with
group link up)	Computer	written modes
Radio	Quantitative data	Quantitative data
Video conferences	Electronic mail	

These can be used in combinations; for instance, a written report used as input to a large group meeting, in which the speaker illustrates his points with slides, and takes questions on a one-to-one basis from members of the audience.

What are the factors that determine the selection of channel and mode? How far are these selections influenced by cultural values? How far does his or her need to communicate with minimal unnecessary ambiguity moderate the cross-cultural manager's selections? These questions are answered below.

5.2.1 Non-Cultural Factors that Influence Selection

Non-cultural factors include:

- number of receivers;
- identities and needs of receivers;
- relationship with receivers;
- complexity of the message function;
- importance of the message and need for impact;
- routine/original quality of the message;
- complexity of the language used;
- need for pictorial/quantitative data;
- function of the message (to persuade, buy/sell, etc.);
- distance: geographical location of the receiver;
- need for speed: urgency;
- need for accuracy;
- need for legal protection;
- need for receiver feedback;
- availability of communication technology;
- cost;
- precedent.

The literature devoted to business communication plays down culture. It describes the efficient use of the various modes but has less to say about criteria governing the selection of mode. It tends to reflect these Anglo communication priorities:

(a) Speed and efficiency as criteria of performance.
(b) Relatively high individualism and narrow power distances.
(c) A legalistic approach to relationships.
(d) The importance of planning the future.

But even in the Anglo cultures, this mechanistic approach to channels and modes is increasingly misleading. It presupposes command-and-control organizational models and over-simplifies the complexity of communication needs in modern organizations. It ignores the capacity of technological innovation, including information technology, to create qualitative and not merely quantitative changes in organizations.

A very different literature deals with organizational communication, where problems of change are central. Unfortunately, the psychologists and sociologists who produce it tend to operate at a relatively high level of abstraction. Modes are dealt with parenthetically. The focus is on communication strategy and few texts attempt detailed analysis of actual instances of the channel used to realize the strategy.

These two approaches might be usefully combined. Sociological and psychological models might be applied to show the relationship between function and medium and how communicative strategy determines and is modified by operational factors. But few attempts have been made in this direction.[1]

Such a literature would be well placed to go on to see how cultural priorities influence management priorities in selecting the communication mode. We deal below with some of the issues.

5.3   CULTURE, CHANNEL AND MODE

Cultural factors can vitally influence selection of the channel and the mode. For instance, it is normal in the United States to telephone a stranger with whom you want to do business:

> 'Hi, you don't know me but my name's John Doe and I'm CEO of Doe Consulting. I read today in the *Chicago Tribune* about your marketing problems and I think we have the services you need . . .'

In Japan, this direct approach would be perceived as over-aggressive and would almost certainly ruin your chances of doing business. Instead you need to find a mutual acquaintance who can vouch for your credibility and make a formal introduction. (The non-Japanese who has no Japanese business connections should seek the help of the Japanese External Trade Organization or JETRO, a Japanese Chamber of Commerce or a Japanese bank.)

That is, a mode (telephoning) appropriate within one culture (American) to perform the function of achieving an introduction is entirely inappropriate within another culture (Japanese).

Culture influences selection of channel and mode in two respects. We see here how variances across cultures are determined by

1   The values associated with the PRODUCTION of a message using a particular channel.
2   The values associated with the EFFECT of using a particular channel and mode. Effects are predicted and analyzed by MODE ANALYSIS.

5.3.1   How Cultural Values Influence Mode Selection

The selection and use of a mode is partly influenced by values associated with written and oral language. A strong oral culture has a tradition of transmitting its history, diffusing current news, and doing business by word of mouth (even though it may have a long-established written system).

The notion of an oral culture is illustrated by the image of villagers grouped around the village story-teller. This activity both reflects and reinforces collective ties. The literary cultures are often also the more individualist with more distant trade links. Modern banking procedures (including letters of credit, double-entry book-keeping, cheques) were invented in the north of Italy in order to facilitate long-distance trade. They were then massively developed in the even more individualist United Kingdom and The Netherlands in the course of imperial expansion. These procedures depend upon monetary value associated with pieces of paper inscribed, guaranteed and realized by different individuals removed in space and time who do not need to know of each other's existence.

Every modern culture (and its sub-culture expressed in management) contains the residue of the traditional culture from which it has sprung. The implication for management communication is that cultures with oral traditions are more likely to choose an oral mode where this is a viable alternative, and to depend heavily on personal contacts and word-of-mouth recommendations when developing business partners. Cultures with literary traditions still give greater priority to textual modes.

For instance, the American who hopes to start a business in Indonesia and comes armed with letters of recommendation from a prominent New York bank may be shocked to discover that these count for less than would an acquaintance with the potential partner's cousin. Conversely, the Indonesian hoping to negotiate a deal in the United States should get his paper work in order.

Second, members of oral cultures tend to construct written text as though composing oral communications. The 'oral' manager writes a report as though speaking it; the presenter of a spoken report builds in extensive verbal redundancy and repetition in order to keep reminding the listener of what has been said and where the argument is moving. A spoken message is linear in time, in the sense that the time the receiver spends in decoding the message corresponds exactly to the time spent in transmission. The sender cannot depend upon the reader's capability to move backwards and forwards in the text as he or she wishes, mentally editing it to suit particular needs.

This is illustrated by the following exchange of letters between an Australian company wishing to modify a joint venture and its Malaysian partner. The Australian letter is analytical to the point of seeming legal; the writer tries to cover all loopholes and the possibilities for feedback and two-way communication are severely restricted. There is very little redundancy. The style reflects a literary tradition. It reads in part:

'I am writing today to inform you that we are forced to modify the terms of the agreement under which we supply you with technical consultants. At present we are sending three technical experts a year, each for a period of two months, with responsibilities for

(a)   training your staff in plant operation and maintenance;
(b)   proposing modifications to plant.

While I regret the need for a revision, I believe that it is necessary in light of the strains which are now being placed on our staff by the current financial situation. Specifically, we can only guarantee two experts a year, each for a period of no more than six weeks, with corresponding modifications to their responsibilities.

While I realize that this will be as much of a disappointment to you as it is to me, I feel it most appropriate to confront the problem realistically rather than to allow us to drift into a state of under-performance which threatens to be mutually detrimental.

With all this said, I hope that we will be able to continue cordial relations and to cooperate in other aspects as fully as possible. . . .'

The Malaysian answer is made not by the managing director, to whom the original letter was addressed, but by a member of the board. He has no executive responsibilities, but as a retired diplomat greatly respected in the Malay community he carries high status:

'I consider it both a privilege and an opportunity to write to you on behalf of the *** Company. This is a privilege in that the entire board and the management staff have asked me to write asking you to continue officially supporting our development program. And I consider it an opportunity to assist in our growth and to help you make a contribution that will reflect the purpose of our national development.

As a diplomat who retired in 19 , and served in your country in 19   to 19 , I am particularly sensitive to the excellent progress that will come from our international participation. I and all other members of our company are proud of our work and your assistance. . . . We hope that you understand that our company is still developing; therefore the assistance from a leading Australian company working in the same field is invaluable. All of us still hope for your kind consideration to assist our company for further development, which is meaningful not only to individuals but also to the country as a whole. . . .'

The Malaysian letter is organized very differently from the concise, factual Australian message. It contains a high degree of redundancy and keeps returning to the same points; pride in association, the need for company and national development, the values of international links. It reflects the writer's prestige and the collective nature of the organization. It appeals on a personal basis and by ignoring the Australian's legal obligations, avoids provoking conflict.

No facts and figures are given to demonstrate the mutual benefits of the existing relationship. The sensitive and potentially face-damaging topic of the communication (the proposal to modify their relationship) is referred to only indirectly. All in all, the letter reflects an oral tradition and strong interpersonal values.

These two letters reflect very different cultural priorities. In its own terms, each is rational. In fact, the Malaysian went on to appeal to contacts within the Australian government, who were able to persuade the Australian company to revise its plans. So the strategy worked.

Two further examples underline the importance of culture in this respect.

In Muslim cultures, Arabic is revered as the language of the Koran and is held to have divine origins. It is believed to be precise and hence no useful distinction can be drawn between the dictionary definition of a word and its significance. The reader is not trained to interact with the text as in Anglo cultures, mentally editing and disputing points. He or she does not easily distinguish more or less significant points. This reverence for written texts extends to newspapers.

This is significant in education. Muslim schools rely heavily upon rote learning, and students are not encouraged to question the conventional meaning of a text. At university level, students pass examinations by learning and regurgitating set texts and notes. These students are unlikely to change their attitude to text when they take up business careers and assume responsibilities for writing and interpreting contracts.

In Chinese culture, written text is revered as the vehicle of knowledge. You show yourself disrespectful and boorish by sitting on a piece of printed paper (including newspaper) or by kicking it.

5.3.2   The Effect of Channel/Mode Selection, and Mode Analysis

Values associated with the interpersonal *effect* of choosing one channel or mode rather than another also vary across cultures.

The effects of using a particular mode are predicted and analyzed by mode analysis. This shows how the mode can be used most effectively within a given situational and cultural context. It also provides a framework for mode selection; that is, for justifying the use of a particular mode in preference to the alternatives.

The model consists of seven parameters, the first six of which are directly derived from the situational variables discussed in Chapter 4.

The parameter of EXPENSE provides a comparative tool for auditing the mode selection. No matter how skillfully you employ a mode, your skills are misplaced if another mode serves your purpose as efficiently, *all other things being equal.*

This condition is important. The more expensive mode may still be preferable when symbolic value is associated with its use within the particular cultural context, and this value is not associated with the use of alternative,

---

MODE ANALYSIS MODEL

Relationship: values associated with WHO communicates the message, and to whom
Topic: WHAT message is communicated
Message structure: HOW the message is communicated
Situation: WHERE the message is communicated
Time: WHEN the message is communicated and the speed of communication
Purpose: WHY the message is communicated
Expense:
    (a) the costs involved in the specific application, taking into account
- mode performance costs
- opportunity costs
- costs incurred by inefficient coding
- costs incurred by inefficient decoding
- needs for legal protection

    (b) the costs of other modes appropriate to communicating this message
    (c) the costs involved in using this mode when compared with the costs of using alternatives.

---

less expensive modes. This implies that the expense parameter has variable significance, which is influenced by the cultural context.

5.3.3   Applying the MODE ANALYSIS MODEL: 1

The model serves a range of functions which include:

- selecting between modes to communicate a given message;
- planning an application of a mode;
- evaluating alternative applications of a mode;
- defining the learner's needs for skills acquisition.

A simple example is used here to demonstrate the first function. The second and third are demonstrated in the next section. Skills learning is discussed in Chapter 12.

Assume that you wish to deliver a short message to an executive colleague in a neighboring office. The message is routine and it is not important that you should use a text form in order to secure legal protection. The telephone system is dependable. Your options are to

(a)   write a short note and have a messenger deliver it;

(b) telephone;
(c) deliver the message verbally, in person.

A simple application of the model provides criteria for selection. The use of each option is profiled as shown in Table 5.1.

Table 5.1

Parameter	Option (a)	Option (b)	Option (c)
Relationship	Low	Medium	High
Topic	Routine	Routine	Routine
Message structure		(analysis of the encoded forms)	
Situation	His office	Both offices	His office
Time	Low	Medium	High
Purpose	Routine	Routine	Routine
Expense	Low	Medium	High

The significant factors are RELATIONSHIP, TIME, and EXPENSE. Option (a) provides the least personal contact; the interaction is in text form only. Option (b) provides intermediate personal contact; the interaction is spoken but not face-to-face. Your travel time is saved but still time is spent in social pleasantries. The expense is correspondingly less. Option (c) costs most time, given your time taken in walking to his office and the cost to both of you of time taken in social pleasantries framing the message. This option provides the highest personal contact.

When the efficient use of time is given priority, the first option is chosen, but when maintaining personal links is most important, the third option is most desirable.

The cross-cultural manager from a collectivist culture may place a priority on good peer relationships at the expense of speed and cost, and decide to deliver the message in person. That is, personal contact and the *relationship* counts for more than time and expense in this instance. But in an efficiency-conscious individualist context, where *time* and *expense* count for more than maintaining the relationship, his courtesy may be perceived as inappropriate. The receiver interrupts other work in order to take time participating in the interaction, and the sender is perceived to be wasting his or her own time.

A further example shows an individualist manager paying more attention to time and expense, when she should have focused on her relationship with her collectivist boss.

Judith, a New Zealander, was working as a consultant for a traditional Chinese family business in Taiwan. She invested considerable time in writing memos to her manager, which she gave to his secretary for delivery. In her terms, the written form had the function of signifying that the message was substantial and deserved greater attention than would a spoken message. Also, she felt insecure about working in this new environment and wanted to avoid ambiguity. The written medium seemed to give greater protection against misunderstanding.

He never mentioned these memos, and so she redoubled her efforts, producing more of increasing complexity. But even her most urgent messages failed to receive feedback. Finally she asked the advice of a Chinese colleague.

In this cultural context, the employee has a paramount need to secure a good personal relationship with his or her employer. When she had an important message to convey she should have discussed it with him first, and only then suggest recording it in writing. First, this gives a priority to personal contact and so reflects the non-bureaucratic nature of a patron–client relationship. Second, it makes tacit acknowledgement of the wide power differences and of *his* right to decide what is important.

In his terms, the stream of written memos unsupported by personal contact seemed discourteous and suggested that she was deliberately distancing herself.

In terms of her Anglo priorities, this constituted an inefficient use of time, and she had chosen instead to invest her energies in work other than fostering a good relationship with her boss. This meant that he felt unable to trust her. Thus he delayed taking decisions on her output and responding to her memos and so, paradoxically, time was wasted rather than saved.

5.4   USING MODES APPROPRIATELY

Recognizing the effects of using a particular channel and mode within a given situational and cultural context is a communication skill. The message achieves its persuasive function only when these effects are taken into account. However, because the business communication literature is predominantly aimed at an Anglo (usually American) market, it tends to take for granted Anglo cultural constraints on acquiring and using skills.

For instance, we have seen above that members of a culture with a strong oral tradition are not naturally inclined to using the typical abbreviated 'bullet' memo. My informal research with Thai management students indicated, however, that they were receptive to the notion that different memo styles were appropriate to different audiences and relationships. Shown alternatives giving the same information, one student commented that the bullet form was suited to an American or multinational company; but that, if he used it in a family business, his father would think he was mad: 'It is too dry and cold. The [discursive alternative] is better. It is like a story . . . like talking together at dinner.'

Second, business communication texts often deal at length with teaching speed-reading techniques, including pre-reading, skimming, scanning, etc. But in any cultural context, these supposedly time-saving and high-efficiency reading techniques require considerable mental effort and are more frequently practiced inside the communications classroom than outside.

These techniques presuppose an ability to deduce and select the correct meaning of each skimmed word from a minimum of contextual clues. This selection process involves the reader in a highly interactive relationship with the text. But non-native speakers of the language lack the linguistic and cultural experience necessary to make these selections. They lack the confidence to decide their interpretation of a text on the basis of highly speculative guesswork. Applying these techniques causes particular difficulties in cultures which are conditioned to reading at the same level of intensity from the start to the end of a text.

This section shows how cross-cultural contexts have to be taken into account when planning the acquisition and application of skills. The skills needed can only be distinguished when the mode has been analyzed, and this involves applying our basic model. This application is shown by examples from two modes: spoken presentations, and telex communication.

The spoken and listening skills required in face-to-face communication are dealt with in the next two chapters. Face-to-face communication is (usually) crucial in cross-cultural relationships and merits detailed discussion.

5.4.1 Presentations

The spoken mode of the management presentation is used to perform a range of persuasive functions, including reporting, selling, or giving instructions. The presentation may be accompanied by textual and pictorial material. It involves at least one sender and one receiver; usually there are a number of receivers. The presenter uses mostly monologue, although this may be interrupted, or concluded by, a question and answer phase.

5.4.2 Applying the MODE ANALYSIS MODEL: 2

Assume that you have to plan a management presentation. The mode analysis model serves its second function of planning an application of a mode. For this function, each parameter is glossed by a list of factors, and the context determines whether and how a particular factor should apply. The lists given are exemplificatory only; they can be extended indefinitely to meet different situational, professional and cultural contexts.

FACTOR LISTS (not exhaustive)

Relationship   Speaker
Other speaker
Chairperson
Questioners from the audience
Audience
  superiors/peers/subordinates
  insiders/outsiders
  previously known to the speaker/unknown
  antagonistic/neutral/supportive
  knowledgeable/ignorant
  shared culture/different cultures
  number
  expectations and needs

Topic   Main topic (for example)
  strategy
  market opportunities
  internal reorganization

Message structure   Formal/informal presentation
Prepared/unprepared
Context of other events, presentations, etc.
Introduction by some other speaker
Question time
  supporting text
  pictorials/visual aids/etc.
Speaker's first/second language
Audience's first/second language
Rhetorical type (including):
  analytical
  problem-solving
  one-sided/two-sided
  descriptive
  argument to recommendation/vice versa
Rhetorical structure (including):
  introduction
  definition
  exemplification
  rebuttal and refutation
  cause and effect
  explanation
  conclusion

Message structure
   (*cont.*)

	Logical connectors (grammatical forms)
	Style
	Standing/sitting
Situation	Physical setting (including):
	room size
	speaker's table/podium
	sight lines
	acoustics
	Microphone
	Possibilities for speaker's movement
	Recording equipment
Time	Time of day
	Length of time available for presentation
	Length of time needed
	Context of other events
Purpose	Persuasion (including):
	to empathize with the speaker
	to believe, understand
	to perform, change/improve behavior
Expense	Costs incurred in giving the presentation (including the times of presenter and audience, and all other opportunity costs)
	Costs incurred by inefficient presenting and/or receiving
	Costs incurred by the message not being given and/or adequately understood
	Costs of other modes appropriate to communicating this message
	The comparative savings/expense involved in using a presentation relative to the alternatives.

The selections you make for any one parameter affect the others. For instance, your knowledge of your audience affects the degree of formality and the rhetorical structure you adopt: a sophisticated audience asked to accept a difficult argument is often best persuaded by a two-sided argument giving both the pros and cons, but if you are asking a group to make a non-complex decision a one-sided argument may be more appropriate.

Whether or not a period for questions is programmed influences your selection of material and argument, and how much data you can afford to omit from the main body of the presentation in the hope of working it into answers. Whether or not you have access to visual materials determines the amount of quantitative data you can use and may determine the rhetorical complexity.

5.4.3 Cross-Cultural Presentations

Where speaker and audience belong to different cultures, variable relationships between these parameters are further complicated. The lack of a common first language is clearly going to have a major influence on the rhetorical type and structure of your argument and on your needs for supporting visual and textual material. The lack of common cultural priorities and perceptions is more subtly significant. You cannot so easily estimate the characteristics of your audience and the appropriate level of formality or informality, use of humor and jokes, appeals to sentiment, conscience, reason, and so on. What balance of speech, and visual and textual material is most likely to fit their cultural priorities?

Cultural differences are most apparent during question time. The relationship between speaker and audience is very different from that during the presentation, in which the speaker delivers a monologue and controls its content. Question time gives the audience an opportunity for active vocal interaction. The speaker is forced into a new relationship with every new questioner, each of whom may introduce an experience or idea outside the speaker's competence or ask for information which he or she is unable to give.

Question time also affects relationships between different members of the audience. If the speaker is generally perceived to deal discourteously with a questioner or to answer inadequately, the individual wins sympathy from fellow audience members. When speaker and questioners are reflecting different cultural priorities, differences of opinion or emphasis are underlined within the public setting. Thus the speaker is particularly bound to follow norms of courtesy, and this means the other culture's norms.

A speaker from an individualist culture speaking to a collectivist culture group is wary of making any comment which appears to be holding an individual within that audience up to ridicule and thus causing him or her to lose face. You may also find that individuals are reticent to ask questions and so stand out from their group. If you cannot expect to be asked questions for clarification, which might be interpreted to suggest an inadequacy in your presentation and thus cause you to lose face, you are under a greater obligation to make the message clear.

Conversely, if you come from a collectivist culture and are speaking to an individualist audience, you cannot expect to get away without questions.

The authority you derive from your role as speaker is less than at home; do not be surprised by aggressive questioning.

5.4.4   Telex Communication

This example serves to illustrate the problem of deciding how and when to abbreviate the message. In the long term we can expect telex to decline in use: newer technologies including FAX give greater accuracy and are cheaper.

In the less developed countries, particularly, many firms do not yet have access to the newest technology. The growth in international trade means that the actual number of telex users and telex messages sent continues to increase. In 1985 one consulting company calculated that there were then almost two million telex users in 200 countries and that users were increasing at the rate of 10 percent a year.

Telex communication is a *writing skill* insofar as messages are conveyed in a written medium and sender and receiver can exploit neither a shared situation nor non-verbal cues when encoding and decoding. It is a *conversational skill* insofar as the sender responds to and gives feedback to earlier messages.

A telex has the advantage over a letter of being fast (but time-zone differences slow international telex communication). It has advantages over the non-FAX telephone in that it provides hard copy — and hence some protection against misinterpretation — and does not enforce the participation of receiver at an inconvenient hour: a telephone call made from New York at two in the afternoon catches the Malaysian receiver at two in the night.

Communicating by telex has the disadvantage of being relatively expensive. Messages tend to be brief; the sender cannot usually afford the luxury of creating an extensive textual context which makes meaning unambiguous. This brevity has the disadvantage that rhetorical purposes (for instance, giving advice, making a query) are often incorrectly signaled and understood. A misunderstood message can result in massive losses to the organization; at the least it generates additional expensive messages querying its meaning.

Managers attempt to overcome the cost disadvantage by resorting to grammatical and word abbreviations; for instance, ATTN for 'attention', U for 'you', PFOMNC for 'performance', SCHRG for 'surcharge', PRBLM for 'problem'. The use of abbreviations increases the dangers of misunderstanding.

For instance, the head office of a British company learnt that a department of the Peruvian government was about to invite bids on a construction project. A telex sent to its nearest local branch, in Brazil, included the following sentence:

TAKING CONSULTANTS ADVICE, SUGGEST PREPARE COSTINGS.

This might be interpreted as any of the following:

'We are taking the advice of consultants, which is that we should prepare costings.'
'We suggest that we should prepare costings which will be based on our consultants' advice.'
'We are taking the advice of consultants, which is that you should prepare costings.'
'We suggest that you prepare costings, taking into account your consultants' advice'.

Abbreviation causes misunderstandings because:

1 There is no commonly agreed set of abbreviations: use between sender and receiver is often inconsistent.
2 Telex operators fail to understand abbreviated forms and mistype them. (The business section of one international hotel chain calculates that nearly 75 percent of all telex errors arise from mistyping, and has a policy of not using abbreviations.)
3 Telex operators attempt to 'correct' abbreviations they do not understand, which produces garbled messages.
4 For purposes of security an organization may use its in-house abbreviations. A member of the organization uses these with an outsider who cannot understand them.
5 When sender and receiver speak different first languages, the likelihood of misunderstandings arising from errors, inconsistencies, and complex abbreviations is multiplied.

In order to write successful telexes at a moderate cost the manager needs to spend a considerable time in revising and editing. A good short telex is harder to write than a letter.

5.4.5   Applying the MODE ANALYSIS MODEL: 3

The MODE ANALYSIS MODEL is applied here to serve its third function, evaluating alternative applications of a mode. The examples used come from international telex messages.

EXPENSE (the cost of transmission) is very significant in determining telex use. But under what conditions is this *not* decisive in influencing message form? When is a full grammatical and vocabulary form selected in preference to an abbreviated form?

CONDITIONS FOR NOT ABBREVIATING	
Relationship	Formal Receiver not previously known to the sender Different organizations Different professions Different cultures
Topic	Complex Non-routine/new to receiver Urgent Legal/contractual
Message structure	Detailed Sender's second language Receiver's second language Complex rhetorical structure
Situation	Telex transmitted from new situation, where operators do not share the sender's first language and/or do not know the abbreviation system (e.g. in a hotel business section)
Time	Not usually significant
Purpose	Complex
Expense	Cost of transmission, not a constraint Cost of misunderstanding, a constraint.

When these conditions apply, the decisive influence of the cost of transmission declines and abbreviation is less.

5.4.6   Cross-Cultural Telexes

Two examples are used here to illustrate the mode analysis model and demonstrate how the factor of cultural difference can become a priority in determining the form of telex communication.

The first example shows the importance of RELATIONSHIP. The telex is sent by a German consultant engineer to a Filipino civil servant, whom he has not met in person:

```
FRANKFURT, 16.07.85
ATT: MR R*** V***, DIRECTOR OF THE MECHANICAL DIVISION.

DEAR SIR,
DUE TO THE POSTPONEMENT OF THE DISCUSSIONS CONCERNING THE
ELECTRIFICATION STUDY IN THE 25TH WEEK, I REGRET I AM NOT IN
A POSITION TO COME TO MANILLA IN AUGUST AS PREVIOUSLY SUG-
GESTED. I SHALL SEND MR DIPLOMAINGENIEUR K*** G***, MY AS-
SISTANT DIRECTOR, AS OUR COMPANY REPRESENTATIVE. HE IS
PERFECTLY INFORMED AS HE SUPERVISED THE PILOT STUDY.

SINCERELY,
KIND REGARDS,
H. G. D***
MANAGING DIRECTOR.
```

All the RELATIONSHIP conditions for not abbreviating the message apply. The message expresses a formal relationship and reads like a letter. Full forms are used in greeting and leave-taking. The writer explains his non-attendance and the identity of his replacement. By investing the cost of sending the letter in telex form, the sender pays the receiver a subtle compliment.

The topic conditions do not apply here; it is simple. Were the RELATIONSHIP conditions not significant, the message could be drastically reduced, for instance to the following: 'cannot visit Manilla August sending K*** G***'. The MESSAGE STRUCTURE conditions are significant in that neither sender nor receiver use the language of the telex (English) as their first language. So the possibilities for misunderstanding are reduced as far as possible and neither grammar nor vocabulary is abbreviated.

The second example comes from a telex sent to a member of the same culture group but describing a second-culture situation. The American manager of a Bangkok branch is telexing his New York headquarters:

```
TO: B D ***
FR: H M***
SJ: BANGKOK CONDITIONS

STORM LAST EVENING AND TODAY HAS PRODUCED GRAVE WEATHER
CONDITIONS. TRAVEL TO AND FROM SUKUMVIT AND KLONGTON
(plants) GETTING WORSE. EMPLOYEES ARE SHOWING UP FOR WORK.
ATTENDANCE TODAY IS 65 PERCENT AT SUKUMVIT AND 85 PCT AT
KLONGTON. FUTURE ATTENDANCE DEPENDS ON WHAT HAPPENS NEXT
TWO DAYS. TROPICAL DEPRESSION HAS EXHAUSTED, HOWEVER MANY
```

OF EMPLOYEES HOMES AND FAMILIES ARE IN FLOOD ENDANGERED
AREAS IN SURROUNDING PROVINCES.

MY RECOMMENDATION IS TO CLOSE THESE PLANTS TOMORROW, AP-
PRAISE THE SITUATION ON FRIDAY FOR FURTHER COMMITMENT. THE
TWO PRODUCTS WHERE SCHEDULES WILL BE IMPACTED ARE CAR-
TRIDGES AND DK'S. WE SHLD HAVE NO PROBLEM RECOVERING DURING
THE QUARTER.

YOUR REPLY AND COUNSEL URGENTLY REQUIRED.

RGS

Again, EXPENSE (cost of transmission) is not treated as a constraint and the message is only very lightly abbreviated. But here, none of the RELATIONSHIP conditions for abbreviating apply. The lack of abbreviation is justified by EXPENSE (cost of misunderstanding — in terms of labor relations), TOPIC and MESSAGE STRUCTURE factors. The topic is complex and is fully explained to a receiver who may have no experience of these weather conditions in a society where families are extended and the culture places a priority on protecting family interests.

This explanation justifies a detailed MESSAGE STRUCTURE, which sets out the complex reasons for the recommendation; by implication, the need to protect employees' interests and thus maintain good labor relations outweighs costs of lost production.

Also note the vocabulary items used. Terms relating to the weather conditions do not belong to the routine jargon of the business, and so the sender cannot assume that the receiver will recognize abbreviated forms.

These two examples show how the mode analysis model is used to evaluate different functions of telex messages. For reasons associated with cultural difference, neither is significantly abbreviated. In the first the sender's need to establish good cross-cultural relationships is significant. In the second the sender addresses a colleague and compatriot, but who needs to have explained local conditions and their social impact.

5.5   IMPLICATIONS FOR THE MANAGER

In your home culture and the local culture, different factors may determine your selection of the channel and the mode used to communicate a particular message.

- Be prepared to make a different selection of channel and mode in the local culture.

(a) Look for the values associated with the use of a particular channel and mode in message PRODUCTION.
(b) Look for the values associated with the EFFECTS of using a particular channel and mode.

• In what respects do (1) a strong literary tradition and (2) a strong oral tradition influence selection of channel and mode?

(a) How are these influences reflected in oral style and written style?
(b) How far is text written as though spoken?

• Use the mode analysis model to

(a) Select between channels and modes when deciding how to communicate a particular message.
(b) Plan your application of a selected mode.
(c) Evaluate alternative applications of a mode. How can you use a mode most appropriately in order to (i) communicate with a member of the local culture, and (ii) communicate about local conditions with a member of your own culture?

5.6 SUMMARY

This chapter has discussed the selection of an appropriate channel and mode to communicate a message. In Section 5.2 different channels and modes and the factors determining their selection were discussed. It is a mistake to assume that Anglo priorities in mode selection are appropriate in other cultures. Section 5.3 looked at the part played by culture in influencing both the productive values associated with using a particular channel and mode and with the effects of a selection. A MODE ANALYSIS MODEL was described with functions including:

1 selecting between modes to communicate a given message;
2 planning an application of a mode;
3 evaluating alternative applications of a mode;
4 defining the learner's needs for skills acquisitions (this is discussed in Chapter 12).

Section 5.4 discussed what is involved in using modes appropriately, and illustrated uses of the second and third functions by a framework for planning management presentations and an analysis of telex communications.

EXERCISES

Exercise 1

Examine recent written messages in which you have been involved as sender or receiver; examples are a memo, a report, a telex, a letter, or an advertisement/notice.

(a)   What essential information is conveyed by each?
(b)   Could this information have been effectively communicated using an alternative mode (spoken or written)? If YES, why was this alternative not used? If NO, why not?
(c)   If these messages were produced in a high power distance culture, would the same mode have been used in a low power distance culture where, typically, the following conditions apply:
   • subordinates prefer a consultative decision-making style which gives them some opportunities to participate;
   • peers are relatively willing to cooperate with each other?
(d)   If these messages were produced in a low power distance culture, would the same mode have been used in a high power distance culture where, typically, the following conditions apply:
   • subordinates are more willing to accept an autocratic and paternalistic decision-making style;
   • peers are relatively unwilling to trust each other?
(e)   If these messages were produced in a highly collectivist culture, would the same mode have been used in an individualist culture, where, typically, the following conditions apply:
   • individual decisions are considered better than group decisions;
   • peers are less likely to agree on important topics?
(f)   If these messages were produced in a highly individualist culture, would the same mode have been used in a collectivist culture where, typically, the following conditions apply:
   • group decisions are considered better than individual decisions;
   • peers are more likely to agree on important topics?

Exercise 2

Make notes of short spoken interactions in which you have been involved. If possible, use the notes you have written in your communications diary (see Chapters 3 and 4). For instance, use notes of a telephone conversation, a group meeting, and a one-to-one interaction.

(a)   What functions were expressed in each? How much emphasis was given to the following (express the emphasis on a scale of 1 to 5)?
   • persuading;
   • greetings and leave-taking;
   • expressing conflict;
   • resolving conflict;
   • asking for information;
   • giving information;
   • asking for opinions;
   • giving opinions.

(b)   Which of these functions could have been as well or better communicated using an alternative mode (spoken or written)? Why was this alternative not used?

(c)   If these messages were produced in a high power distance culture, would the same mode have been used in a low power distance culture where, typically, the conditions listed in Exercise 1(c) apply?

(d)   If these messages were produced in a low power distance culture, would the same mode have been used in a high power distance culture where, typically, the conditions listed in Exercise 1(d) apply?

(e)   If these messages were produced in a highly collectivist culture, would the same mode have been used in an individualist culture where, typically, the conditions listed in Exercise 1(e) apply?

(f)   If these messages were produced in a highly individualist culture, would the same mode have been used in a collectivist culture where, typically, the conditions listed in Exercise 1(f) apply?

NOTE

1   An attempt to combine these two approaches is made by Timm, P.R. (1980) *Managerial Communication: A Finger on the Pulse*. Prentice Hall, Englewood Cliffs, NJ.

6
Relationships in Face-to-Face Communication

6.1 INTRODUCTION

An Israeli engineer was invited to speak at a seminar in South Africa. All seats in the seminar hall had microphones controlled by a technician in a corner box. The speaker's microphone had yellow lights that flashed ten minutes before he or she was due to finish, and red lights four minutes before. Then at the precise moment the microphone was cut off, whether or not the speaker had finished. In practice, all speakers made a point of finishing in time.

But in one session, the Israeli wished to continue in order to lead a group discussion of the issues. He was told that this was not possible; although the schedule showed a free hour following this session, the schedule had been set and could not be changed.

The Israeli felt frustrated by his failure to establish a less formal relationship with his audience. He explained:

'They're extremely disciplined and hierarchical. That wouldn't work in Israel, we would refuse to stop talking.'

(What wouldn't work?)

'Having a guy in the corner cutting you off, a subordinate.'

(But if the culture is so hierarchical, why do senior people allow a subordinate to cut them off?)

'Because he's not making the rules, he's only enforcing them. Everyone respects the discipline, they're disciplined throughout society. This would never work in Israel. We're very democratic.'

This shows a problem in trying to communicate in one sort of relationship when social norms enforce a different sort of interaction. In this chapter, we deal with the problems of expressing management relationships across cultures. In a culture where management relationships are generally formal, trying to create less formal relationships may be counter-productive. Similarly, if you come from a formal management culture, you may need to adapt to a less formal mode when working in a normally informal culture.

We focus here on spoken communication at the micro level, and examine the expression of one-to-one relationships as a means of exerting influence. The speaker is more likely to be persuasive when he or she chooses a style that expresses the relationship with the other person appropriately.

6.2 HOW ADDRESS TERMS SIGNAL THE RELATIONSHIP

More or less formal relationships are signaled by how people address each other. Here we deal with

- address terms (e.g. first name, family name, title);
- pronoun systems (e.g. 'you', 'vous' or 'tu' in French).

Why are address terms and pronoun systems important? They reflect your relationship with the other person and help to create it. If you cease addressing your business acquaintance as Mr Smith and start calling him John, you signal a closer relationship which implies a different level of trust. Across cultures this switch may be more or less welcomed for different reasons.

In Anglo cultures, all the alternatives below are (or in recent history, have been) appropriate in different relationships. Those at the top of the list tend to imply more formal relationships, and so in most situations are more formal, and those at the bottom imply closer relationships and so are less formal. However, use differs in different cultures and sub-cultures, and so a precise ordering is not possible.

[without a name] Sir/Master/Madam (not in the US)/Maam/Miss/
    Missus/(in the UK, working-class connotations) Mister/Miz
Mr John Smith/Mrs John Smith/Mrs Ann Smith/Ms Ann Smith/Miss
    Ann Smith/Messrs Smith (for plural of Mr; in written text only)
Mr Smith/Mrs Smith/Ms Smith/Miss Smith
John Smith/Ann Smith
Smith

John/Ann
Mr John/Mrs Ann/Ms Ann/Mz Ann
man/woman/lady/boy (often derogatory in the US)/girl/[plural forms]
[nicknames] Jacko/Dimpy/etc.
[terms of endearment] Love/Honey/etc.
[family titles] Daddy/Mummy/etc.

Even in the individualist and narrow power distance Anglo cultures, the subordinate generally uses a more formal address term when speaking up to his superior than the superior uses down. For instance, at work the janitor addresses the manager as 'Mr Smith' and the manager responds with 'Charley'.

6.2.1   Address Terms Across Cultures

The cross-cultural manager cannot assume that his or her own address system is appropriate in the other culture. Some Anglo cultures pride themselves on their openness and equality in forming business relationships. The American or Australian manager may use first-name terms when meeting with a negotiating partner for the first time ('Just call me John'). But when the other culture does not share this trusting and optimistic view of human nature, approaching too quickly has an effect opposite to that described. Instead of creating closeness it generates unease and suspicion.

An American manager working in his firm's British subsidiary asked to be transferred back home. When asked why, he explained that he found his British colleagues too 'reserved'. On his first day he had made clear that he expected to be called Chuck, but after six months they still insisted on referring to him by his family name or given name, Charles. The more he tried to break through their reserve the more they seemed to resent it and keep an emotional distance, and he could not be confident of his working relationships with them.

He had adopted a wrong strategy. His attempts to break down barriers too quickly had merely fortified them. If you are working in a cultural context more formal than your own, continue to use the formal term of address until your opposite number makes it clear that first names are now appropriate. Conversely, if you have come to a less formal culture, expect your colleagues to quickly adopt first name or nickname terms. If you resist this informality, you appear to be cold and untrusting.

Second, the cross-cultural manager cannot assume that the equivalent address term is appropriate in the other culture, even where power distances are equivalent. For instance, a Thai manager may have a title and full name of Khun Paron Kesboonchoo. ('Khun' is used with both men and women and so is equivalent to all of Mr, Mrs, Miss, Ms. Paron is a male name, and so here Khun translates as Mr.) But he is known generally as Khun Paron.

The Anglo manager, who expects to be called Mr Smith or John and never Mr John, may find this odd. But no Thai would refer to his colleague as Khun Kesboonchoo and only very close associates by his first name or nickname without the title Khun.

Third, the cross-cultural manager cannot assume that a form not used in his or her home management culture is meaningless in the other culture. Anglos do not normally use family titles in the workplace, but in India the family titles 'uncle' or 'aunty' may be used to denote a client relationship with a patron who is not a member of the immediate family. The young executive who announces that he is going to make a complaint to 'uncle', who happens to be the CEO, is demonstrating both his status within a patronage network and his informal power in relation to third parties who do not belong to the network.

A young Indian may be brought up to use these terms for all friends of the parents. However, precise titles are used to denote family relationships. One Indian executive commented: 'When I first came to the United States, I was amazed how Americans call even their distant cousins uncle and aunt.'

6.2.2   Formality and Situation

How we address each other also depends on the situation. In different situations we use different terms to address the same person.

In the Anglo cultures, address terms can vary widely between the same two persons, in different situations. For instance, in the workplace the manager and janitor choose terms that signal their power difference. The manager addresses 'John' and the janitor replies to 'Mr Brown'. But suppose that they belong to the same social club or worship at the same church; in that context, where they enjoy equal status, they are more likely to use a less formal differential: 'John' and 'David'. This reflects the fact that, in these cultures, status and power earned within the workplace does not apply outside (compared, for instance, with France).

A reasonably open Anglo company might accept a secretarial assistant greeting a boss by first name and introducing the topic of conversation — perhaps even a non-work related topic. But in a culture where power differences are much greater, the junior might never start a casual conversation. The following is far more likely to occur in a Western office on a Monday morning than in a Taiwanese office between Chinese boss and assistant:

Assistant: 'Hi Jess, how was the golf?'
Boss: 'Awful.'

But even in the West, would a secretarial assistant greet the CEO so casually? A new boss? The head of state? At what point would he or she substitute 'Good morning, Sir'? And how would the choice of greeting be affected by the presence of other people?

In the Anglo office, the manager and assistant of opposite sexes sometimes use pet names which are otherwise associated with an intimate relationship. But even when it occurs this use does not extend to outsiders. An American secretary writes to a syndicated agony column:[1]

> 'Currently, I work in a professional office where clients, whom I call Mr, Mrs, Sir, Ma'am, or by their names, occasionally call me 'Honey' — but only once. They are told, either by me or by my superior, that I will not tolerate such familiarity. They may be annoyed momentarily, but they never have to be told twice, and I usually get an apology.
>
> Pet names belong only between the closest friends and family. Please tell all those people who claim it's "just a habit", and have conned themselves into thinking it's cute or more informal, that it is nothing of the kind. It's extremely presumptuous and offensive, and they should not be surprised when someone is annoyed by it.'

The Anglo cultures are this flexible in their use of address terms because different areas of activity tend to be treated as distinct, and superiority in one area probably does not translate into another. In cultures where authority in the work place does apply in non-work activities, the address differential is more likely maintained.

The cross-cultural manager working in an Anglo culture learns to adjust to its address norms, but this does not mean that he wishes to continue them when back home.

Hiroki Kato explains[2] that a Japanese businessman who has learned American ways may ask his American colleague to call him by his first name or nickname when in the United States. But it makes him acutely uncomfortable if you use the same form of address in Japan, particularly when he is surrounded by colleagues:

> 'The usual expectation of the Japanese is that everyone calls everyone else by their last name plus '-san', '-sensi', or by their title (e.g. Kacho, 'section chief').
>
> It made an interesting news item in Japan when then Prime Minister Nakasone reportedly mentioned that he dealt with President Reagan on a first-name basis and termed the two men's relationship as the "Ron–Yasu Relationship". (The Prime Minister's first name is Yasuhiro.) The fact remains, however, that no one, including his cabinet ministers, ever called him by his first name in Japan.'

In Japan, rules of status apply even to relationships between business partners. Buyers are assumed to have greater importance than sellers, and a seller says 'onsha' (your great company) whereas the buyer replies 'otaku' (your company).

6.2.3 Pronoun Systems

Modern English uses second person 'you' to denote both singular and plural, and it is neutral as regards the relationship between speaker and addressee. (A possible exception may be the Southern United States form 'you all' abbreviated to 'y'all', which can be used with either singular or plural audience and indicates the speaker's solidarity.)

In other languages, the selection of second person pronoun serves the same function as the address term. Where the language offers two alternatives, the plural form may be used to address one person. Whether you use singular or plural form is determined by the receiver's sex, age, superiority/inferiority to yourself, and the closeness or distance of the relationship.[3] In French, the singular form 'tu' is intimate, and when addressing even one person with whom you are not on intimate terms, use the polite form, plural 'vous'. Equivalents in Spanish are 'usted' and 'tu', and in German 'sie' and 'du'.

Many oriental languages have even more complex systems. Japanese has fourteen synonyms for 'you', and the appropriate choice depends on the other person's sex, age, occupation, social and professional status.

6.3 EXPRESSING THE RELATIONSHIP

The new British manager of a Brazilian subsidiary arranged a first meeting with his senior staff. He discussed aims, congratulated them on their work, then said that he could already see the evidence of their determination to further improve productivity by the stack of reports on his desk. 'It seems you want me to take all the decisions around here. If this goes on I can see that I'm not going to see much of my family at weekends.' His audience laughed politely. The meeting broke up in a mood of good humor.

Two weeks later, the mood had changed. He complained bitterly that still too many minor decisions were coming to him. He had hoped by now to see some signs that routine problems were being resolved at lower levels. Why had nothing been done to prioritize decision-making processes?

The local managers were aghast. If this was what he had wanted why had he not made it clear? Of course the issue had been raised before, but in the form of a joke. Because it was accompanied by humor and a reference to his family needs, they had not taken it seriously. His style in making an important announcement had been inappropriate.

This section looks at the problem of style in spoken communication, and how it is expressed.

A formal style creates a sense of power and authority, but at the same time it marks the speaker as more committed to the topic than to the relationship, and creates emotional distance between him or her and the hearer. An informal and casual style down-plays authority and distances the speaker from the topic, but has the effect of making a closer relationship. The example above showed an important message misinterpreted because it came in the form of a joke.

Which style you use depends on

- who you are addressing;
- how you wish the other person to react;
- the cultural context — in this context, what style is most appropriate?

6.3.1 Style and Relationship

You create a closer relationship with the other person by using expressions of concern and admiration, a similarity in experience and needs, sympathy and understanding, and common views.

Assume that in a neutral situation in an Anglo culture, your boss asks about your weekend golf, then goes on to joke about his own poor performance. You interpret this choice of a non-task related topic and his self-disclosure and humor as an expression of personal interest and perhaps a willingness to create a closer relationship.

The subordinate does not expect to be called to his boss's office (which is a relatively formal and non-neutral situation) in order to talk only about golf, although this topic may serve to reduce the distance between them before moving on to the main topic.

The superior generally has greater freedom in deciding what topic is appropriate. In the office, a business-related topic conveys an impression of authority, reflects his or her power, and shows that the speaker has a clear objective in communicating. A change in the relationship towards a closer tie generally has to be initiated by the higher status person.

Style varies according to the situation. The manager adopts a more formal and distant style when addressing the same colleague in the board meeting than on the golf course, perhaps when communicating the same information. Whether or not other people are present may also affect style.

This means that if you wish to modify your relationship with a subordinate by changing the communicative style, make sure the style is appropriate to the situation.

6.3.2 Expressing Power by Direct and Indirect Requests

A powerful style reflects and helps assert wide power distances when the speaker is perceived to have the authority to enforce his or her will in this particular situation. A powerful style is direct, as in this example:

(a) Supervisor: 'Please complete this project by Friday.'
     Employee: 'Sure.'

In a flatter, more 'democratic' organization, the supervisor may feel it necessary to explain why the directive is justified, and a more indirect style is appropriate:[4]

(b) Supervisor: 'Working on anything interesting now?'
     Employee: 'Not really.'
     Supervisor: 'Would you like to take on a project for me then?'
     Employee: 'Sure.'

In (a) the supervisor is much more committed to the project than in (b), and hence much more likely to lose face if the employee refuses the job. If the organization is hierarchical, the employee is far less likely to refuse it, and perhaps can do so only at risk to his job. In (b) the employee can refuse and the supervisor does not lose face. Now consider:

(c) Supervisor: 'Working on anything interesting now?'
     Employee: 'Yup, they sure keep us busy.'
     Supervisor: 'That's good, we like to keep you challenged.'

The direct style is as inappropriate in the democratic situation as the indirect style is in the hierarchical style. The imperative leaves the 'democratic' employee feeling bruised: 'Why can't he ask me politely?' The indirect form leaves the 'hierarchical' employee with the feeling that the supervisor is weak and indecisive: 'If he wants me to do a job why can't he come out and say it?'

In an Anglo culture where organizations are flatter, giving a reason for a request seems more likely to win compliance. For example, when interrupting a colleague at the photocopier, the first request below stands a better chance of success:[5]

'Excuse me, I have five pages. May I use the machine because I'm in a rush?'
'Excuse me I have five pages. May I use the machine?'

The clauses 'Excuse me, I have five pages' and '. . . because I'm in a rush' *frame* the core request 'May I use the machine'. In different situations and cultural contexts framing is more or less needed to signal politeness and avoid sounding peremptory.

In a wide power distance context, the relative statuses of the sender and receiver play the major part in determining whether a request is successful. This means that the superior may need to use little or no framing, and excessive framing sounds apologetic and causes him to appear weak or insincere. The subordinate uses more convincing frames, or risks being perceived as impertinent.

6.3.3 Expressing Distance and Closeness

The first in each pair of adjectives below expresses a more distant relationship but also carries greater credibility and effectiveness. The second in each pair expresses a more casual style and reflects a closer relationship:

(a) non-abbreviated/abbreviated style;
(b) self-monitored/casual style;
(c) elaborated/simple grammar.

These are dealt with below.

6.3.4 Non-Abbreviated/Abbreviated Style

In a formal relationship, where sender and receiver are separated by power distances and/or a distant personal relationship, the speaker uses more complete forms, even when shared understanding of the context makes the full form redundant. Assume that the assistant is on his first day at work for a much older manager:

Assistant: 'Excuse me sir, do you want to take this telephone call?'
Manager: 'No I'm busy. Could you take a message please.'
Assistant 'Yes sir.'

In a wide power distance culture when complete forms are associated with politeness and formality, the subordinate is under particular constraints to use complete forms when addressing a superior. In a less formal context an abbreviated form is appropriate:

Assistant: 'Telephone?'
Manager: 'I'm busy.'
Assistant: 'Okay.'

Abbreviation also takes place at the word level. 'It's' for 'it is', 'can't' for 'cannot', 'rep' for 'reputation' all reflect informal contexts.

6.3.5 Self-Monitored/Casual Style

The speaker conveys authority when he or she seems to be choosing the words with care. The speaker monitors the message and speaks clearly. Immediacy also conveys power, and is expressed by personal reference to what he or she wants done. Personal reference is more effective when it appears earlier rather than later in the message. Probability ('X will happen') is more powerful than possibility ('X may happen').

A casual style indicates a closer relationship with the receiver but may also signal less control over the content. Extreme forms may suggest the speaker's uncertainty and even powerlessness. These features typify a casual style and are generally not appropriate in formal situations:

(a)   slurring and running words into each other, and a lack of pausing;
(b)   overuse of intensifiers — 'very', 'totally', etc.;
(c)   empty modifiers — 'kinda/kind of', 'sorta/sort of', etc.;
(d)   empty adjectives — 'cute', 'super'.

Anglos, in particular Americans, favor hyperbolic forms to give emphasis: 'I love those people', 'I hate it', 'I'm going to kill Bruce'. But these forms can lead to considerable confusion if used with Orientals not used to this style. Most Oriental cultures avoid these hyperbolic extremes in casual conversation and these forms may be taken literally.

6.3.6   Elaborated/Simple Grammar

In English, hyper-correct grammar conveys authority within a formal context, but in an informal context sounds inappropriate, and fails to exert the power that the speaker obviously wants. Hyper-correct forms include:

(a)   super-polite forms — 'Would you be so kind as to close the window please';
(b)   grammatical forms suited to written rather than spoken modes — '. . . to whom I wrote' as opposed to '. . . whom I wrote to', or even the strictly inaccurate '. . . who I wrote to';
(c)   elaborated verbal forms — 'I would have gone if I had been able' as opposed to 'I would have gone if I could'.

The use of elaborated verbal forms offers the competent speaker a wide range of varieties in expression, and it typifies educated English. This style is sometimes difficult to handle. But although English modal forms ('can', 'might', etc.) tend to be more complex than in some Asian languages, for instance, where even future and past time markers are not always compulsory, they are considerably less complex than in Portuguese and Spanish. These languages have a far wider range of subjunctive expressions (expressing wishes, hopes, uncertainties, under different conditions) which are regularly used even in informal contexts.

6.3.7   Style and Culture

Stylistic differences are often associated with culture groups, and groups tend to stereotype each other in terms of their spoken style. Many Americans perceive British spoken style as over-formal, whereas the British may think American speech over-casual and think this reflects their behavior.

New Yorkers are perceived to be 'pushy' because they produce utterances which overlap with utterances produced by the other speaker and do not appear to wait to hear what is being said. For instance:

George: 'John changed his schedule again and I thought that explains a lot | about him.'
Bill: | 'What, that he works different from the others or thinks he's | smarter or more important, or something?'
George: | 'It's not smarter or more important, it's different priorities.'

Bill interrupts George, and is interrupted in turn.

Overlapping shows that you are listening. But members of cultures educated to think that only one person should speak at a time find this difficult to handle. Tannen[6] comments on data of interactions produced by speakers who overlapped their utterances and speakers who did not:

> '. . . when an overlap-avoiding speaker began to speak to show listenership, an overlap-avoiding speaker interpreted this as an interruption and stopped talking. The irony is that from the point of view of the culturally different speakers, each one thought the other created the interruption: the overlap-avoiding speaker thought the overlapper intended to interrupt, but the cooperative overlapper cannot understand why the speaker interrupted himself by stopping.'

Similarly, many Asians perceive Anglos to be aggressive because they ask too many questions in a machine-gun style. And Anglos think that the Indian's laughter when a potentially embarrassing subject is broached indicates lack of seriousness.

These stereotypes of style are particularly damaging because they are usually formed unconsciously and so are difficult to recognize and uproot. The cross-cultural manager needs to recognize when the speaker's stylistic choices reflect cultural priorities rather than decisions about the relationship.

In general, the cross-cultural manager should use the more formal or distant address form and style. Only switch to a less formal and less distant style with peers when the other person indicates that this is acceptable. Switching prematurely may be interpreted as presumptuous and 'pushy'.

6.4   HOW THE TOPIC IS DEVELOPED

How you develop your point of view significantly reflects your perceptions of your relationship with the other person, and modifies that relationship. We deal with topic development here in terms of

- tight/loose development;
- argument/narrative.

6.4.1 Tight/Loose Development

How a speaker develops a topic is clearest in a monologue presentation. The presentation speaker creates a sense of authority and control by moving through the topic point by point, making clear that it has been planned and signposted at each stage ('That's all I have to say about X; I now want to move on to Y.') The speaker who slides between points and gives the impression of developing the ideas as he or she goes along conveys less authority, but may create a sense of informal closeness.

The same applies in face-to-face interaction. If an agenda is prepared for a meeting, this shows that it is expected to be more formal. When the chairperson uses the agenda items to impose structure on the interactions, he or she gives the meeting a sense of direction and formality, but at the expense of inhibiting unstructured brainstorming.

In an informal meeting, the development of ideas is looser and the style more casual. The direction is less obviously planned. The participants brainstorm with little concern for tight cohesion. They shift between different topics and make frequent side sequences, departing from the primary topic to a secondary topic, then back to the primary topic.[7] For instance:

Manager: 'Have Registration said anything about the income file yet?'
Assistant: 'Yes, Jonah phoned after lunch. By the way, they need another programmer.'
Manager: 'Again? I'll see who we've got.'
Assistant: 'Yes, the new one has to relocate. Anyhow, they want some clarification on the resale figures . . .'

In this example, the move out to the side sequence is marked by 'By the way . . .', which suggests a lack of formal planning, and the move back by 'Anyhow . . .'.

Side sequences also occur in monologues. The presentation speaker uses them in order to introduce a relaxed mood and to 'soft-sell' an idea. But too many side-sequences risk confusing or frustrating the receiver who wants direction in the interaction.

In a cross-cultural context, the manager should be careful of shifting topics and using side sequences. When members of the other culture use the language only as a second language, non-linear topic development can be very confusing, even when topic shifts and side sequences are heavily marked.

6.4.2 Arguing the Point

Efficient planning, control, and decision making depends upon rational thinking directed to mapping out the future. Until recently it was generally accepted that this thinking process is best communicated by a rational, logical argument.

A logical argument makes a claim, that such-and-such is true or ought to be done. This claim is expressed by a 'therefore' statement. In order to justify this 'therefore', the argument also presents a 'given' statement, which provides factual support, and a 'since' statement,[8] which explains the relationship between the 'given' and the 'therefore'. Here are two examples.

GIVEN:	SINCE:	THEREFORE:
By innovating, our competitors have increased their market share.	This demonstrates the value of innovating.	We should also innovate.

The 'since' statement here justifies the relationship between 'given' and 'therefore' by emphasizing the general value of the 'given'.

GIVEN:	SINCE:	THEREFORE:
Advertising rates have increased by 10 percent.	Higher rates increase our sales costs.	We should increase prices.

The 'since' statement here shows the cause and effect relationship between the 'given' and 'therefore'.

This form of verbal logic can become complicated, using other types of 'sinces' including 'unless' statements, and replicated throughout the argument. Similar relationships between 'givens', 'sinces', and 'therefores' are then created between sub-topics and topics.

A logical argument provides clear and persuasive justification for adopting a particular interpretation or policy. It reflects Western intellectual traditions of precise, scientific detachment, and appeals to an abstract sense of reason existing outside the relationship between the speaker and hearer. Thus it has the effect of establishing the distance between them. It is potentially divisive; the speaker is concerned with winning an argument, and this implies a possibility of conflict. However logical the argument presented, therefore, it is not persuasive when the hearer places a priority on a close relationship.

The Western cross-cultural manager cannot depend over-much on this form of logic when working in a culture where decision-making processes are based more on intuition and emotion as in Japan and Korea, and where members of the group are searching for consensus that unites them in a relationship rather than around an abstract idea, and so minimizes personal conflict.

Contrarily, the non-Western cross-cultural manager working in a Western scientific culture is liable to experience problems in adjusting away from his or her usual techniques of controlling and persuading. Appeals to emotion may not only fail, but create a resistance which damages relationships in the future.

6.4.3   Narration as a Form of Argument

A Canadian company was considering erecting a late-night entertainment center in a middle-class suburb. When plans were discussed in a board meeting, a fierce dispute broke out over whether much resistance could be expected from local residents. Figures produced by a marketing analyst could be interpreted ambiguously. Eventually an American board member described the history of the Chicago Cubs' move to introduce late play to the Wrigley Field ball-park and the unexpected opposition.

This use of narration rescued the argument from the logical *cul de sac* where it was stuck. The analogy did not fit precisely, as supporters of the scheme pointed out; but it threw the whole problem into a different light, the sense of nose-to-nose conflict lifted, and the board reached a decision.

Using narration as a means of argument includes using analogy and metaphor. It means reinterpreting basic human characteristics and appeals to a common sense of values and social coherence. It provides guidelines for action when insufficient data are available and logical argument is inadequate.

Narrative and analogous argument is a traditional form of reasoning, and the cross-cultural manager experiences it in societies where oral traditions are still strong. Chapter 5 gave an example of a Malaysian letter which included narrative elements used to avoid conflict, and showed how it differed from the 'logical' Australian letter to which it responded.

Analogous and non-logical reasoning is also a powerful tool in Western organizations, and new thinking on management communication indicates that its importance as a primary means of creating organizational coherence should be more widely recognized. Weick and Browning writes:[9]

> 'The implied advice for managers who try to solve problems is that, when they try to be rational, they may overemphasize logic and forget that there are multiple logics and multiple rationalities and that stories incorporate much of what argument leaves out. If the manager can argue logically with facts and then cover the same points using stories that ring true and hold together, then he or she has understood the issue more thoroughly.'

The cross-cultural manager similarly uses both analogous and logical arguments, balancing them to appeal most effectively to the other-culture receivers.

6.4.4   Proverbs

Among educated people in Anglo cultures, it is seldom considered sophisticated to use proverbs and maxims; no British business person says 'A stitch in time saves nine' in order to explain a renovation policy, for instance. In general, the cross-cultural manager working in an Anglo culture should avoid them. But in Oriental cultures, proverbs are quoted frequently. The Westerner can use those from his or her own culture (but be prepared to explain them), and better yet, show your empathy by citing proverbs from the host culture. For instance:[10]

- from Burma, 'A man can practice virtue only when his stomach is full' — which seems to support Maslow's hierarchy of needs.
- from Thailand, 'Aim at a definite end' — the value of management by objectives.
- from Vietnam, 'Force binds for a time; education binds forever' — applicable to McGregor's theory X and theory Y.
- from the Philippines, 'The prompt man beats the industrious one.'

6.5   LISTENING

This chapter deals with communication at the micro level of style. The features discussed operate very subtly to express power and solidarity relationships, and degrees of formality and informality. They reflect cultural perceptions about social status and responsibility.

A member of the other culture does not share your perceptions and so does not respond in the same way as do members of your culture to the stylistic features that you use. And he or she does not produce the same stylistic features with the same meanings in the same contexts. These differences create difficulties in cross-cultural communication. The cross-cultural manager needs to cultivate communication skills at a more sophisticated level than might be necessary when interacting within his or her own culture.

An effective communicator encodes and sends appropriate messages that are persuasive to the receiver. He or she *also* has to be efficient in decoding and receiving messages; if you cannot decode efficiently, you cannot give good feedback. In order to produce messages that the receiver can understand, the cross-cultural manager has to facilitate that person's listening; and in turn, to decode and understand messages coming back, he or she has to develop listening skills.

A good listener develops the following habits:

1 Adopt an inquiring attitude. The other person is telling you something he or she perceives to be of interest.
2 Evaluate the meaning of the words. Even when different cultures use the same first language, the same words have different meanings.
3 Evaluate the use of stylistic devices, including ambiguity.
4 Listen for what is *not* said; that is, for what the sender thinks is so obvious as to be redundant or what is so new as to be outside his or her experience. This means processing the message in terms of the differences between your and the speaker's personal and cultural priorities.
5 Ask questions to check your understanding.
6 Give feedback based on the message and to check mutual understanding. If necessary, paraphrase the message in your feedback.
7 Do not jump to conclusions; listen for the whole message.
8 Give yourself time to think before replying. Make clear when you are adopting listening and speaking roles, and make the shift between roles clean-cut.

Remember that the other person has the same problems recognizing your cultural priorities and how they are expressed in the communication. Facilitate his or her listening so far as you can:

(a) Speak slowly and carefully when using your language. You cannot make a non-native speaker understand by shouting.
(b) So far as possible, avoid idioms, slang, metaphors, jargon.
(c) If necessary, explain complex words, but make clear that you are giving an explanation and not presenting an alternative message or adding a qualification.
(d) Use stylistic devices that are appropriate in the situational and cultural contexts (e.g. a declarative request rather than an imperative form); but keep them simple.
(e) Check that you are being understood as you go along.
(f) You may have to spell out the message and its purpose more clearly than you would with a member of your own culture, who could be expected to pick up the clues. So be prepared to explain not only WHAT you want done and WHAT you think important, but WHY you want it done and WHY it is important.
(g) Make clear those features in the context that demonstrate your purpose.

Bad listening was shown by the American manager of a British subsidiary. He had the habit of assessing the communications of his British subordinates on the basis of the first few words he heard and interrupting to answer within these terms. This meant that he often missed the important, new information that the speaker might have packaged at the end. His interruptions were perceived as aggressive and the faulty communication generated both resentment and expensive misunderstandings.

Listening is often assumed to be an automatic skill synonymous with hearing. This is a false assumption. Developing effective listening skills is particularly important when you or the other receivers are using a second language.

At first, this communicative elaboration may not seem easy or natural. This is a small price to pay when measured against the costs in terms of human relations, management efficiency, and profits that may be incurred by a communications breakdown. As your relationship develops and each of you learns to recognize the other's personal and cultural priorities, you will know when to drop the elaboration.

6.6   IMPLICATIONS FOR THE MANAGER

In a cross-cultural setting the manager needs to develop skills of recognizing how relationships are expressed in face-to-face communication.

- In the other culture, how are formal relationships signaled in spoken communication? How are informal relationships signaled?
(a)   Compare address terms used with superiors/peers/subordinates.
(b)   In what situation are more or less formal terms used to address the same people?

- For what communicative purposes does the superior adopt a more *formal* style when addressing subordinates? When does he or she need to communicate authority and distance? How is this formality expressed in spoken language?

- For what communicative purposes does the superior adopt a *casual* and *less formal* style when addressing subordinates?
(a)   When does he or she need to communicate relaxed authority and closeness?
(b)   How is this informality expressed in spoken language?

- For what communicative purposes does the subordinate adopt a more *formal* style when addressing superiors? When does he or she need to communicate acceptance of authority? How is this formality expressed in spoken language?

- For what communicative purposes does the subordinate adopt a *casual* and *less formal* style when addressing superiors?

(a)   When does he or she need to communicate closeness?

(b)   How is this informality expressed in spoken language?

- The cross-cultural manager needs to recognize when different types of topic development are appropriate.

(a)   In what situations is a tight topic development more appropriate? When is a loose topic development better?

(b)   In what situations is logical argument an appropriate way of persuading other people? When is a narrative style more appropriate?

- Develop the listening skills described in section 6.4.5.

Developing a Diary: 3

Develop the diary started in Chapters 3 and 4. Take notes of how you and members of the other culture express and create relationships. Pay attention to levels of formality/informality, authority, distance/closeness as expressed in

(a)   address forms;

(b)   style;

(c)   topic and argument development.

Apply this information as in Chapters 3 and 4.

6.7   SUMMARY

This chapter has discussed ways of expressing and creating relationships in face-to-face communication. It has dealt with formal and informal/casual styles of communicating. Formal styles convey authority but distance the speaker from the other person. Informal styles form and recreate closer relationships but convey relaxed authority and confidence.

Section 6.2 showed the importance of address terms in signaling the relationship. These differ according to the person and the situation, and vary across cultures. Section 6.3 showed how stylistic features express relationships. Section 6.4 dealt with topic development and showed how different forms may be more or less appropriate according to the context. Section 6.5 looked at the importance of listening skills.

EXERCISES

Exercise 1

This exercise examines the factors which determine the appropriate term of address.
  In your culture, what terms of address do the following use in these situations? If there is more than one alternative, what factors determine the selection?

(a) The CEO and clerk meet outside the office elevator. How might the CEO appropriately address the clerk?
    Mr John/John/John Smith/Mr Smith/Smith/Sir
(b) In this situation how might the clerk address the CEO?
    Mr Herb/Herb/Herb Miller/Mr Miller/Miller/Sir
(c) The CEO calls a middle-ranking executive to his office in order to congratulate him. Which does he choose?
    Mr Peter/Peter/Peter Fogg/Mr Fogg/Fogg/Sir
(d) How does the executive reply?
(e) The CEO calls the same executive to his office in order to reprimand him. Which does he choose now?
(f) How does the executive reply?

In these other situations, assume the same people meet and discuss topics unrelated to business. What address terms do they use now?

• at the office party;
• at the golf club;
• in the supermarket.

Answer these questions for some other culture that you know. If there are differences, why?

Exercise 2

This exercise looks at factors determining how topics are selected and developed appropriately.
  You have recently moved to your branch in the Kingdom of Darana to work as executive assistant to the managing director. He and all other members of staff are local Daranese. For each of these situations, decide whether local behavior is appropriate or inappropriate in terms of *your* culture, and why.

(a) On your first day, your boss (whom you have only met once before, at the airport on arrival) walks into your office unannounced, sits down, and asks how you and your family are settling in. You tell him everything is fine. You then suggest discussing your responsibilities. He looks surprised, says there is plenty of time for that, and leaves.
(b) At an office party, your immediate subordinate asks you detailed questions about how plans for a new project are progressing.

(c) You suggest to two of your local colleagues, on about the same level of seniority, that you would prefer them to call you by your nickname. They insist on using title and family name (e.g. Mr/Ms Smith). They become even more distant and formal when you use their first names.
(d) Your boss calls you and these colleagues to a meeting where he explains his marketing strategy. This monologue is delivered in an authoritative and formal style. Twice you try to interrupt with comments. He looks pained and makes clear that you should keep quiet until he has finished.

NOTES

1   Dear Abby. *Bangkok Post*, 2 October, 1988.
2   Hiroki Kato (1988) From FOBs to SOBs: Japanese vary too. *Newsaction* (Northwestern University, Ill.) **3**(1), 30.
3   For pronouns, address systems and power, see the famous paper by Brown, R. and Gilman, A. (1960) The pronouns of power and solidarity. In *Style in Language* (ed. T.A. Seboek). MIT Press, Mass., pp. 253–76.
4   This and the following example come from Hewitt, J.P. and Stokes, R. (1975) Disclaimers. *American Sociological Review*, **40**, 1–11.
5   These examples come from research by Langer, E.J., Blank, A. and Chanowitz, B. (1978) The mindlessness of ostensibly thoughtful action. *Journal of Personality and Social Psychology*, **36**, 635–42.
6   Tannen, D. (1985) Cross-cultural communication. In *Handbook of Discourse Analysis* (ed. T. Van Dijk), vol. 4. London, Academic Press, pp. 203–15.
7   See Jefferson, G. (1972) Side sequences. In *Studies in Social Interaction* (ed. D. Sudnow). Free Press/Macmillan, New York, pp. 294–338.
8   For descriptions of 'since' statements (the most problematic), see Micheli, L. McJ., Cespedes, F.V., Byker, D. and Raymond, T.J.C. (1984) *Managerial Communication*. Scott, Foresman and Co., Glenview, Ill.
9   Weick, K.E. and Browning, L.D. (1986) Argument and narration in organizational communication. In *Yearly Review of Management of the Journal of Management* (eds. J.G. Hunt and J.D. Blair), **12**(2), 243–59 (see 255).
10 Managing across cultures. *World Executive Digest*, February 1988.

7
Ambiguity in Spoken Communication

7.1 INTRODUCTION

A newspaper tells the story:[1]

> 'Nearly two decades later, the words of Eisaku Sato still glisten in the annals of Japanese verbal befuddlement.
>
> As Prime Minister in 1969, Mr Sato visited Washington to deflect American anger over a flood of textile imports from Japan, a hot trade issue at the time. The Japanese must exercise restraint in exports, President Richard M. Nixon insisted.
>
> To which Mr Sato replied as he looked ceilingward, "Zensho shimasu." Literally, the phrase means "I will do my best", and that's how the interpreter translated it.
>
> What it really means to most Japanese is, "No way."
>
> ### Many obfuscations
>
> Mr Nixon thought he had an agreement, however, and when Japan continued on its merry export way, he reportedly denounced Mr Sato as a liar.
>
> The interrelated worlds of Japanese politics and business are chockablock with obfuscations of this sort . . .'

Mr Sato intended to say that he refused, but his message suggested literally that he would try to find a solution. Thus form and function did not correspond; indeed they were contradictory. Most Japanese understand what he was really saying; within the context of their shared culture the relationship between form and function was clear. But in terms of American culture it was not.

This chapter focuses on spoken communication, and sees why spoken messages so often fail to achieve their purpose. It looks first at the problems of interpreting the function of a message when this only indirectly corresponds to its form. Message function is defined here as the purpose which it is designed to achieve. When the form is indirect and does not make the function explicit, the message may be ambiguous and only imperfectly understood by the receiver.

An ambiguous message is defined here as one that can be interpreted in more than one way. Ambiguity is frequent in cross-cultural situations. The cross-cultural manager does not share the cultural perceptions which determine why a member of the other culture chooses an indirect message form and how to interpret it. Similarly, the manager may be at a loss to understand why his or her messages have been interpreted other than as intended.

On the other hand, the sender may deliberately build ambiguity into the message in order to give the receiver greater flexibility in decoding, thus satisfying politeness norms.

7.2 FORM AND FUNCTION

The newspaper story quoted above suggests that the Japanese are particularly prone to express messages obscurely, in forms which may be perfectly grammatical but only very indirectly relate to the speaker's real intention. In fact, all cultures regularly trade in similarly obfuscating messages.

How many times have you said 'I agree up to a point' when you don't agree at all, or 'I've enjoyed meeting you. Let's have lunch some time' when you have not intention of meeting the other person again? But an honest statement, 'Talking to you has bored and depressed me and I have no intention of repeating the experience', is obviously unacceptable.

All cultures respect the need for good manners, even when they violate strict truth. But what passes for good manners in one culture might elsewhere be taken at face value or perceived as insincere.

When Americans say 'Let's have lunch some time' this expresses and is interpreted as a statement of goodwill, not a definite invitation. If you want to interpret it as an invitation pull out your diary and settle the date and time. But Hall suggests that an Indian interprets it literally.[2] In his terms he does you honor by accepting, and arrives at your office expecting lunch. You are irritated to have been given no warning when you have other plans and the Indian is insulted by the awkwardness that this creates.

7.2.1   Terminology

In order that the meaning of a verbal message is correctly interpreted the sender and receiver must share an understanding of the terminology used. That is, the message must consist of words that the receiver understands in the professional, cultural and situational contexts within which he or she interprets it. Nonsense words such as in 'Pass me the whatsit' make sense only when the situational context is obvious. Technical terms and jargon only succeed when both sender and receiver share the specialist area of information.

Problems occur in cross-cultural situations when there is a 'vocabulary gap' between culture A and culture B. This occurs when a concept in culture A is not expressed in culture B, or is expressed only imprecisely, or by a vocabulary item that has a range of alternative meanings in culture B but not in culture A.

Cultures develop vocabularies and grammatical systems that reflect their needs and experiences. Eskimos have about ninety words for different types of snow; other cultures, which seldom if ever see snow, may manage with one. Problems occur when a society is forced by rapid development and outside pressure to adapt to concepts for which it has no means of referring. It either borrows a term from some other language or invents. For instance, Malaysia has a Language and Literature Agency with a brief to create Malay-language terminologies in technical areas (management, law, medicine, physics, etc.).

In business, this lack of correspondence in vocabularies may arise from the historical fact that the conceptual structure of modern management originated in the West and has been imprecisely rendered in other languages. Lee[3] reports research in which 96 bilingual Pakistani graduate business students were asked to write down synonyms in Urdu for 'authority', 'responsibility', and 'grievance'. They gave 17 different synonyms for authority, six for responsibility, and 16 for grievance; these included pain, sorrow, uneasiness, bad blood, grief, unhappiness, hardship, difficulty, brawl, malice, and worry.

The implications are clear. Suppose a manager requests his staff to report their grievances. They list their family disputes, bad debts, unemployed offspring. The manager expects work-related complaints only and reacts impatiently. The Pakistanis, on the other hand, wonder why the manager pretends to take an interest in their welfare when obviously he has no intention of doing anything about it.

But sharing a vocabulary is not in itself sufficient to guarantee that the purpose is conveyed, as the introductory story shows.

7.2.2   Incomplete Forms

When the sender and receiver interpret the context similarly, incomplete forms may be sufficient. In an appropriate context, this interaction, discussed in Chapter 6, makes sense:

Assistant: 'Telephone?'
Manager: 'I'm busy.'
Assistant: 'Okay.'

Taken in isolation and when context-free, these utterances ('telephone'; 'I'm busy'; 'okay') mean very little. But the full interaction makes sense when the following conditions apply. The assistant takes a telephone call for the manager and asks whether she wishes to speak. The manager replies that she does not and asks him to take a message, to which he agrees.

This shared contextual understanding includes understanding of their relationship and roles. The abbreviated forms reflect a relatively informal relationship, which is more likely to occur where power distances are narrow.

This interaction takes on slightly different meanings in different situations; for instance, when the speakers are in different rooms and the assistant thinks that the manager has not heard the telephone ringing, or between spouses at home.

Speakers do not normally refer to what is obvious and taken for granted in their context; bread bakers do not often need to refer to 'bread', although they may have to distinguish types ('the rolls', 'the pans', etc.). Thus experience of the context determines what is included or excluded in relevant messages. Where shared cultural values determine contextual priorities, this poses problems for the newcomer to the culture, for instance the cross-cultural manager, whose perceptions of significance do not match that of the locals.

7.2.3   Ambiguity

We have seen that a message may be ambiguous when it is incomplete or inaccurately coded — although in an appropriate setting of which both sender and receiver share an appropriate understanding these features may not cause problems. Ambiguity also arises when the receiver does not know how to interpret the message and cannot decide what action is required, even though it may be well-formed and grammatically complete.

Even a grammatically correct and complete utterance can carry different meanings in different contexts, which further shows the importance of shared cultural understanding. Consider this:

Manager (to assistant):   'I haven't seen the Amex report yet.'

This utterance may have at least any one of these functions:

- It gives information with a primary objective of maintaining a relation-ship and similar remarks might be 'It looks like being another fine day', 'the traffic was light this morning'. The assistant is not expected to take any action and need only show polite interest: 'No, nor have I', 'It's got some good points', etc.
- It asks whether the assistant has seen it.
- It asks where the report is.
- It directs the assistant to acquire a copy.

How the assistant interprets the utterance is shown by his or her choice of feedback response. The range of feedback responses includes:

(a) 'Hm.'
     'That's good.'
     'Sorry to hear that.'
(b) 'No, nor have I.'
     'I liked it.'
(c) 'It's behind you on the shelf.'
     'Here it is.'
(d) 'Yes. I'll get one now.' (GOES TO GET IT)
     'I'll get them to send you one up.' (ORGANIZES ACTION)

So taken out of context this short declarative sentence is highly ambiguous. Answers (a) above (e.g. 'Hm') make non-committed responses that interpret the declarative sentence as having declarative function, a neutral comment intended only to maintain the relationship. We term this relationship be-tween this declarative form and its declarative function as CORRESPONDING.

But answers (b)–(d) demonstrate that very often the relationship between grammatical form and function is NON-CORRESPONDING. These show that the declarative sentence is interpreted as something other than a neutral com-ment and the assistant is expected to do something more, either by provid-ing more information or by acquiring a copy.

If he decides that it is not intended as a neutral comment, it is a little less ambiguous. He still has to choose between responses (b)–(d), but *not* (a) (e.g. 'Hm'). These non-committed answers do not respond appropriately to a function asking for commitment.

If the assistant deduces that the statement is intended as a wh– question asking where the report is (or who . . . , what . . . , how . . . , when . . . , why . . .) then answer (b) (e.g. 'No, nor have I') is no longer appropriate, and he has to decide between (c) and (d) (e.g. 'It's behind you on the shelf', 'Yes, I'll get one now' — GOES TO GET IT). If he decides that the manager really intends a direction equivalent to 'Please get me the Amex report', then the only appropriate answers belong in (d), which consist of a verbal response and activity which satisfies the order.

This shows that the declarative sentence can function correspondingly with the declarative meaning, or non-correspondingly as a yes/no question, a wh– question, or a declarative. A yes/no question form cannot usually make declarative meaning; it asks for a yes/no answer, a wh– answer or for a direction to be implemented. Similarly, a wh– question asks for a wh– answer or a direction to be implemented. And an order is unambiguous; the receiver is told what to do and cannot pretend not to understand the function of the sentence. Figure 7.1 shows possible alternatives.[4]

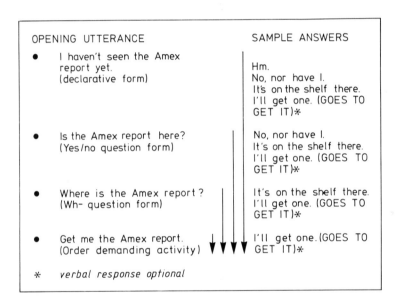

Figure 7.1

So an opening utterance at any level (A, B, C, D) can be answered at the corresponding level or at any level below. But note that an opening utterance cannot usually be answered at a level above without violating social norms. For instance, the assistant's answering 'It's on the shelf there' unaccompanied by any activity in response to a direct order might be interpreted as equivalent to 'I'm not going to get it, you can get it yourself from the shelf there.' This courts a sanction.

We now go on to see how ambiguous utterances such as this can be interpreted, and then examine examples illustrating the causes of ambiguity in cross-cultural situations.

7.2.4 Interpreting Ambiguity

In the example above, the assistant can only respond correctly if he makes an appropriate interpretation of the manager's declarative form, 'I haven't seen the Amex report yet.' But how does he make the correct interpretation?

He may be helped by the context of other language; in the context of any one of the following the function is less ambiguous:

Manager: (a) 'The pressure seems
                  to be off for now.'
             (b) 'I don't know where   'I haven't seen the Amex
                  the new clerk puts   report yet.'
                  things.'
             (c) 'Could you do
                  something for me?'

He is helped by obvious situational clues; for instance, where are they? If on the golf course then he is not expected to drop his clubs and immediately go off to implement a direction. Is the manager apparently under stress, and needing help? Their relationship is constrained by cultural factors. How wide is the power distance between them? How is an assistant expected to service his boss's needs? Is it normally his function to supply documentation, or to organize other people to do so?

Consider this interaction between a visitor to the office and the receptionist.

Visitor: 'Is Mr A's secretary in?'
Receptionist: 'It's five o'clock.'

At first sight, the receptionist's answer does not provide a logical answer to the query. It can only make sense when we bring situational and cultural factors into consideration. The visitor needs to distinguish between three rational possible interpretations:

(a)   the secretary is in;
(b)   the secretary is not in;
(c)   I don't know/cannot say whether she's in or not.

If it is normal for this secretary to still be at work at five, or for all secretaries in this organization and/or this culture to be at work, then interpretation (a) applies. If it is normal that she/they leave by this time, then (b) applies. If the receptionist only begins work at five then (c) applies.

The receptionist's answer presupposes that the visitor knows enough about this individual and/or the culture to make the correct interpretation.

That is, it presupposes shared experiences and perceptions. In cross-cultural situations, this presupposition may not be justified.

7.3 AMBIGUITY IN CROSS-CULTURAL INTERACTIONS

In his or her home culture the manager experiences no great difficulty in identifying the function of an utterance. But in a cross-cultural context, where different values and perceptions of the situational context are applied in creating and interpreting messages, serious problems can arise. An inaccurate interpretation of the real meaning of an utterance can cause damaging misunderstandings.

A few days after starting work for the very traditional Indonesian director of an Indonesian organization, Jack, a New Zealander, was waiting for him to arrive at his office in order to resume a meeting interrupted the day before. He had requested his secretary to report his boss's arrival and meanwhile was working on papers. Later the secretary came in.

Secretary: 'The Director's here.'
Jack: 'Thank you.' (CONTINUES WORKING)
Secretary: 'No, he's here now.'
Jack: 'Yes, I'll be along a few minutes.'
Secretary: (EMBARRASSED) 'No no, he wants to see you now.'
Jack: 'Okay.' (GOES TO THE DIRECTOR)

Jack erred in supposing the message to be information in response to his request on which he could act at any time that suited him. In fact, it was meant as a message relaying a directive from the director equivalent in function to 'Come to see me/the director'. In terms of Figure 7.1, the mistake arose because he interpreted the secretary's declarative form as having corresponding declarative function at level A whereas it was intended to function as an order, at level D.

Such a misunderstanding creates embarrassment and reinforces cross-cultural inhibitions against communication. The effects can be immediately more expensive. This is shown by the case of a Taiwanese assistant working for a British manager. The manager asked her to prepare a list of employees whose performance merited bonus payments. The regulations setting out the criteria for bonus payments were open-ended, but she applied them as in the past and shortly produced a list. He scanned it and the following interaction took place:

Manager: 'There are more names here than I expected. This is going to be expensive.'

Assistant: 'Yes sir.' (EXITS)

The assistant spent three days redefining the criteria and pruning the list. She was acutely aware that several deserving employees were going to be disappointed, and that morale would suffer. When she took back the revised list, she hesitantly expressed her doubts. The manager was surprised that she had wasted so much time. He had intended his remark as a comment, not as a direction that the list be revised, and had not intended that she give it further attention.

He had intended his declarative to be interpreted on level A; she had interpreted it as equivalent to level D. She had followed an interpretive strategy that applies in any hierarchical situation, and particularly in her wide power distance culture; her superior had expressed dissatisfaction, therefore it was her responsibility as a loyal subordinate to remove the difficulty. The subordinate is wise to try interpreting a declarative statement made by a superior at the lowest possible level (D), as an order, and only if this interpretation is inappropriate at successive levels above, first as a wh–question (C), then as a yes/no question (B), and only if this is inappropriate as a statement.

When speaking English, it is usual to use 'yes' as a marker meaning 'I hear/understand what you say'. This use sometimes becomes confused with the standard meaning expressing assent (or 'I agree') if the speaker is not a native English speaker and uses an inappropriate tone. Difficulties arise when a Japanese, for instance, uses 'yes' marking understanding and it is interpreted by the native English speaker as 'yes' meaning 'I agree'. For example:

Australian: 'Are you interested in buying my plant?'
Japanese: 'Yes' (meaning 'I understand you/I will consider that' *but not* 'I'm interested in buying your plant')
Australian   'Good. Well let's talk details . . .'

If you think that your cross-cultural interaction is becoming confused by this ambiguity, move your question down from a yes/no form (level B) to a wh– form (level C), framing it as politely as possible:

Australian: 'I wonder if you could give me some advice. If I decide to sell my plant, WHAT terms might interest you?'

If you still receive a 'yes' answer (inappropriate as a commitment response at this level) then you know that 'yes' is signaling understanding only.

7.3.1   Why Don't They Say What They Mean?

Why do communicators eschew clear-cut forms which admit only one meaning and instead use ambiguous forms which can be misinterpreted?

One obvious reason is communicative incompetence. When the message sender has failed to think through the implications of his or her message form and the possible alternative interpretations that can be made of it, confusion results.

In the charge of the light brigade at the Battle of Balaclava, history provides a dramatic example of extraordinary costs resulting from a mistaken reading of a carelessly coded message. The British cavalry were told to seize the artillery positions. This was assumed to mean attacking Russian artillery positions, rather than to protect British guns against a Russian detachment trying to carry them off. Sent in the wrong direction, the light brigade lost over 500 men.

But the cross-cultural manager should beware of assuming that communicative incompetence explains all ambiguous messages sent by members of the other culture, and of stigmatizing them as naturally bad communicators. What is ambiguous to the manager may be crystal clear to them (and vice versa).

Cultural perceptions determine not only priorities in the situation but also *how* a message is phrased.

At one extreme, American culture values blunt and direct speaking. Saying exactly what you mean is counted a virtue. Cutting directly to the heart of the matter and giving it emphasis has positive rather than negative connotations. For example, a Los Angeles doctor describes injuries caused by gang warfare:[5]

'Dr Stanley R. Klein, the director of trauma services at Harbor Hospital, said "These are war injuries. Period. End of discussion." '

American verbal culture has a low toleration of ambiguity and the American expects to interpret and be interpreted pretty much at face value. But Pascale and Athos argue that this insistence on removing ambiguity may not always be desirable:[6]

'There is too much American trust in increasing the clarity of communication between people, especially when disagreements are substantive. Getting a currently hopeless impasse clear is often unwise and likely to make things worse.'

Cultures that place a higher priority on avoiding conflict prefer to obscure substantive differences. Ambiguity, which serves this function, is associated with politeness. It gives the other person greater latitude in interpreting your utterance, and does not so strictly limit the range of responses. And blunt speaking which removes all ambiguity from the message implies that the receiver is incapable of making a sophisticated analysis of alternative meanings, and this constitutes rudeness.

In many Oriental cultures, an order phrased at level D and stripped of all ambiguity ('Get me the Amex report') is likely to be issued only to a very junior subordinate and is highly aggressive when used with a peer or a senior subordinate. And similarly, negative comments that imply disagreements are avoided.

In a negotiation, the Anglo's preference for bluntness reflects a desire to move to the fundamental point of a negotiation relatively fast. Other cultures spend more time in sizing up the situation and creating rapport before getting down to essentials. In practice, this may mean that the Anglo is better served by backing off from demanding direct answers until the other party feels prepared to give them unprompted. Conversational tactics which create unnecessary stress for the other party damage what might otherwise be a fruitful relationship.

7.3.2   Examples From Japan

This tendency to avoid direct comment is particularly marked in Japan. The introductory story gives an example, and Masaaki Imai shows why Mr Sato's response to Mr Nixon is typical:[7]

> 'A newcomer to Japan may never be able to recover from the initial culture shock of finding out that "yes" does not always mean "yes" in Japan until he realizes that there are some sixteen ways to avoid saying "no" and that to call a spade a spade is not in the Japanese tradition.'

Cross-cultural confusion arises when the Japanese is doing business with a hard-selling Anglo; for instance:

Anglo: 'Are you going to buy my product?'
Japanese: 'I shall give it careful consideration.'

The Japanese intends a negative; the answer is intended to discourage further discussion of the topic. But the Anglo interprets the Japanese answer as an invitation to push further, and he continues:

Anglo: 'Okay so let's look at the details again. Where do you have questions?'

This confuses the Japanese who believes that he has already declined the deal and has indicated that the topic should be dropped. His unwillingness to respond in turn confuses the Anglo, who thinks that the deal is still very much alive.

In a parallel situation, the Anglo has no difficulties in refusing:

Japanese: 'You might like to consider buying our product.'
Anglo: 'No, that's just not possible.'

The Japanese finds this unnecessarily offensive, and backs off from any further involvement. Hence a potentially profitable business relationship breaks down in confusion.

Even a welcomed suggestion might at first be received with apparent lack of commitment. A British businessman working in Japan explains why: 'A Japanese businessman says "perhaps" because he can't make a decision on his own. First he has to form a consensus with other people in the company.'

If forced into a corner, the Japanese (and Asian) business person will tend to give an answer that satisfies the questioner, even when this bends the truth. Hall and Whyte give an example of the American who is too direct in demanding details of his Japanese partner's performance:[8]

> 'What the American did not know was that in Japanese culture one avoids the direct question unless the questioner is absolutely certain that the answer will not embarrass the Japanese businessman in any way whatsoever. In Japan for one to admit being unable to perform a given operation or measure up to a given standard means a bitter loss of face. Given a foreigner who is so stupid, ignorant, or insensitive as to ask an embarrassing question, the Japanese is likely to choose what appears to him the lesser of two evils.'

That is, he gives the answer most likely to please. When his projections prove inaccurate and his promises over-optimistic, the foreigner has only himself to blame for the resulting confusion.

7.3.3   Interpersonal Ambiguity

In summary, unambiguous and ambiguous messages offer both advantages and disadvantages within an interaction. The unambiguous message (e.g. 'Get me the Amex report', in which grammatical form corresponds to function) is that whose meaning is relatively clear and the possibilities for misinterpretation are reduced. The disadvantages are that the lack of interpretive options given to the other person reflect rudeness.

Where the grammatical form is open to a wide range of interpretations (as in 'I haven't seen the Amex review'), the intended function is less apparent. The advantages of an ambiguous message are that it gives the other person options in how to interpret and respond, thus reflects politeness, and may disguise an unpleasant truth. The disadvantages are that it can be misinterpreted in circumstances where a mistake is costly.

Hence there is a trade-off between directness, which gets your purpose across but can create resentment and hence be less persuasive, and indirectness, which maintains a cordial relationship but at the risk of misunderstanding.

7.4   STRATEGIC AMBIGUITY

We have been dealing with examples of ambiguity which show what happens in interpersonal relationships when an individual has a choice of meanings which can be derived from a single message. Ambiguity also arises when different individuals derive different and perhaps contradictory meanings from one or more messages.

When the organization consists of individuals or groups with different interests, the manager may use ambiguity as a deliberate and strategic tool to create unified diversity:[9]

'Strategic ambiguity is essential to organizing because it allows for multiple interpretations to exist among people who contend that they are attending to the same message — i.e. perceive the message to be clear. It is a political necessity to engage in strategic ambiguity so that different constituent groups may apply different interpretations to the symbol.

This defines ambiguity in terms of conflict between individual receivers' interests, and implies that each individual has a clear understanding of his or her interests, interprets the message to fit these interests, and is unaware that other receivers deduce a different message. This is successful for as long as the different receivers do not come together and discover how far their interpretations differ.

The manager may also choose ambiguity as a strategy in order to make it easier to deny interpretations placed upon messages when these latter turn out to be undesirable, and to save face.

The case below shows both the short-term benefits of strategic ambiguity can backfire over time.

7.4.1   Ambiguity in Singapore

A two-year international R & D project in Singapore was set up to develop materials for technical teacher education. The team consisted of two groups, five contracted British research experts and twelve seconded Singaporean Chinese technical instructors. The manager was a Canadian development expert.

The Britons were chiefly interested in creating a sound research basis before designing the development package. They were designated consultants and took their superior status for granted. The Chinese, who had wide general experience of their society, were impatient of detailed analysis which seemed to them redundant, and wanted to proceed immediately to writing the materials. The senior Chinese were appointed team leaders and were directed to coordinate with the consultants. Because they represented the host institution, a ministry, they assumed that they had superior status.

The manager realized very quickly that the contradictions between these different interests threatened immediate disaster. The only hope of saving the project seemed to lie in papering over immediate differences and trusting that over time solutions would arise empirically. Questions of status and what constituted 'coordination' were left vague; the consultants were given the final say in research activities and the instructors in implementation. Project activities were anchored on decisions reached in weekly meetings.

For the first nine months, formal meetings were devoted to discussing R & D outlines. These were dominated by the more voluble consultants. The manager followed each meeting by holding informal teaching seminars, with the theoretically inexperienced instructors. These were supposedly to explain the research issues aired in the formal meetings. In practice, they developed into detailed discussions of specific proposals.

Each group interpreted the concept of 'research' differently, the consultants in terms of analytical constructs and the instructors in terms of application. Further, the consultants assumed that the formal meetings were pre-eminent in determining project development because they followed a recognizable bureaucratic model, were formal and minuted. The instructors took for granted the greater importance of the informal meetings which were producing the concrete proposals demanded by their ministry.

During this first phase, progress on these two fronts was rapid. Each group worked on its own particular interests, and needs for interaction were relatively slight. Then the project reached the second phase when it became necessary to translate the research outlines into a teaching syllabus.

The instructors insisted that they had already completed the necessary materials; the syllabus need consist only of a framework grading and linking them. The consultants replied that the completed materials were useful only as illustrations of theory discussed; the syllabus could only now begin to be designed, and should be governed by the research findings. Each group claimed that superior status justified their interpretation of the concept.

The manager's strategy had held the team together throughout the first stage of its work but she was unable to develop this in order to cope with the new contradictions. For several weeks the two groups were at loggerheads, each pursuing its interpretation of the project aims and claiming the support of the project leader. But gradually, lines of informal communication were reconstructed.

When the two groups exchanged notes on their interpretations of the ambiguous points, they began to understand how the confusion had arisen.

They no longer felt able to trust the manager. They perceived her fostering an ambiguous situation not as a strategy to further superordinate goals but in personal terms, as manipulation. This was greatly resented. Her personal authority and capacity to lead the project slumped.

7.4.2 Strategic Ambiguity in a Cross-Cultural Context

This case illustrates three types of ambiguity, in the structure of the group, the organization, and the task. This strategic ambiguity succeeded in postponing major problems in the first phase, but could not be adapted to answering the new questions posed by the second phase. Far from protecting her position, it endangered it.

Whether or not strategic ambiguity resolves more problems than it generates depends on:

1 The organizational relationships of the individuals and groups.
2 Informal communication networks.
3 The tasks performed by the different individuals and how they interrelate.
4 Time: for how long can ambiguity be tolerated, and contradictions maintained at a passive level? When will the need to resolve contradictions become so pressing that their continuance becomes actively destructive?

In this case, the contradictions arising from a policy of strategic ambiguity were made worse by the cross-cultural context. The outsider consultants experienced personal needs to orientate themselves in their new environment, and these feelings reinforced their professional needs to research. The insider instructors took their environment for granted and were chiefly concerned to satisfy their local employer, to whom they would return when the project was finished.

The manager of a complex organization frequently needs to resort to strategic ambiguity in order to ensure the cooperation of different groups. The risks are multiplied in mixed-culture work groups, which are inherently ambiguous. Different individuals have different priorities and different reasons for belonging to the group, and have loyalties outside it. The cross-cultural manager may need to develop strategic ambiguities in order to nullify the cultural contradictions. The case shows that when cultural contradictions correspond with and reinforce strategic ambiguities, the mix can be destructive.

7.5   IMPLICATIONS FOR THE MANAGER

In a cross-cultural setting the manager needs to develop more sensitive skills of interpreting the context.

- Develop a sensitivity to how you express important functions.

(a)   What vocabulary words common in your profession may be ambiguous to a member of the other culture?

(b)   What grammatical forms do you frequently use that might be ambiguous to a member of the other culture, when
  - giving instructions;
  - negotiating a deal;
  - evaluating performance;
  - offering an opinion?

(c)   What alternatives might you use that are less ambiguous and will not cause offence?

(d)   What grammatical forms do you frequently use in these activities which are direct and unambiguous but are likely to cause offence?

(e)   What alternatives might you use that are less likely to cause offence and will be interpreted appropriately?

- If you are working in a culture where a lack of directness is valued as a sign of politeness,

(a)   Try rephrasing yes/no questions, wh– requests for a content answer, and commands at a high level — even at the level of a declarative statement. Try using these forms:

> I'm interested in . . .
> Perhaps you can tell me . . .
> I wonder if . . .
> For instance:
>   'I'm interested in getting the Amex review.'
>   'Perhaps you can tell me where the Amex review is.'
>   'I wonder if you could get me the Amex review.'

(b)   Try using frames to explain your messages.

- If you are working in a culture where bluntness and directness is valued, try rephrasing elaborated messages more directly.

- When you are managing a complex organization in which different individuals/groups have different interests:

(a) How far do these individuals/groups correspond to different cultural groups?

(b) Under what conditions is strategic ambiguity likely to ameliorate or exacerbate ambiguities in the cultural context? Take into account:

- organizational relationships — do work groups correspond to or overlap culture groups?
- informal communication networks — do these function between work groups? Between culture groups? Is networking between groups likely to resolve contradictions or to activate them?
- the tasks performed by the different work/culture groups and how they interrelate
- time — for how long can ambiguity be tolerated?

Developing a Diary: 4

Develop the diary started in Chapters 3, 4 and 6, in order to take account of the new material presented in this chapter.

Take notes of the verbal forms you use to communicate the functions you have already listed.

1 How does each reflect the context (relationships with the receivers, power distances, the task to be performed, the topic)?
2 How do you rate each in terms of directness/indirectness?
3 How persuasive was each, in terms of how far did it cause the other person to change his or her perception of the situation and behavior, on a scale of 1 to 10?

Take notes of the forms used by members of the other culture to communicate the same functions. How persuasive are they? What modifications do you need to make to your choice of language forms? What modifications might they make to theirs?

7.6 SUMMARY

This chapter has dealt with ambiguity and clarity of purpose in spoken communication, and shows that ambiguity does not necessarily reflect indecision. It has focused on the problem of expressing purpose by using forms which can be clearly understood but do not cause offence by transgressing social norms of politeness.

Section 7.2 showed that the form of a message may only indirectly reflect its function and what is meant. The context provides the clues by which ambiguity can be resolved. Section 7.3 showed that in cross-cultural interactions the manager has problems in identifying how members of the other culture interpret the situation because he or she does not share their cultural perceptions and priorities. These perceptions determine norms of when more or less formal and informal styles are appropriate.

EXERCISES

These exercises give practice in interpreting ambiguity.

Exercise 1

Read the story below. Then, for each of the episodes (a)–(f) decide which answer (i)–(iv) is most appropriate in your culture. Explain your answers using Hofstede's analysis.

Modern Electronics is a manufacturing company in your home city. All the persons who work for the company are members of your culture. Mr Aaba is the CEO. Mr Beede is Executive Assistant to the CEO, and has held this post for about eight months. They have an amicable working relationship, but are not close friends.

(a)   Yesterday they met to discuss company policy. They were unable to complete this business and agreed to continue their discussions when Mr Aaba arrived back from a lunch date today. It is now 2.00 p.m. Mr Beede is working through some routine papers. He needs another five minutes to complete the task. Mr Aaba's secretary comes to his office.

Secretary: 'Mr Aaba has just come in.'
Mr Beede: (i) 'Hm.' (CONTINUES TO COMPLETE THE TASK)
          (ii) 'Okay.' (GOES TO MR AABA'S OFFICE)
          (iii) 'Okay, I'll be along shortly.' (CONTINUES TO COMPLETE THE TASK)
          (iv) 'Okay, five minutes.' (CONTINUES TO COMPLETE THE TASK)

(b)   When Mr Aaba and Mr Beede get together, they recommence their discussion of general policy issues. Mr Aaba refers in passing to the work of the off-site R & D department. Mr Beede has no immediate responsibility for its work and has only met the manager, Mr Fifo, a few times at company functions.

Mr Aaba: 'Their monthly report is usually out by now. I haven't received it yet.'
          [THAT MORNING MR BEEDE HAD NOTICED THAT THE RE-PORTS HAD JUST BEEN DELIVERED TO THE POST ROOM ON THE FLOOR BELOW.]
Mr Beede: (i) 'They're here, yes.'
          (ii) 'Admin got them this morning.'
          (iii) 'Haven't you?'
          (iv) 'I'll get you one now.' (LEAVES THE ROOM TO FETCH A COPY)

(c)   When a copy is found, Mr Aaba starts leafing through it.

Mr Aaba: 'The resale figures aren't in the obvious place.'

[MR BEEDE SAW THE RESALE FIGURES WHEN GLANCING
THROUGH A COPY IN THE POST ROOM THAT MORNING.]

Mr Beede: (i) 'Yes I know, it's been badly edited.'
            (ii) 'Oh really.'
            (iii) 'Yes if I can show you.' (TAKES THE COPY AND FINDS THE
            FIGURES)
            (iv) 'I think you'll find them at the end.'

(d)   When the resale figures have been located, Mr Aaba begins reading them and
then shows some surprise — as did Mr Beede this morning until he realized that a
loan repayment was included.

Mr Aaba: 'They're 20 percent down on last month, they're terrible.'
Mr Beede: (i) 'Yes, they look bad.'
            (ii) 'Yes, they look bad but of course they include that loan
            repayment.'
            (iii) 'Well no, they're not bad when you count in the loan repayment.'
            (iv) 'Hm. Do they.'

(e)   Mr Aaba decides he wants to talk to Mr Fifo about R & D's expenses. He dials a
direct line. There is no answer.

Mr Aaba: 'He isn't in his office.'
Mr Beede: (i) 'Okay.' (REACHES FOR A SECOND TELEPHONE AND BEGINS
            RINGING AROUND OTHER OFFICES WHERE MR FIFO
            MIGHT BE)
            (ii) 'He could be talking to production about the gauge switch, or
            with the trainer's meeting. Or the library.'
            (iii) 'I'm not sure where he is.'
            (iv) 'Yes, I see.'

(f)   Mr Fifo cannot be found. Mr Aaba and Mr Beede conclude their meeting. The
next day Mr Aaba stops by Mr Beede's office.

Mr Aaba: 'I read more of that R & D report. This problem seems to be serious. I
            think we'll have to tell Mr Fifo to go.'
Mr Beede: (i) 'Yes, I understand what you mean.'
            (ii) 'We can dismiss him next week.'
            (iii) 'Yes, I think we might have to.'
            (iv) 'Okay, I'll fix it.' (GOES TO PERSONNEL DEPARTMENT AND
            ORDERS DOCUMENTATION FOR MR FIFO'S DISMISSAL)

Exercise 2

Suppose that the story in Exercise 1 above happened in some other culture. Use
Hofstede's analysis discussed in Chapter 2 to choose another culture that is very
different from your own. Now read the story again and for each of the episodes (a)–
(f) select the answer (i)–(iv) which you think would be most appropriate in this other
culture.

NOTES

1   Haberman, C. (1988) Some Japanese (one) urge plain speaking. *The New York Times*, 27 March.

2   This example is also discussed in Hall, E.T. (1960) The silent language in overseas business, *Harvard Business Review*, May–June, 87–96.

3   Lee, J.A. (1966) Cultural analysis in overseas operations. *Harvard Business Review*, March–April, 106–114 (see 109).

4   This simplifies a discourse model first developed by Sinclair, J.McH. (1980) Discourse in relation to language structure and semiotics. In *Studies in English Linguistics for Randolph Quirk* (eds. S. Greenbaum, G. Leech, and J. Svartvik). Longman, London, pp. 110–24.

5   Gross, J. (1989) To aid victims of US urban violence, it's trench medicine. *International Herald Tribune*, 22 February.

6   Pascale, R.T. and Athos, A.G. (1981) *The Art of Japanese Management*. Warner Books, New York, p. 146.

7   Masaaki Imai (1975) *Never Take Yes For An Answer*. Simul Press, Tokyo.

8   Hall, E.T. and Whyte, W. (1961) Intercultural communication: a guide to men of action. *Human Organization*, **19**(1), 5–12 (see 6–7).

9   Eisenberg, E.M. (1984) Ambiguity as strategy in organizational communication. In *Communication Monographs*, Vol. 51, pp. 227–42 (see 231).

8

Non-Verbal Communication

8.1   INTRODUCTION

At a reception given in an Arab embassy in London, a Briton was introduced to an Egyptian. They had common business interests and it was clearly to their mutual advantage that they should strike a deal. The Egyptian stood up close to the Briton, speaking directly into his face. The Briton automatically moved to one side so that they now stood at an angle of ninety degrees, and about four feet away. The Egyptian again moved up within 18 inches of the Briton, who again moved to one side. They continued this movement around each other throughout the evening.

Both went home disappointed. The prospects for business had seemed very promising, but each felt he could not trust the other. Neither could explain his suspicions, but neither was prepared to take the negotiations any further.

The Briton had adopted a stance and distance that conformed to the norm favored by his culture in polite conversation between males. But this communicated distance and reserve to the Egyptian, who had followed his cultural norm of standing close and so projecting emotional sincerity. This was too close for the Briton, who perceived the Egyptian to be crowding him.

This shows a cross-cultural negotiation breaking down because each participant was behaving according to cultural norms to which the other was unaccustomed; and because each was behaving and responding to the other unconsciously, they could not explain their feelings of suspicion. Each wanted agreement and trust, but projected messages which the other was bound to misinterpret.

143

This chapter discusses non-verbal communication and how messages are sent by means other than by using language. Different cultures invest different meanings in non-verbal signals when sending, and also interpret signals differently. The manager needs to understand the extent and importance of variations.

Unlike language forms, which can be described by grammars, non-verbal forms are very difficult to codify. When did you last see a dictionary of hand gestures? (A comprehensive dictionary would be almost impossible to write, or to use; by one estimate the human body is capable of over 270 000 discrete gestures.) However, this problem of description should not blind us to their importance. Only about 30 percent of what is communicated in a conversation is verbal.

Differences in the non-verbal forms used by different cultures are important to the cross-cultural manager for the following reasons:

1   He or she must be sensitive to the fact that they occur, and are significant.
2   He or she must recognize that non-verbal signals made by the other person may have a different significance.
3   He or she must recognize that his or her own non-verbal signals may be interpreted other than as intended or expected by a member of another culture.
4   The non-verbal means of signaling discussed here operate at varying degrees below the conscious threshold. As the introductory story shows, the sender is not usually conscious of an intended effect when taking a particular stance, and the receiver is not usually conscious of the reasons for his or her reaction to it. As for timing and dressing, the sender is aware of a decision to make an appointment at a particular time or to choose a particular suit for a meeting, but is far less likely to be aware of the message communicated by this decision within the context.

For instance, the Japanese 'salaryman' who wears a dark shiny suit to work like all other salarymen, does not have to ask himself why he chooses to communicate an appearance of collective uniformity when he dresses himself in the morning.
5   Because these messages operate below the conscious threshold, they generate feelings which are difficult to recognize and hence difficult to rationalize and reject. Non-verbal signaling is therefore an extremely powerful means of conveying feelings and extremely difficult to control.

8.2 TIME

Perceptions of time, how it can be divided and how used, vary across cultures. Chapter 4 showed that WHEN business is communicated varies widely. Here we deal with four important temporal concepts:

- appointment time;
- schedule time;
- discussion time;
- acquaintance time.

These dimensions were first postulated by Hall and Whyte, and are also discussed elsewhere in Hall's work.[1]

8.2.1   Appointment Time

This section deals with the issue of punctuality. What constitutes punctuality in one culture may be perceived in another as bad-mannered tardiness, or at the opposite extreme, as unnecessary precision and a lack of concern for more important aspects of the relationship.

In the Anglo cultures, the manager may be up to five minutes late for an appointment without feeling it necessary to apologize; after five minutes demands an apology and perhaps an explanation ('the traffic . . .'). Appointment time for a social occasion varies depending on its nature: twenty minutes late for a formal dinner might be considered excessive, whereas your arriving an hour after the appointed time for a casual drinks party may still be acceptable. (The implication is that in these cultures you should always make sure of what sort of social occasion it is that you have been invited to.)

In Swedish terms the Anglo allowance of five minutes for an appointment is lax. Swedes are more particular; an appointment at ten o'clock means ten o'clock on the dot.

In these cultures early arrival for a business appointment may mean your waiting. Early arrival for a social occasion may cause your host or hostess embarrassment, and is not acceptable.

The Middle Eastern and Latin American cultures attach less urgency to appointment time, and have fewer inhibitions about making multiple appointments and talking with casual visitors at the same time. An American manager studying at a Spanish University was frustrated to discover that her lecturer did not arrive for a 1.00 p.m. lecture until 1.20 p.m. Gradually she realized that this caused no inconvenience to her Spanish co-students, who timed their own entrances at 1.20 p.m. When she had learned this cultural interpretation of the appointment time, she found no difficulties adjusting.

In Latin America, an invitation for a party at eight means that you can arrive at any time between eight and ten or even eleven at night without being 'late'.

How do you excuse lateness? In most cultures a short lateness can be excused by bad traffic conditions or a car breakdown. In Japan an appeal to family loyalty is effective ('Just as we were leaving the house, my uncle phoned'). In India, the claim 'I tried telephoning to say I had been delayed but the telephone wasn't working' is usually credible.

8.2.2 Schedule Time

Schedule time refers to the time when a job should be finished. Anglo cultures place a premium on completing work by the time appointed. Cultures which are less optimistic about the possibilities of controlling future time and planning its use give much less importance to scheduling.

Hall and Whyte ask how you get a job completed within a satisfactory time when the concepts of a deadline is weak and non-existent. They relate how an Arab gets his car fixed, by applying constant pressure:[2]

> 'First, I go to the garage and tell the mechanic what is wrong with my car. I wouldn't want to give him the idea that I don't know. After that, I leave the car and walk around the block. When I come back to the garage, I ask him if he has started to work yet. On my way home from lunch I stop in and ask him how things are going. When I go back to the office I stop by again. In the evening, I return and peer over his shoulder for a while. If I didn't keep this up, he'd be off working on someone else's car.'

In Anglo cultures this constant needling is usually interpreted as bad manners. The irritation it arouses is more likely to cause delays than to hasten the process; a Chicago auto repair shop carries a sign 'labor $24 an hour, and $48 an hour if you watch'. The Arab business person is not advised to try the same tactic in these cultures (unless, perhaps, more than one deadline has already been passed and a lapse in manners is justified).

8.2.3 Discussion Time

How much time should be spent in a discussion? In Anglo cultures, it is generally supposed that a meeting which crisply covers the main points in as short a time as possible without 'time wasting' is more successful than a long drawn-out ramble. This means omitting non-essential details and aspects of the personal, non-business relationship.

But this needs some qualification. The length of discussion also depends upon the gravity of the topic, the preparations involved in calling the meeting, and the relative statuses of the persons involved. In Anglo cultures a five minute meeting on topic X may be acceptable when the other participants only have to walk down the corridor from their own offices, or if the person calling the meeting is of much higher status and therefore perceived

to possess more valuable time. It may not be acceptable if the other participants have to make elaborate preparations to attend.

A British businessman operating in South East Asia returned to his London base for a series of exploratory talks. He had previously arranged to
meet a senior executive in Scotland, and took an overnight train to Glasgow
to keep the date. He was met by an aide, who regretted that her boss was ill,
and that she herself could only spare fifteen minutes. When he reported
back to his partners, they immediately assumed this particular discussion to
have been a failure, without checking what had been agreed in it. They
based their assumption on the shortness of discussion time given the pre-
planning, the extensive travel involved, and the junior status of the other
person.

In general, collectivist cultures invest more time in discussion time, but
Hong Kong is an exception. In some respects, attitudes are more extreme
than in the Anglo cultures, and your choice of a non-work related topic may
be perceived as a symptom of inefficiency.

In Latin cultures, this emphasis on 'the shorter the better' appears to treat
time as an end in itself rather than as a means to an end. Hall and Whyte
argue[3] that the Latin Americans treat discussion as

> '. . . part of the spice of life. Just as he tends not to be overly concerned about
> reserving you your specific segment of time, he tends not as rigidly to separate
> business from non-business. He runs it all together and wants to make some-
> thing of a social event out of what you [the American] regard as strictly
> business.'

One businessman reports that in Brazil you must expect to spend at least
two hours in general discussion before mentioning the topic of your business, and in Bolivia, three hours.

Similarly, the Greek shows good will and good faith *not* by cutting the
discussion to the main points but by examining every detail. This lengthen-
ing of discussion time in order to develop the relationship signifies good
manners, not the reverse as in the Anglo cultures.

In Asian cultures, the impatience of Anglos to get to the crucial point of a
negotiation is well-known, and may be consciously exploited. An interpreter
from the People's Republic of China told me:

> 'We know that Americans are always very impatient to get an agreement so
> that they can go on somewhere else. So we make them wait. We take days off
> and send them on trips to factories. They get frustrated and so eventually try to
> settle as quickly as possible. That way we get a good deal.'

8.2.4 Acquaintance Time

By this, Hall and Whyte refer to the length of time you need to know a person before you are prepared to do business.

In the United States acquaintance time may be very short. This is particularly true if you represent a company which is well-known. A representative of IBM, for instance, can walk in off the street, show his business card, be immediately shown into your office, and perhaps walk out with an order after a few minutes' discussion fixing details of delivery and payment.

In Arab cultures, acquaintance with the individual is usually more important than with the organization he or she represents. One Anglo businessman commented:

'In Saudi Arabia you can expect two or three weeks foreplay. Your moral standing is more important than your business card. You're just waltzing around, talking about your family, life at home, where you've been in the world, then the decision is suddenly made, just like that.'

This 'foreplay' is necessary in order to build a relationship of personal trust, for which knowledge of the abstract organization cannot substitute.

8.3   SPACE

The work space and its arrangement have symbolic values, which vary across cultures. Where the individual works, the access or lack of it that this affords other people, and how the space is organized, communicate messages of power and status. Hence the space is used symbolically to exert control over subordinates and impress visitors.

In Anglo cultures, the most prestigious office is generally reckoned to be the largest, and in a multi-floor building, the highest. The metaphor 'from the top down' describing a communication process seems to reflect this physical arrangement as much as the organizational chart. The CEO typically occupies a large top-floor corner office. Access is controlled by a secretary stationed in an outer office.

In these cultures, the symbolic value of the high, inaccessible office outweighs its main practical disadvantage of distance from a workforce which occupies a ground-floor office or a separate building. The more important the aide to the CEO, the closer his or her office to the CEO's.

One American manager reports her experiences of working as a junior in a communal office where seniority and years of experience was indicated by the area allotted to the individual. Each area was demarcated by movable partitions:

'We were told how much space we could have to the nearest inch. The people who had worked there a year longer than me had two inches more. This had no practical value. But everyone took it very seriously. Occasionally someone might try to increase their space by coming in early and moving the partitions an inch or two. This was a very unpopular thing to do.'

This reflects the relatively narrow power distances typical of an American organization. Because power distances are narrow does not mean that they are unimportant. On the contrary, because they are so narrow, those with greater power are all the more determined to make their superiority overt. And when resources such as work spaces are allotted more generously to superiors than subordinates they serve a useful symbolic function of manifesting differences in power.

In a wide power difference culture, the superior demonstrates his or her authority in relations with subordinates; perhaps they lower their eyes when speaking and remain standing, sit in obedient silence at meetings and negotiations, show deference at every opportunity. Then the superior has far less need to symbolize authority by size and position of office space.

The Oriental manager may regard as adequate or even spacious office conditions that would be perceived as crowded in the West. So the Western cross-cultural manager shown into a poky little office that would be given to a junior secretary at home should not make the mistake of assuming that its occupant has no importance.

In a Japanese office, managers and subordinates share the same room. Desks are arranged in columns, and the departmental head uses the front central desk, flanked on either side by his senior aides. (He may use a separate individual office, situated at the end of a corridor, only to receive honored visitors.) The front desk in each column is occupied by a senior manager, with his subordinates ranked behind him.

The column closest to the windows running up the side of the office is occupied by the 'window people'. They may have imposing titles but are given little responsibility. In this collectivist culture, where employment may be guaranteed for life, they cannot be dismissed without creating loss of face and conflict. Nevertheless, the employee moved to a window desk is being discreetly told that his or her services are no longer crucial, and that if he or she should decide to find some other job in preference to fruitless hours spent staring out of the window, this would not be regretted.

In the past, French companies were modeled on the family business, and closeness to the workforce was given priority. The manager took a central office which gave him a view of the workforce. Thus the central office acquired symbolic value. American norms are now widely copied, but the traditional pattern can still be seen.

8.3.1   Furnishing the Space

In narrow power distance cultures the selection and arrangement of furniture in the office space symbolize rank as powerfully as does the size and position of the space itself. The more important the person, the more luxurious the furniture. The furniture permitted each individual is often used to precisely reflect his or her rank.

An American manager working for the Ohio branch of a New York based finance company explains what happened when a second Ohio branch was closed:

> 'There was all this furniture, desks and chairs, and we said we needed it. But if it came to us then the New York people would complain. It would mean our junior managers might get an extra chair each, when people in New York were stuck with their usual quota. Head office didn't want the conflict. They sold off the furniture, almost gave it away, rather than have that problem.'

The CEO arranges his or her furniture in order to accommodate a range of communicative situations. Chairs positioned in front of the main desk may be used in short formal meetings by subordinates, perhaps when reprimanded. The subordinate invited to join the CEO in easy chairs around a low coffee table to one side of the room is being made aware that the atmosphere is lighter. The meeting is less formal.

A group of subordinates led to a round table are being signaled by the CEO that he or she does not intend to pull rank. All participants share the same furniture, and are not separated (as they would be if the meeting were held around the CEO's desk). In this more democratic setting, ideas can be freely exchanged and the agenda negotiated. On the other hand, if the CEO shows them to a conference table and seats himself in the most powerful position at the end of the table or in the middle of one side, this signals strongly that the meeting is formal and that he intends to enforce a particular agenda.

Hence this flexibility in the use of office space has important symbolic connotations. It indicates the range of activities for which the manager is responsible; by implication, the wider the range, the more important.

It is normal in many Western cultures to push furniture out to the edges of the room. In the East, furniture may be positioned in the center.

In Japan, you may be shown into a meeting room which has an alcove in the wall opposite the door, containing such art objects as ceramics and scrolls. As an important person you will be seated with your back to this, which makes a picturesque backdrop reflecting your importance to the other people. Your host is seated to one side, and the least important person is closest to the door. When entertaining Japanese visitors in your office, never ask them to sit near the door and make sure the leader of the team is furthest from it.

8.3.2   Computers as Symbolic Furniture

Because of its powerful instrumental functions, the personal computer has taken on symbolic significance as an item of furniture.

In Anglo management cultures efficiency is assumed to be a priority, and is often signaled by the replacement of paper by the computer. When personal computers were first introduced they had important symbolic value, and every CEO boasted one in his or her office (even if unable to use it). But now that computers are used so widely, and by all ranks, superiors often now prefer to distinguish themselves from subordinate ranks by *not* having one in the office.

In less developed countries, this new technology has not yet become so common as to have lost its symbolic importance. In countries where labor is cheap and production is labor-intensive, the use of computers may complement rather than surplant paperwork, and the manager may still signal his or her efficiency by the amount of paper that has to be dealt with. An Indian executive commented that 'you need paper to show your bosses [not visitors] that you are busy. The higher up you are [in the organization] the less need for paper.'

8.4   MATERIAL POSSESSIONS

In many cultures, power is symbolized by material possessions, and these may be prominently displayed in the manager's office. In different cultures, different possessions fill this function. In the West, the manager might put valuable pictures on the wall. In Eastern countries including Japan, decorative fish are valued; carp can cost up to $10 000 each.

In Arabic countries, it is bad manners to admire another person's possession; rules of courtesy bind the owner to give it to you. An Australian manager made the mistake of admiring his Arab host's new silk tie. The man immediately took it off and insisted that his guest should have it. The Australian was only able to get out of this embarrassing situation by accepting the tie graciously, but adding that if he wore it he should no longer be able to see it; therefore he preferred that his friend should take it back on loan to wear whenever he wished, in order that its new owner might then have a better opportunity to enjoy it. This made a neat escape. But in other situations you may find it much harder to excuse yourself from accepting the unwanted gift. So do not make your admiration obvious.

In Japan, you may admire your host's possessions but not effusively, or he or she may feel obliged to present it to you.

The Anglo manager often has family photographs on his desk. One American junior manager explained that she liked to see these because they 'show stability and tell me that this person has something other in life that's important besides work'. This is much less common among Japanese managers, whose families are expected to take second place to work loyalties.

The custom of displaying sporting trophies, perhaps to communicate individual competitive abilities and good health besides non-work interests, seems to have started in the United States, but is increasingly common everywhere.

An older Thai manager shows his or her religious and cultural affinity by displaying a Buddhist shrine in one corner of the office, and perhaps starts each day by praying before it. A portrait of a respected monk may hang on the wall.

8.5 DRESS

In different cultures, styles of dress signal degrees of formality and informality.

In Malaysia, a good-quality long-sleeved batik shirt is often used as formal dress and in some situations may be preferable to a Western suit. A Western shirt and tie is less formal, but preferable to a short-sleeved batik shirt.

In India, status is attached to wearing simple dress. The top manager may go tieless in situations where his subordinates wear ties. At a formal meeting senior managers may wear safari suits whereas their juniors come in pants and jackets.

In the individualist Anglo cultures, a suit is always considered more formal, but may not be considered appropriate in certain occupations. In the early days of the computer industry, executives communicated the radical nature of their business by dressing in a uniform of denim. This is now changing, and front people dealing with customers often wear suits.

IBM is frequently noted for requiring its salesmen to be uniformily dressed (blue suits and white shirt, often buttoned down). Similarly, in the 1950s and before the influence of President Kennedy made a more informal style acceptable, Arthur Anderson consultants were expected to wear hats. But these examples of uniformity are well-known because they are so exceptional in a culture where dress expresses individualism.

Westerners tend to dress more informally in hot weather. This is not the case in Asian countries, where despite the heat shirts and ties are worn by male office workers, and only manual workers and foreign tourists dress in shorts and loose shirts.

Among the traditional upper classes of some European countries, wealth and class is coded in dress, in a form only accessible to persons with the same education and experience. The English aristocrat arrives for a meeting dressed in a much-worn tweed suit and wearing a tie of unfashionable width. Only someone with a similar background recognizes that the tweed is the best that money can buy and that the design on the tie indicates that its wearer once served in an elite guards regiment. The aristocrat does not dress in a new blue silk suit that would impress the middle classes because he sees no need to impress them.

The cross-cultural manager needs to dress for each occasion at the level of formality expected of him as an outsider. This does not necessarily mean giving up his wardrobe; in some cultures the outsider who adopts local dress is perceived as offensively patronizing.

8.6   BUSINESS CARDS

In many cultures, an important element of dressing for business is a supply of business cards. These should be printed in both the language of the other culture and (if necessary, on the reverse) your own language. If you are expecting to visit more than one foreign country with a different language, have a new set of cards made for each. For instance, never make the mistake of presenting a Chinese with a card printed in not only Chinese but also Japanese and Korean.

Try to have your cards translated and printed before you leave your own country; you may be expected to present cards as soon as you meet your opposite number when landing at the airport. If necessary, seek the advice of the other country's embassy or chamber of commerce on where to find an efficient translator and printer.

Have your title translated in terms of an appropriate equivalent rank in the other culture. Titles such as 'Vice President' can be ambiguous and cause confusion. An American company employing 500 people might have 20 or 30 VPs, each representing the interests of a single department at the highest levels; this reflects the culture of a market bureaucracy. But a Japanese company of similar size may have only two or three VPs, who may feel they lose face if introduced to a junior American VP as though their ranks were equivalent. In this case, the American 'VP of Computer Services' would be advised to have his or her title translated in Japanese as equivalent to 'Head of the Computer Services Department'.

Every German business person has a card giving his or her academic and professional qualifications, and should be addressed by his title on the card.

Etiquette is involved in giving and receiving cards. Wherever you are, give your card with the other person's language face up, and always take care to spend a few seconds reading the other person's card carefully. In Korea, give the card with your right hand and extend your left hand to take that of the other person. If his or her card shows a company rank, draw breath and nod admiringly. In Japan, present your *meishi* (card) using both hands so that the other person can read it.

Anglos tend to produce their cards at the end of a meeting, to serve as reminders. In Japan, formally present your card when first introduced to the other person, even before speaking. When teams meet, everyone presents a card to everyone else, the top person in each team presenting his or hers first. You can expect to use a great number of cards in even a short trip. Because you should never be without them, take a generous supply with you and if you do run out, ask your hotel for help; most first-class hotels offer their own *meishi* printing services.

Wherever you are it is not normal to present your card at a second meeting unless the information on it has changed; for instance you have a new title. Presenting the same card twice may suggest that you have forgotten the first meeting, which can cause serious offence.

Never write on the other person's card or use it for notes. The Japanese only ever writes on his own card, on the obverse side, when giving it to be used in lieu of a personal introduction ('This introduces my good friend . . .').

8.7   ENTERTAINMENT

Giving entertainment and hospitality is more or less important in different cultures. Almaney describes its significance in Arab cultures:[4]

> 'To a foreigner, the Arab's outstanding trait may well be hospitality. . . . A guest is considered almost a sacred trust to be treated as well as or better than one's immediate family.'

The style of entertainment offered to a guest signals the importance given to the guest and the meeting.

In Hong Kong an international educational agency hosted a tea for its local teachers. All were invited, but the entertainment was restricted by the limited funds, and the director was later disappointed to learn that the cake and beverage provided for each guest was perceived to indicate the poverty and low standing of the organization.

He would have done better by channeling the funds into a much more expensive dinner reserved for a handful of top people. This would signal their importance, both to themselves and to other members. Although uninvited, the latter would be proud to belong to an organization which was able to entertain in such lavish style. In this hierarchical context, democratic principles do not apply to entertainment.

Hari Bedi emphasizes the importance of encouraging employees of different nationalities to mix in informal situations:[5]

'I recall an evening river cruise in Bangkok at which expatriate managers took up one side of the boat and Thai employees the other. There was a lot of drinking, the band played old Western favourites, and the affair turned into a private party for the expatriates. The Thais felt left out and were thoroughly dispirited.'

He urges that social occasions should not be rigidly planned like board meetings; group spirit is built by informal rather than formal parties; and conversation should be uninhibited:

'Most expatriates, following Western etiquette, won't talk about religion or politics at social gatherings. But Asians don't observe such taboos. So these occasions can provide opportunities for visitors to learn about cultures, customs, politics, and current events, turning the evening — providing employees know they can speak freely — into a stimulating experience.'

Food has symbolic value in all cultures. You may be offered a dish that is accounted ordinary, or even distasteful, in your own culture; but you will cause deep offence if it has importance in the other culture and you reject it. In the recent past honored guests in Saudi Arabia were offered sheep's eyes. The mushroom is not usually considered a delicacy in the Anglo cultures; but in Japan, matsutake mushrooms are especially prized — a single well-shaped mushroom may cost as much as $80, and even an average specimen runs to $40 a stem.[6]

In the People's Republic of China, you may be entertained at a formal banquet. You note that, unlike in the West, the place to the right of the host is *not* considered more prestigious, and you may be seated at either left or right. The banquet may be completed much faster than you would expect at home; dinner is not valued as an opportunity for lengthy conversation as it is elsewhere. You decide to reciprocate, but do not make the mistake of providing a return banquet which is significantly more expensive. This appears to criticize the initial banquet and causes offence.

A Chinese interpreter took an American visitor to a top Shanghai restaurant. In order to show his appreciation of the quality and abundance of the food, he asked at the end if he might have a doggy-bag to take the remains home. The interpreter commented: 'I was very embarrassed. The Chinese see using a doggy bag as [a sign of being] mean. Who wants to eat yesterday's food?'

Some cultures prefer to entertain business colleagues at home, some in a restaurant. A Thai explained why her Western manager's attempt to arrange a dinner party for his Thai staff at his house was considered a failure: 'In a restaurant we know where to sit [in order of importance] and who to talk to. We are very embarrassed going to a home for a business dinner, particularly a Western house. We don't know how to behave.'

Similarly, an American journalist had been at college with the son of a prominent Columbian businessman. He visited the country many times thereafter, meeting his friend's family. But only after two years was he invited to the family home. He explained: 'That was very important. It showed I was treated and trusted as one of the family. It's not a casual thing, as in the States.'

In Germany, the host always suggests and pays for the dinner. The visitor is only able to repay the courtesy by inviting his or her host to make a return visit.

When entertaining members of another culture in your country you have to make a decision as to whether to take them to a restaurant serving your cuisine or theirs.

When the cuisines are very different (for instance, German as against Korean) and the other persons are visiting your country for the first time you are always safer to choose their cuisine. They may be literally unable to stomach food radically different from that to which they are used.

This also gets over the problem of food taboos: Muslims and Jews do not eat pork and may object to eating food prepared in utensils used for pork, and Hindus do not eat beef.

Take your guests to a restaurant serving your local specialties if:
• your and their cuisines are similar;
• food taboos do not apply;
• they have some experience of your cuisine and/or indicate a desire to try it.

Westerners used to using a knife and fork may be unused to using chopsticks in an Oriental culture. If this is your problem, make sure you practice before leaving home. Etiquette demands more than that you should simply be skilled at transferring food from your bowl or plate to your mouth. When eating with Chinese, never point your chopsticks at another person and never stick them upright in a bowl of rice. At a Korean meal, show that you have finished by laying them on the table; atop your bowl signals that you are merely pausing. At a Japanese meal, make sure that when laid down on the bowl or chopstick rest, they are not pointed at another guest.

Orientals dining in the West should not despair of the permutations in use of knife, fork and spoon; learn what you can before, and watch your hosts.

Slurping noises and burps which may be considered good manners at home as a signal that you are enjoying the food should be avoided.

8.8   STANCE, DISTANCE, AND GESTURES

The story that introduced this chapter showed the importance of stance and distance. By adopting a particular stance and using particular gestures, you communicate feelings and an attitude about the relationship, and similarly interpret the stance adopted by the other person. The messages thus communicated are powerful because they are usually sent and received subconsciously, and therefore cannot be easily controlled. (This also applies to messages signaled by eye movements and voice quality, discussed below.)

Gestures made during conversation are almost always synchronized with verbal elements. For instance, a hand gesture falls on a stressed word rather than on an unstressed word, and the body shifting forward synchronizes with that part of the message to which the speaker gives particular emphasis. Gestures are used as a non-cognitive sub-text to underline the rhythms and meanings of the cognitive spoken message.

Furthermore, a participant in a conversation relates his or her gestures (and eye movements) to those made by the other, and to the creation of the joint discourse. Here is a simple example. A speaker leans forward to emphasize a point, the hearer leans back, then turns his head away, to indicate that he disagrees, or is breaking off his hearing activity and wants to make a verbal contribution.

None of this means that all speakers gesture equally, or that the more you gesture the more effective a speaker you are; a small hand movement can be most powerful if it contrasts with otherwise stillness. Nor does it mean that the same gesture means the same thing in different cultures.

Researchers are unable to agree on how far particular forms of non-verbal physical behavior are universal and how far they are constrained by cultural features, and therefore differ. For instance, shortening the upper lip and bearing the teeth is generally reckoned to be aggressive and akin to animals signaling conflict. But there are startling variances, and the cross-cultural manager is wise to assume cultural differences until the evidence proves otherwise.

For example, Anglos usually assume that a smile indicates pleasure and good humor and that its meaning is universal; this is not the case. The Japanese are taught to smile as a matter of etiquette: an appearance of happiness avoids inflicting sorrow on the other person. Klineberg cites a story[7] of a Japanese woman servant who

'. . . smilingly asked her mistress if she might go to her husband's funeral.

> Later she returned with his ashes in a vase and said, actually laughing, 'Here is my husband'. Her white mistress regarded her as a cynical creature; Hearn [1894] suggests that this may have been pure heroism.'

In other Asian cultures, too, a smile may indicate a need to disguise embarrassment. The Westerner who interprets a smile raised in response to a proposition as an invitation to continue the topic may be making a grave mistake; instead, perhaps the topic should be dropped.

Anglos often betray uncertainty by such involuntary gestures as touching their faces and twitching their feet. If this is your problem, make a conscious effort to keep your hands away from your face and make sure your feet are out of the other person's field of vision. On the other hand, try to position yourself so that you can observe the other person's feet and check when he or she is under pressure.

Our introductory example showed that Arabs are happiest speaking straight to the other person and at about 18 inches distance. If you observe two Anglos talking like this, you can usually assume (without hearing a word spoken) that the communication is emotionally tense. By one estimation, Anglos become uncomfortable when sitting at a nose-to-nose distance of less than five and a half feet;[8] and it is common in an Anglo office to see people talking to each other leaning against opposite walls of a corridor. Hall suggests that Americans will not stand closer than 18 to 20 inches away when talking to a stranger of the same sex.[9]

Some cultures use touching as a means of showing trust and affection. An Italian visiting a factory in Canton suddenly placed his arm around the shoulders of his Chinese opposite number to indicate to the other people present the closeness of their relationship. Chinese do not touch in this way for this purpose, and the man was caused deep embarrassment. In Indonesia, make sure never to touch the other person, and this includes clapping him or her on the back.

In Oriental countries, from the Indian sub-continent eastwards, it is considered disrespectful to show the soles of your feet to another person. The American habit of leaning back in the chair with your feet up on your desk is therefore to be avoided in these cultures. Do not use your feet to point, particularly not at another person. In Thailand, never hit another person on the head, where the spirit is supposed to reside. In Malaysia, do not cross your legs when sitting in front of a superior person: sit with your knees and legs together.

8.8.1   Gestures of Greeting

In those cultures where physical contact is associated with intimate relationships and is therefore eschewed between business colleagues and in public, informal and physical greetings create embarrassment and animosity. An Asian newspaper writes:[10]

'Australians have reached the conclusion that "G'day mate, how's it going", followed by a hearty slap on the back, is no way to do business in Asia.

The blunt greeting has in the past been an endearing formula for winning contracts in many parts of the world. But in Asia it can be as insulting as a slap in the face.

Australians are now being encouraged to try the more subtle approach of learning Asian languages and culture.'

Even handshaking is avoided. In many South East Asian cultures members greet each other by placing their hands together in front of your face and making a slight bow. Complex social rituals determine who makes this salute to whom first (usually the junior to the senior), at what level, and how deep the bow. This salute serves the useful function of allowing an individual to respectfully greet a crowd of people when it would not be possible to acknowledge them all individually. A newscaster might start the news program by thus saluting an audience of millions.

Managers from these cultures may expect to shake hands with the Westerner. Nevertheless, the Western cross-cultural manager can make a good impression by returning this gesture with the Oriental gesture, made appropriately. Similarly, the Oriental manager working in the West has to overcome his or her inhibitions about shaking hands and in addition may have to put up with some friendly back-slapping.

In Anglo cultures, a firm handshake is associated with strength of character and commitment and is valued. Other cultures (for instance in the Middle East) are used to giving a much lighter handshake.

In India, middle-class business people are now more used to shaking hands than making the traditional *namaste* (hands together). However, a male should not expect to shake hands with a female unless she makes the gesture first. If she chooses not to shake hands, a smile or verbal greeting is sufficient.

The Anglo is inhibited about public kissing, particularly between men. In Latin cultures, a kiss on both cheeks is common; in Latin America, the kiss is accompanied by placing a hand on the other person's shoulder and is known as the *abrazzo*.

The Japanese and Koreans bow in greeting, and the depth of the bow indicates the degree of respect shown. Displays of public emotion are avoided, even within the family; husband and wife bow to each other, and a son returning from completing his education overseas is greeted at the airport not by embraces but by bows, a little deeper than usual.

In the Oriental cultures, kissing, particularly mouth-to-mouth, is considered a private sexual act. Public kissing is thought obscene and should be avoided.

8.8.2 Signaling Agreement and Disagreement

The New Zealand Maori signal 'yes' by raising the head and chin; Sicilians use the same gesture to signal 'no'. In Iranian Azerbaijani, a nod forwards indicates 'yes' and a nod backwards indicates 'no'. La Barre reports that a Bengali servant in Calcutta expresses the same function by rocking his head rapidly in an arc from shoulder to shoulder, usually four times.[11] This is prevalent throughout southern India.

8.8.3 Receiving an Object

An important object, for instance a gift, is received in Sri Lanka and Thailand by the right hand, with the left hand supporting the right elbow. In the Arab cultures never use the 'unclean' left hand to receive an object — nor to serve food, nor to take food (and never show the palm of your left hand).

Do not try to out-give the Japanese; it causes embarrassment and obliges the recipient to reciprocate. Here and elsewhere in the Orient it is considered impolite to unwrap a gift in front of the donor; by words, gesture, eyes, you may betray disappointment. (Equally, it is considered impolite to make an important gift that is not wrapped.) In Anglo cultures, it is usually considered impolite *not* to unwrap the gift.

8.9   EYES

It is a physiological phenomenon that when you are interested in the other person or the topic of communication, your pupils dilate. When you are bored, or antagonistic, your pupils contract. Some cultures recognize the importance of the eyes and the involuntary messages that they express. The Arab, for instance, stands so close in conversation in order to 'read' the eyes of the other person; Yassir Arafat, chairman of the Palestine Liberation Organization, used to wear dark lenses indoors, not from an affectation but in order to mask his true thoughts.

Similarly, Thais are taught to look for personality as expressed in the eyes. A Thai language teacher commented critically of her Western students: 'They are cold-hearted, they don't tell me anything with their eyes. They don't look at me when they talk.'

The Indian woman does not look into the eyes of a man to whom she is not related. She may look into the eyes of male family members with the exception of her maternal uncle, who, if unmarried, is an eligible marriage partner. In Indian and Middle Eastern cultures, a subordinate commonly looks down and away from a superior in order to show respect. This can create misunderstandings if the superior is an Anglo; in Anglo cultures this avoidance of gaze is commonly interpreted as a sign of evasiveness and untrustworthiness.

In fact, research carried out in the United States suggests that Americans maintain eye contact with the other person more when listening than speaking, in a ratio of about 2.5 or 3 to 1. Length of gaze increases with distance from 5.5 seconds at two feet to 8.8 seconds at six feet and 9.6 seconds at 10 feet.[12] In Anglo cultures, a superior may signal power by not maintaining eye contact when a junior is speaking; but a failure by the junior to maintain eye contact may suggest evasiveness.

One of the functions of making and breaking eye contact seems to be to tell your conversational partner when you have finished your turn and you wish him or her to make a contribution. Typically you break contact as you finish, then give a sustained gaze. This synchronization between eye movement and speech (and perhaps also gesture) shows how non-verbal signals communicate non-cognitive meaning.

What happens if you do not conform to the norms of your culture in making or breaking eye contact? (All the research shows wide differences between individuals.) In Anglo cultures an individual who makes abnormally long eye contact may be perceived as over-aggressive; a person who makes too little eye contact is hiding something. These perceptions are made unconsciously — you come away from a negotiation with feelings that, for some reason you cannot clarify, the other person is untrustworthy.

They are particularly dangerous when the other person belongs to another culture. He or she may be conforming to the norms of that culture, which happen not to correspond to your norms. This demonstrates the importance of understanding how much non-verbal behavior is determined or modified by culture. The cross-cultural manager may not always understand the meaning of specific non-verbal signals used by the other culture; but it must always be borne in mind that such differences exist, and that the meanings of signals may not correspond.

8.10   VOICE

Scholars have distinguished a range of features associated with the human voice and how it is used, which communicate meaning. These include:

- voice quality — for instance, its harshness, hardness, stridency, breathiness, thinness, strength, nasality;
- tempo;

- pitch variation;
- volume.

These are obviously influenced by physiological characteristics; for instance, pouting forwards of the lips affects the vocal tract and thus affects voice quality. But it is also significant that these features are stereotyped within the culture, and this influences their production. If the natural features of your voice are associated positively in your culture, you stress them. If they are associated negatively, you quickly learn to disguise them and seek remedies, for instance by learning from a speech therapist.

A voice feature that is stereotyped positively in one culture may strike the outsider very differently. The listener reacts in terms of his or her own cultural preferences, and hence is in danger of stereotyping the speaker on the basis of voice.

For example, in Anglo cultures a deep male voice is associated with masculinity and is favored, and a high-pitched male voice may be scorned. This opinion does not hold true elsewhere. In West Africa, males are freer to speak across a wide pitch range. A high-pitched voice is thought to be expressive of emotion, and in cultures which encourage the expression of emotion by males this is very acceptable. In Iran, females are expected to be relatively unemotional, and to speak within a more restricted pitch. It is acceptable for Anglo females to speak at a lower pitch than, for instance, Japanese females.

Hall suggests that, in terms of American stereotypes, Arabs, Spaniards, Indians and Russians speak too loudly; but to Britons, South East Asians and Japanese, the Americans are loud.[13]

Among Arabs, loudness is associated with sincerity and forcefulness, but not when speaking to a superior, with whom a softer tone must be used. Americans may speak loudly as a means of indicating that the other person should speak up. Hence, an Arab may adopt a relatively soft tone as a sign of respect when addressing an American. The American speaks up, signaling that the Arab should too; reacting to this expression of power (in his terms), the Arab reacts by speaking even softer. By the end of the conversation the Arab is shocked by the American's apparent bullying and the American equally annoyed by the Arab's seeming lack of forcefulness.

8.11 IMPLICATIONS FOR THE MANAGER

The cross-cultural manager needs to remember:

1 A greater part (perhaps 70 percent) of the meaning conveyed by a spoken message is communicated non-verbally.

2 Non-verbal communication is non-cognitive, and provides a powerful sub-text to the cognitive spoken message.
3 The message *sender* is often unconscious of sending these cognitive messages, and the *receiver* is unconscious of how and why they convey specific impressions.
4 Because so much of the process of non-verbal communication is unconscious, it creates impressions which work below the conscious threshold, are difficult to rationalize and uproot, and are hence extremely potent.
5 Much non-verbal communication is culturally conditioned. How the message is sent and how interpreted is determined by cultural values.
6 A non-verbal signal may communicate one message in culture A and a different message in culture B.

Hence the cross-cultural manager needs to be sensitive to the possibility that his or her behavior is communicating messages in the other culture that are not intended; and the interpretations placed upon non-verbal messages sent by members of the other culture may not correspond to what is intended.

We have touched on only a very few of the signal types by which cultures communicate non-verbal meaning. Others not discussed include facial expressions, values associated with smell (including the use of perfume), color symbolism, social rituals, graphic symbols. The manager needs to look for differences in the use and interpretation of these in other cultures and to apply the same principles to their identification and analysis.

8.12 SUMMARY

The purpose of this chapter has been to indicate the range of non-verbal message types used to communicate meaning, their importance, and the extent to which they vary across cultures.

Behavior we commonly think of as 'natural' may not be natural to a member of another culture. That is, our instinctive and non-verbal reactions to events are partly determined by social norms.

In a short chapter only a few non-verbal signal types can be dealt with, even briefly. We have discussed notions of time (section 8.2), space (section 8.3), material possessions in the workplace (section 8.4), dress (section 8.5), business cards (section 8.6), entertainment offered by and to the manager (section 8.7), stance, distance, and gesture (section 8.8), eye movements and contact (section 8.9), and voice features (section 8.10).

EXERCISES

Exercise 1

This examines how non-verbal behavior in groups reflects cultural priorities.

A large group of engineering instructors drawn from one country were attending a seminar held in the palatial conference center of an international agency. For one session they were divided into a number of small groups, each consisting of about 15 persons. They met in separate rooms on the second floor of the building. When the session ended, the groups left their rooms and walked down a broad central staircase to the coffee shop on the first floor.

The first group to come down descended the staircase in ranks of about three abreast. They descended in close formation, looking ahead of them and talking softly. The front rank consisted of a white-haired man (older than any other person in either group), accompanied on either side by a much younger man listening in respectful silence.

The second group descended in ones, twos and threes, spread the length of the staircase. Those at the front looked back, apparently unsure where to go. Those behind were shouting, calling jokes, talking among themselves.

(a) How do you explain the behavioral differences?
(b) Where do you think the seminar participants came from: (i) Australia, or (ii) Bangladesh, or (iii) Switzerland. Explain your answer.

Exercise 2

This exercise looks at how meaning is communicated non-verbally.

(a) Use a video recorder to record a television political discussion involving a number of people. Make sure you are out of the room or cannot hear it when the recording is made. Then play it back with the volume turned right down.
(b) What does their non-verbal behavior tell you about the communication? Note your answers to these questions:
  • At what points do the participants (i) agree, or (ii) disagree?
  • Who is most forceful?
  • At what points is each speaker most defensive? Look for indicators of uncertainty such as touching the face, covering the mouth, clenching the jaw, and looking away from the other person.
  • Who are you most inclined to trust, and why?
(c) Now rewind the video, turn up the volume, and check your answers. How successfully did you infer the communication from the non-verbal signals?
(d) Show the recording to a member of another culture, and compare your reactions to the silent play. At what points do your interpretations differ? If they differ, why?

NOTES

1 Hall, E.T. and Whyte, W.F. (1961) Intercultural communciation: a guide to men of action. *Human Organization*, **19**(1), 5–12.

2 *Ibid.*, p. 9.

3 *Ibid.*, p. 8.

4 Almaney, A.J. (1981) Cultural traits of the Arabs: growing interest for international management. *Management International Review*, **21**(3), 10–18 (see 12).

5 Bedi, H. (1987) Management: 'Fun' at the boss's table. *Asiaweek*, 7 June.

6 Shipiro, M. (1988) Waiter, is that gold or lead in my mushroom? *International Herald Tribune*, 23 November.

7 Klineberg, O. (1935) *Race Differences*. New York. See also Hearn, L. (1894) The Japanese smile, in *Glimpses of Unfamiliar Japan*, New York.

8 Sommer, R. (1959) Studies in personal space. *Sociometry*, **22**, 247–60.

9 Hall, E.T. (1955) The anthropology of manners. *Scientific American*, **192**, 84–90.

10 'G'day mate' not working in Asia. *Nation* (Bangkok), 5 January 1989.

11 For these and other examples of non-verbal communication, see La Barre, W. (1947) The cultural basis of emotions and gestures. *Journal of Personality*, **16**, 49–68.

12 Argyle, M. and Dean, J. (1965) Eye contact, distance and affiliation. *Sociometry*, **28**, 289–304.

13 See Hall, E.T. (1972) Silent assumptions in social communication. Reprinted in *Communication in Face to Face Interaction* (eds. J. Laver and S. Hutcheson). Harmondsworth, pp. 274–88 (see 279).

9
Preparing for Cross-Cultural Negotiations

9.1 INTRODUCTION

A New Zealand team negotiated a deal with a small family business in Malaysia. The Malaysian team was led by their president, a young graduate of the London School of Economics. Discussions were amicable, and on the third day an informal agreement was reached. At a celebratory banquet, the president said that after sorting out a few last details he would sign the deal, probably within 24 hours. The New Zealanders had no reason to doubt his obvious sincerity. They congratulated themselves on so rapidly concluding, and telexed the good news home.

For the next two days they heard no more from the president, and telephone calls failed to reach him. Then a younger brother appeared. He greatly regretted that no deal could be made. Their widowed mother had refused her elder son permission to sign. The New Zealanders had neither seen or heard of the lady before. They discovered that although she held no office in the company, her family authority translated into absolute rights of veto over the company's business.

This exemplifies the problems that occur when the negotiator is not the person with authority to take decisions on the negotiated agreement. Because they assumed that the company president enjoyed full control, the New Zealand team had failed to prepare for the possibility that they would need to satisfy the needs of some person other than those present at the negotiation. Because he had failed to make clear the restrictions on his authority, the president lost face by so abruptly breaking off talks.

166

DATA YOU NEED ON THE COMPANY

- Products: characteristics, life cycles, development, differentiation, hierarchy. R & D policy.
- Pricing strategy: objectives, elasticity.
- Profits and profitability.
- Purchasing strategy.
- Markets (local and international). Customers. Sources of materials. Demand: market share. Competitors. Marketing strategy. Advertising and promotional strategies/agents.
- Channels of distribution and distributors. Transportation.
- Labor relations. Recruitment policies. Training facilities. Salary structures and fringe benefits. Labor relations between locals and members of your culture.
- Financial data. Financial statements and other reports. Debt ratios.
- Communication facilities.
- Type of company: legal status. Importance of family ties. Patron–client relationships.
- Organizational structure, and strategies for change. Structures of control and communication. Structures for planning, motivation, and resolving conflict. How decisions are made, communicated, and implemented. Organizational culture.
- Technology and plant.
- Record in negotiating and in implementing negotiations: delivery and quality performance. Legal history.

DATA YOU NEED ON THE INDUSTRY

- National and international competition.
- Market growth. Industry forecasts.
- Market research.
- Upstream and downstream industries, local and/or foreign.
- The categories relating to the company, where they apply to the industry.

DATA YOU NEED ON THE NATIONAL ENVIRONMENT

- Economic and financial data: currency, exchange rates and requirements, conditions for repatriation of capital, national and company investment policies, subsidies, tax structure, tariffs, customs duties,

expected time for customs clearance. Inflation rate. GNP. Average incomes.
- Infrastructure: transportation, communication systems.
- Labor resources: skills demanded and supplied, trained manpower, training facilities, educational structure.
- Laws relating to trade and industry. Plant location, pollution and the environment.
- Laws relating to employment, recruitment and dismissal procedures, severence payments, salary structures, fringe benefits.
- Laws relating to ethical problems.
- Laws relating to ownership of land, plant, technology, intellectual property.
- The political system and structures; opposition groups within the political structure and from outside it.
- Country risk.
- Geography and climate. Hot, wet, cold seasons. (When is the best time to negotiate?)
- Public holidays, work hours.
- Names and addresses of contacts.

DATA YOU NEED ON THE CULTURAL ENVIRONMENT

- Typical cultural attitudes towards time, nature, human relationships, modes of activity. Power distances, needs to avoid uncertainty, degree of individualism versus collectivism, degree of masculinity versus femininity. (See Chapter 2.)
- Attitudes towards planning, motivation, conflict, decision making, implementation of decisions. (See the companion volume, *Managing Across Cultures.*)
- Face-to-face relationships in business. (See Chapter 6.)
- Evidence of and attitudes towards cultural change.
- Values associated with innovation and technology.
- Attitudes towards non-members of the culture, and towards members of your culture.
- Degree of legalism in negotiating and implementing negotiations.
- Social, religious, ethnic, economic, political groups. Inter-group conflicts.
- Languages used and language groups. Correlations between language groups and social, religious (etc.) groups.

Checking the limitations on your authority to take decisions in a negotiation is one aspect of preparation, and how you decide to use this authority influences your strategy. This chapter deals with the range of factors influencing the preparation of an effective strategy. Our basic categories (WHO, WHAT, WHY, HOW, WHERE and WHEN) are applied once more.

9.2   BACKGROUND INFORMATION

The first stage of preparing your negotiating strategy consists of preparing and reviewing background technical information. This is essential: PREPARE, PREPARE AGAIN, AND THEN CHECK YOUR PREPARATIONS. Time invested in preparations is never wasted. If you do not apply all the information you collect in a particular negotiation, you may need it again for a future negotiation with this company or some other company within the same country and culture group.

Always invest time in updating your information. Political and economic conditions change so rapidly that data collected even a few weeks before may be outdated by the time you arrive at the negotiation table.

The information you need can be classified under four headings: company data; industry data; data on the national environment; data on the cultural environment.

9.2.1   Sources of Background Information

Many companies are inhibited from developing their international markets and negotiating for foreign contracts by the problems of finding these data. If you are considering trading with a less-developed country which has only recently begun to play a significant role in world markets, the difficulties of securing up-to-date data from reliable sources may seem insurmountable.

Some of the sources listed below supply information freely, but others can be costly (consultants, for example).

1   Your own internal resources. Unknown to you, some other branch of your company may have previously traded with this country or company. Has any individual in your company worked with this country before joining you, or even visited on vacation? Check your records.

2   The other country's embassy and consulates have trade officials who will be happy to offer advice. Check their libraries and reading rooms.

3   Trade missions.

4   Your own country has trade officials who can offer advice, which

perhaps redresses any bias you may be given by other-country sources. Check with your department of commerce/foreign ministry/ministry of overseas trade (etc.).

5   Trade publications, specialist reports (for instance the *Economist* Country Reports), and business journals, including those published in the other country. For other-country journals, check with their embassy and trade missions.

6   Reference directories.[1]

7   Business/financial press; the business and international politics pages of non-specialist newspapers.

8   Financial reports; other company reports.

9   Universities and management schools. They can put you in touch with (a) faculties which consult, and (b) alumni who may have experience of the other country.

10   Other consultants.

11   Banks: international, headquartered in your country, or headquartered in the other country.

12   International organizations: for instance, the International Monetary Fund (IMF), International Trade Administration (ITA), and United Nations agencies.

13   Organizations such as Rotary and Lions, which have international branches and can provide contacts.

14   Other-country foreign trade associations; for instance, the Japanese External Trade Organization (JETRO).

15   Your trade/professional association.

16   Other companies in your country.

17   Government departments in the other country.

18   A local agent or 'fixer'.

The importance of the last two are discussed below.

9.2.2   Government Departments in the Other Country

If you are planning a joint venture or a subsidiary in the other country, contact officials in local government departments as early as possible. They can advise on regulations and legal requirements, and possible subsidies.

Particularly in a highly collectivist culture, government bureaucrats may feel greater loyalty towards their department and superiors than towards the civil administration as a whole. When their responsibilities overlap (for instance, responsibilities for awarding tax exemptions, shared by a Ministry of Finance, Ministry of Trade, Ministry of Development), departmental staff perceive their relations with other departments in terms of competition. If you need to communicate with a range of departments, contact them all individually: you cannot be certain that documents sent to one will be efficiently relayed to the others.

9.2.3   The Agent or 'Fixer'

A good local fixer serves not only as a source of information; he or she can also perform a range of other functions, before, during and after the negotiation. These include:

(a) arranging the negotiation and preparing the groundwork;
(b) advising on the logistical factors (see section 9.5), including booking accommodation;
(c) arranging official documentation (work permits, operating licences, customs clearance, etc.);
(d) suggesting future possibilities for business, and making introductions;
(e) performing normal agency/consulting roles.

In general, the agent 'greases the wheels'.

9.3   WHO ARE THE OTHER PARTIES, WHAT DO THEY WANT, AND WHY?

The next stage of preparing your negotiating strategy involves assessing the needs of both sides. Analyses of the participants, issues and interests proceed concurrently. Here we deal first with their side and then yours; understanding their situation helps you determine how best to advance your case. We deal with four questions:

1   WHO is in their team? What is its size and composition?
2   WHAT company interests are represented? Related to this, are legal interests represented?
3   WHAT authority does their team have to take decisions?
4   WHY are they negotiating?

Your answers affect how you prepare your own tactics — discussed in section 9.4.

9.3.1   Who Represents their Interests?

You are greatly helped by information regarding the identities of their team. In particular, you do not wish to face a team of six active negotiators on your own, or a team of specialists whose skills you cannot balance.

The size and composition of the team is influenced by cultural factors. Greek and Latin American top managers prefer to maintain personal control over all aspects of the negotiation rather than to delegate to subordinates. The Mexican may be selected for his or her rhetorical skills and capacity to impress. The Japanese aim to reach consensus among themselves at all stages, and so bring a large team in order that all interests are represented. The Chinese also bring large teams, but authority is rooted at senior levels.

You hope to discover the names, ranks, and functions of their team members. You cannot expect this information to be easily available, particularly when it is to their disadvantage that you should have it, and in a culture which harbors strong suspicions of outsiders. Research conducted within your own organization, with other companies that have dealt with this company and culture, and with your trade organizations, chamber of commerce, should give you some idea of what to expect.

This initial information will help you to estimate how many of their team will be active in the negotiation. In a collectivist and wide power distance culture, the manager may come to the table with an entourage of aides who are not expected to contribute other than by demonstrating agreement with and loyalty to their boss. This function is symbolic; it shows that the boss has power over the organization and that internal relations are harmonious.

Your knowledge of who comprises their team gives you some idea of what issues they consider important. If their engineering function is heavily represented, then you might decide to include a high-powered engineer on your team. A study by Campbell and associates found that the status or role of the other person was particularly crucial to British sales negotiators, in contrast with the French, Americans, and Germans.[2]

How many of their team play an active role? You cannot take for granted that a silent member of the team is equally silent away from the negotiating table. It is often a clever strategy to bring one team member whose primary function is to listen and to analyze. This member has an important influence during breaks, when the team plans its strategy for the next session.

The composition of the typical American team reflects a concern with technical competence. But a company from a high power distance culture may be represented by its most senior and prestigious members whose presence best reflects its importance, and the importance it ascribes to the negotiation. Faced by a team of experts but of relatively low company status, they may question whether your organization is equally serious.

Assume that an Anglo company sends a young fresh-faced technical expert to negotiate with a Chinese company. The latter is represented by a senior and aged executive. He feels his face threatened by having to deal on equal terms with a much younger person and pulls his organization out of the talks. In this context, the Anglo company would do better to send an older person of equivalent rank.

Do they intend to include a member of their legal staff? If so, then expect an emphasis on legal guarantees, and make sure that your interests are similarly represented. If they do not intend to bring a lawyer, then only include one on your side when you have considered the cultural implications. In cultures which place a premium on trust in negotiating and implementing a contract, including a lawyer might be construed to mean that you do not trust them to keep their word.

For instance, Japanese companies have traditionally emphasized consensus and compromise in reaching agreement on disputes. The legal profession has a much lower status than in the West, and the Japanese used to include a lawyer in their team as a last resort. In response to American negotiating practices this is changing, and the Japanese team is now more likely to include a member of their legal staff.

Make sure you know the titles of all members of their team. These give you some indication of each individual's expertise and authority. But do not expect that the role associated with a title used in another culture corresponds precisely to its role in yours. You should ask if you have any doubts of the functions performed by their 'president', 'general manager', etc.

What can you learn of the personalities of their negotiators, and does this influence your choice of representatives? If you expect them to send a person with a reputation for making threats, then obviously you will be better represented by a person able to counter this particular tactic.

Campbell and associates found that negotiator characteristics are particularly crucial in negotiations between French business people, in contrast with Americans, Germans, and the British.[3] They suggest that, when negotiating sales with the French, choose representatives who are similar in personality and background to the French team.

9.3.2 What Authority Does Their Team Have to Take Decisions?

Claims of limited authority includes:

- limited personal authority ('Only our CEO can decide that');
- policy and financial limitations;
- technological limitations;
- legal and political limitations ('Our laws do not permit us to do that');
- ethical and principled limitations ('Our country is poor, and I would not be acting responsibly if I agreed to divert funds to a project which primarily benefits foreigners').

The first of these concerns us here.

The people playing the most active part in the negotiating process may not be the most active in taking the decisions. The decision makers may not even be present: negotiators may have to satisfy and perhaps buy off a number of absent third-party constituencies, which may include bosses, family members, shareholders, political and governmental authorities, other customers/suppliers, and workers and labor organizations. These parties have a formal or informal interest in the company's business, and in different cultures a constituency may be more or less significant. When you enter the negotiation, can you identify these invisible constituencies and their interests?

In the People's Republic of China, all final decisions have to be delayed until ratified by the relevant political authorities, who have formal authority. Pye writes:[4]

> '. . . negotiating teams tend to be large, but lines of authority can be diffuse and vague. Technical specialists and representatives of end users may aggressively take part in the deliberations but turn out not to have commensurate influence on final decisions.'

In other words, you need to find out whether the negotiators are also the decision makers.

The team negotiating on behalf of a family company in a personnel bureaucracy (defined in Chapter 2) may only feel empowered to sign when they have secured the informal agreement of senior family members. The introductory story gave an example.

Your understanding of the interests and constituencies represented by the negotiators gives you some idea of how they will decide and the time you should expect to allow before the contract is finally signed. The Japanese look for a consensus; Taiwan Chinese firms tend to adopt a 'top-down' narrowly collective process of decision making. Members of a narrow power distance culture are more likely to vote, and in a wide power distance culture the decision is handed down from the top.

Your analysis of their decision-making process helps you decide whose interests you have to satisfy and whose are easier to ignore.

9.3.3   Why Are They Negotiating?

When you have done your background preparation on the company and its environment, and identified the interests of the actual negotiators and of their unseen constituents, you are well-placed to identify their objectives in negotiating. In your assessment, how do they perceive the issues, and what do they want to achieve from the negotiation? Can you identify any issues that are potentially embarrassing to the other side and that they would prefer to avoid? Can you use your knowledge of these issues to your advantage (without, of course, resorting to blackmail or otherwise transgressing ethical norms)?

Now assess their interests. What is the most you expect them to demand and what is the least you expect them to accept? Distinguish between

(a) objectives that they MUST achieve;
(b) those that they HOPE to achieve;
(c) those that they WOULD LIKE to achieve, but are of relatively lesser importance.[5]

The HOPE objectives are less essential than the MUST objectives, and the WOULD LIKE objectives are the least essential of all.

In an international setting, estimating MUSTS, HOPES, and WOULD LIKES is complicated by cultural factors. Their priorities may not correspond to yours. For instance, assume that you are trying to negotiate a labor contract with a union in the other culture. Chapter 2 shows that you cannot expect the labor force to be motivated by the same factors as those that appeal to employees in your home context. Thus you cannot take for granted that the MUSTS, HOPES, and WOULD LIKES expressed by your home-based workforce correspond to those of the local workforce.

Also, look for their BEST Alternative TO a Negotiated Agreement, or BATNA.[6] If they cannot reach agreement with you, then what alternatives are available to them? Suppose that you are negotiating with a foreign manufacturing company to supply machine tools. If talks were to break down, how easily could they find another supplier? If your competition is strong, then they have little to lose by the breakdown, and hence you can expect them to hold out for good terms. If you are alone in the field, then they may be desperate to get the contract signed, and this is to your advantage.

Suppose that you represent management in a labour dispute with your unions and your BATNA is weak; you will have to accept a strike by the workforce. You analyze that this would prove highly damaging to the company. You wish to avoid resorting to this BATNA if you possibly can, and hence you are under considerable pressure to negotiate a satisfactory agreement.

You can only estimate international BATNAs if you understand the international marketplace and the activities of your competitors. This reinforces the need for the careful preparation of background data.

9.3.4   Cooperation and Competition

Every negotiation is an expression of urges towards both cooperation and competition. If you hope to avoid all competition, then you can expect to give away everything the other side demands. If you refuse to cooperate, then you can only expect to gain by force. Both you and the other side enter the negotiation expecting to cooperate at some points and compete at others.

Do not assume that members of a culture that prefers to avoid open conflict will be inhibited from pushing their objectives and will give you an easy time. We have seen that the Japanese dislike for saying 'no' is influenced by a perception of social relationships and courtesy rather than by any lack of competitive spirit. Equally, a good negotiator from a conflict-tolerating culture is cooperative when it is in his or her interests to be so.

All cultures throw up the rare extremes of entirely malevolent and untrustworthy opponents (such as terrorists) and fully cooperative partners who give and expect total honesty. In any culture, the great majority of negotiators are found between these two extremes, prepared to give on certain issues and determined to compete on others.

In general, expect cooperation in the earlier stages of the negotiation when areas of mutual interest are examined, and competition in the later bargaining stages. These stages are examined in the next chapter.

9.4   HOW WILL YOU NEGOTIATE?

The two preparatory activities of assessing the other side's situation and establishing your own interests proceed together. When building your own case, review your background information and assessments of the other side, and answer these questions:

1   How large should your team be?
2   What company interests should be represented?
3   What authority do you have to take decisions?
4   Why are you negotiating, and what do you hope to achieve?

9.4.1   Your Team and Authority

Decide on the composition of your team, taking into account your understanding of how the other side are likely to express their cultural priorities at the negotiating table. How many people should you include and what qualities should they possess? Decide what professional skills you need to have represented, including legal skills, and what levels of seniority. A technical person may be essential as a resource, but how far can he or she be utilized as a negotiator?

Do you need to pay attention to age or sex characteristics? We have already noted that when dealing with a Chinese team you might do better to nominate as leader an older person who carries authority, rather than a younger person, even though the latter may have greater professional expertise. This also applies with other Asian cultures which traditionally respect age. In some cultures, women are not usually thought to be qualified for important business, and a woman on your team may be at a serious disadvantage in Saudi Arabia or Iran.

Check the limits to your formal and informal authority. What third-party constituencies do you have to satisfy? Supposing that conditions are not as you assumed before you left home, or the other side makes unexpected demands, how far are you empowered to make on-the-spot decisions in response? There are two reasons for making certain of your own status. First, it is to your psychological advantage that you should be precisely aware of the limitations on your authority; it gives you certainty and force in your communications. Second, remember that, in the other country, you may not be able to depend upon quick and secure communications if you need to seek instructions.

In the negotiation, as a general rule you will not admit to limitations to your authority unless it is in your interests to do so. The stronger your position appears to be, the more respect you earn. However, do not boast of authority as a matter of pride when you may actually be forced to back down and seek head-office ratification, or when pretending to wait for ratification allows you to play for time and so gives a tactical advantage.

A Danish team negotiating in the People's Republic of China was kept waiting for several weeks after the chief Chinese negotiator had suddenly apologized that the negotiations had taken an unexpected turn and that he needed to consult with his political bosses.

The Danes suspected that this delay was unnecessary and that the delay was only intended to erode their patience; but they curbed their anxiety, and waited for the talks to resume.

When the Chinese team returned to the table, they explained that unfortunately they needed concessions. These were being imposed by their political bosses, who would have to be satisfied if the contract was to be signed.

The Danes turned the tables by regretting that they were not empowered to act in these new conditions and would have to return home for advice. When they returned, several weeks later, they were quickly offered terms very close to those provisionally agreed before the first delay.

Strategy planning issues are dealt with below. This discussion does not include negotiation tactics which are dealt with in the next chapter.

9.4.2 Preparing Issues

What are you negotiating for and what can you offer in return? Commercial negotiations are seldom restricted to a single issue of price for goods. All parties can expect to win something from a good negotiation. Part of the skill of effective negotiating is to create new issues, and so increase the alternatives for each party to benefit. Everyone can win; no one need lose.

Suppose that I offer to sell you 100 widgets for a price which you consider unsatisfactory. If we stop at this point, the deal breaks down and nobody benefits. The price I demand is a MUST HAVE, but I am happy to propose an additional offer of a gross of woggles at reduced price. You accept on condition that I pay freight charges. I respond by asking for an increased downpayment; and so on. These proposals increase the size of the pie to be shared, and give both sides a bigger slice.

How an imaginative solution helps both sides is exemplified by the story of two sisters who argued over possession of an orange.[7] One sister wanted to drink the juice, the other to use the peel in baking a cake. They agreed to divide it in two, and so overlooked an alternative by which both would double their benefits: one take all the peel and the other take all the juice.

As a first stage in increasing the alternatives, *list* the issues over which you expect to negotiate. When negotiating the sale of goods, for instance, these include:

(a) price;
(b) discounts;
(c) quantity;
(d) quality: technical specifications, quality control;
(e) time: delivery dates;
(f) freight and freight insurance;
(g) technology protection.

Then prioritize the issues, and decide whether there are any that you hope to avoid, because they are irrelevant, potentially embarrassing, or would be better delayed to some future occasion.

You may need to range far outside the foregoing conventional list to find the factor that clinches the deal. And finding ways of maximizing joint benefits may be difficult when you are dealing with another culture. It means developing a sophisticated understanding of their needs and problems. You cannot take for granted that your priorities (whether short-term gains, long-term commitment, etc.) correspond to yours.

The problems faced by a Briton when negotiating a deal in the Middle East show the need to use imagination. He reported of his opposite number:

'I couldn't spot what he really wanted. He knew my offer was good but he wasn't really interested. I suggested all the alternatives on payment, delivery, and so on. But he kept referring to his hopes for his son. Then I realized. He wanted me to get the boy a job in the UK. Well, he was a bright boy and that was no problem. My brother's a partner in [a merchant bank in the City of London]. I phoned him and fixed an attachment. I got the deal. My brother was pleased too, he got a useful contact.'

9.4.3   Preparing Interests

Next, identify your interest in each of the issues you have listed. What is the most you can realistically demand from the negotiation (without appearing to be an idiot), and what is the least you will accept? Decide your objectives and list:

(a)   objectives that you MUST achieve;
(b)   those that you HOPE to achieve;
(c)   those that you WOULD LIKE to achieve, but are of relatively lesser importance.

How does your list compare with the priorities you expect the other side to have? In which areas can you hope to cooperate? In which should you expect to compete? What competitive tactics can you expect to be used against you and how can you counter them?

Evaluate your position. How strong is your negotiating position, and what is your BATNA if the talks should break down? What are you prepared to sacrifice in order to prevent breakdown? What concessions are you prepared to make and what will you demand in return for them? On what points are you not prepared to concede?

Do not expect to achieve all your objectives. If you achieve all, you have either asked for too little or the other side is too weak. Both should worry you. If the first applies, you have not properly prepared your data regarding markets and competition. If the other side demonstrates weakness now, how forcefully can you expect them to implement the agreement when pressures from your competitors and from within their organization are exerted at a later stage?

Double-check your technical information. When negotiating with the Chinese, for instance, you can expect to be questioned carefully on technical specifications and you do not want to lose face by showing ignorance.

9.4.4   Preparing by Role-Play

Prepare by role-playing the negotiation within your own organization. If possible, have colleagues who have some experience of the other company and other culture to play devil's advocate and take the roles of the other side. Look for your weak points; what new information do you need?

Base the role-play upon your strategy plan. This helps you to

(a) reinforce your understanding of objectives;
(b) avoid confusion over areas of responsibility and expertise during the negotiation;
(c) avoid unwanted surprises;
(d) prepare fallback positions if you should need to revise your objectives and strategy;
(e) make constructive self-criticism of communication strategies (discussed in the next chapter).

9.4.5   Preparing Documentation

You expect to be given information about

- the other company;
- its industrial and national environment;
- members of the other team.

Make sure you have similar documentation about *your* background to give them. Information about your team members should include their names, ranks, and expertise.

Prepare documentation relating to technical matters. Be ready to provide both hard technical data and glossy brochures which convincingly market your company and product to a casual reader. The latter are useful because you can expect that in time out the other side will discuss the negotiation with family, friends and business acquaintances. They may have only a superficial understanding of the issues involved, yet make up an invisible constituency which powerfully influences the negotiation at a distance. It is a courtesy to have the documentation that you intend giving to the other side printed in their language.

Prepare an agenda of points which you think are negotiable. They may offer an alternative, so be ready to negotiate a joint text.

As you progress through the negotiation, prepare the following:

1 Summaries of points agreed to date — perhaps at the end of each stage or day — and check them with the other side. This makes it harder for them to renege on oral agreements.
2 Your own summaries showing what has been agreed in reference to your objectives. Use this to clarify your thinking and maintain unity within your team.
3 Notes of the other side's proposals, the points at which they appear strong and weak. This helps you analyze their position and identify their MUSTS, HOPES, and WOULD LIKES.

4   Revisions to your strategy plan.

5   Notes updating your background information.

9.5   WHEN AND WHERE: PREPARING THE LOGISTICS

This section deals with logistical factors that you need to prepare before the negotiation. First we examine questions of WHEN and WHERE, and then list general points.

9.5.1   The Investment in Time

How much time should you invest in the negotiation and what are the opportunity costs? On the one hand you may decide that a negotiation is stalled, the possibilities for increasing the size of the pie are negligible, and that you would do better to settle for what you can get and move on to more profitable business elsewhere. This must be weighed against the possibilities that quitting too soon will lose you opportunities for making a better deal and building relationships that will pay off in the future.

Graham and Herberger explain that Americans in particular have an international reputation for taking unnecessarily small profits in order to satisfy head office needs for a deal (almost any deal) and to rush on to the next deal.[8] Their obvious impatience is used against them by negotiators whose cultural concepts of time and its value are much longer term, and who only have to wait in order to get agreement on their own terms.

For instance, when the Americans and North Vietnamese met in Paris to negotiate an end to the Vietnam war, the State Department lodged their delegation in a hotel on a day-by-day basis. The Vietnamese leased a villa for a two-year period, thus demonstrating their readiness to hang on for the conditions they wanted.

With each new deal you need to calculate afresh how much time you can afford to invest. However, one golden rule stands out: DO NOT DISPLAY IMPATIENCE. Indicating that you are prepared to sit and wait is a legitimate form of bluffing, and pays dividends. The example above of the attitude displayed by the Vietnamese, whose military situation at the time scarcely warranted a further two years of bloody conflict, makes this clear. When the other side is not constrained by needs for a rapid agreement, showing your impatience only increases their intransigence.

9.5.2   Checking the Itinerary

If the negotiation involves traveling, plan the precise details of your travel plans. These can have as important an effect on the results of your negotiation as the talking, so get them right. If you have to travel far, you do not wish to be rushed straight into the introductory meeting. Give yourself time to rest after getting off the plane, and insist that this is respected. Plan your flight allowing for time differences and 'jet lag'.

> A Briton was due to negotiate a deal in Singapore. The experience of a colleague suggested that his hosts would want to take him straight from the airport to a reception, and then start talking early the next morning when he was still exhausted.
>
> He therefore arrived two days earlier than expected, giving himself time to recover from the flight. He spent these days taking long walks around the city, getting a feel for the new culture and observing as much as he could.
>
> At the time he was expected to arrive he returned to the airport. He met his hosts, explaining that he had been forced to take an earlier flight but had not wished to disturb their arrangements, and so had not announced himself.
>
> He welcomed the invitation to the reception, and the next morning started the talks in excellent condition.

Can you be certain of being met at the airport and taken to a hotel? If not, check the hotel name and address. If your flight arrives late, when airport banks have closed, check that you have local currency to pay for a taxi. What are the conventions for tipping taxi drivers?

When traveling to a country with which you are unfamiliar, do not make appointments without checking the calendar for public holidays and office and bank hours. In Muslim countries where the population fasts for the holy month of Ramadan, little business may be done in the second half of the day; so check the dates of Ramadan (they vary from year to year). In countries where office staff take a long siesta at midday, you may find you have to fix appointments for the morning or early evening.

9.5.3 Checking the Location

Where are you going to negotiate? Your own office gives you a tactical advantage; and if you have to make a trip, your local branch office or chamber of commerce is obviously preferable to their office. The relatively neutral ground of a hotel may make a satisfactory compromise.

Wherever the meeting, check that you have access to efficient and secure communication links. Check that your team has a room set aside for undisturbed private talk. Check the location of bathrooms. If you need to bring your own secretary and/or translator, what facilities are available for them?

OTHER LOGISTICAL FACTORS

1 Make sure of your visa as early as possible. Check with your sources on the length of time you need to allow for visa processing.
2 You may need specific documentation in support of a visa. For instance, a Westerner from a Christian country may need evidence of Church membership before traveling to some Muslim countries.
3 Check whether your passport is stamped for entry to countries considered unfriendly. For instance, some Muslim countries do not accept passports stamped for entry to Israel. If this is a problem, ask the passport department of your foreign service for an additional passport.
4 What health regulations are enforced? Do you need vaccinations and injections against specific diseases?
5 Make sure of customs regulations in the other country. Are there regulations restricting or banning the import of alcohol, or literature? You do not wish to be embarrassed or to embarrass your hosts by being held at the airport for bringing in a banned girly magazine.
6 How much of the other country's currency can you carry into the country? How will you be affected by exchange control regulations? What credit cards are commonly accepted?
7 If you are carrying medicinal drugs, do you need a doctor's prescription to take them through customs (for instance, when entering the United States)?
8 If you need to send large quantities of display and other material which cannot be carried in your luggage, when will it be delivered, and what facilities exist for checking it through customs?

9.6   IMPLICATIONS FOR THE MANAGER

This section applies the material presented in the chapter in the form of a strategy plan. Design a form which covers the following aspects of your preparation.

1   BACKGROUND INFORMATION

Research and check your background information.

2   YOUR TEAM

List:
  Name(s)

Rank(s)
Responsibilities
Other relevant factors (age, sex, experience of their culture, etc.).
Who has authority to decide on a deal?
Your third parties. What constituents do you have to satisfy in making a deal?

3 THEIR TEAM

List:
  Name(s)
  Rank(s)
  Responsibilities
  Other relevant factors.
Who has authority to decide on a deal?
Their third parties. What constituents do they have to satisfy in making a deal?

4 ISSUES

What do *you* perceive to be at issue?
What do *they* apparently perceive to be at issue?
What additional issues might be negotiated to the mutual benefit of both sides?

5 YOUR INTERESTS

Describe the maximum *you* can hope for.
Describe the minimum *you* can accept.
Describe *your* prioritized objectives:
  Those objectives that you *must* achieve
  Those that you *hope* to achieve
  Those that you *would like* to achieve, but are of relatively lesser importance.
What is *your* Best Alternative To a Negotiated Agreement?
What interests do *your* third parties have? What is the least that will satisfy them?

6 THEIR INTERESTS

Assess the maximum *they* can hope for.
Assess the minimum *they* can accept.
Assess *their* prioritized objectives:
  Those objectives that they *must* achieve
  Those that they *hope* to achieve

Those that they *would like* to achieve, but are of relatively lesser importance.
Assess *their* Best Alternative To a Negotiated Agreement.
Assess the interests of *their* third parties. What is the least that will satisfy them?

7   COOPERATION AND COMPETITION

Over what issues and interests do you expect to cooperate?
Over what issues and interests do you expect to compete?

8   TIME

How much time do you expect to invest in the negotiation?
What is the most time you will invest before breaking off negotiations?

9   PLACE

What advantages does the proposed site offer (i) you, and (ii) the other side?
What communications facilities are available? How do these restrict communications with your head office?

10   OTHER LOGISTICAL FACTORS

What other logistical factors have to be taken into account which may affect your traveling to the site of the negotiation?

9.7   SUMMARY

This chapter has dealt with your needs in preparing for cross-cultural negotiations, particularly when you are negotiating in another country. The sociological parameters of WHO, WHAT, WHY, HOW, WHEN, and WHERE have been applied again.

The first stage in formulating strategy consists in identifying your needs for background information, and section 9.2 discussed different categories of information and sources which can be tapped. Section 9.3 went on to show the strategic importance of analyzing information about the other side: who are the other parties, what do they want, and why? It dealt with needs to assess their team composition, their authority, their concepts of the issues and interests, and the losses they face if the negotiation should fail. Like you, they stand to gain from the negotiation, and have reasons for both cooperating and competing.

Section 9.4 raised similar questions about your side, and showed how the answers determine the broad lines of your negotiating strategy. (Ongoing strategic considerations are dealt with in the next chapter.) Section 9.5 looked at temporal and situational factors. The checklist in section 9.6 illustrated the implications for the manager.

EXERCISES

Exercise 1

This exercise practices preparation.

You represent a department store in your country. You are preparing to travel to three countries, Japan, Thailand, and Germany, in order to negotiate large purchases of costume jewelry. (You hope to make a deal in each of these countries.)

How do you expect them to negotiate? From your knowledge of their cultures, list *four* important points for each that you expect to affect their negotiating behavior. The points you list for any one country should not appear in the lists for the other two.

Exercise 2

This exercise practices analysis of the other side's objectives.

Your head office has to negotiate new contracts with your white-collar employee organizations in branches around the world. All make the same demands (not prioritized):

- a 20 percent rise in basic pay rates;
- massively increased sick pay and pension benefits;
- guaranteed long-term (10 years) employment contracts for all;
- generous awards for individual achievement.

You make a series of preliminary offers (see below). How far is each likely to meet the MUST HAVE objectives of each branch? Use the Chapter 2 material on cultural priorities to justify your answers.

Belgium

- a 20 percent rise in basic pay rates;
- no increased sick pay and pension benefits;
- no guaranteed long-term employment;
- generous awards for individual achievement.

Australia

- a 4 percent rise in basic pay rates;
- moderate increases in sick pay and pension benefits;
- guaranteed long-term (10 years) employment contracts;
- no awards for individual achievement.

Singapore

- basic pay rates raised on a sliding scale: 20 percent for senior staff and 3 percent for the most junior;
- massively increased sick pay and pension benefits;
- guaranteed moderate-term (5 years) employment contracts;
- generous awards for individual achievement.

Denmark

- no rise in basic pay rates;
- sick pay and pension benefits increased on a sliding scale: most benefits for senior employees;
- no guaranteed long-term employment;
- only junior employees to be rewarded for individual achievement.

NOTES

1 See, for instance, Tygier, C. (1983) *Basic Handbook of Foreign Exchange*. Euromoney Publications, London. Also Roberts, G. (ed.) (1985) *Guide to World Commodity Markets*. Economist Books, Kogan Page, London/Nichols Publishing, New York. Also *International Marketing Data and Statistics* (annual editions). Euromonitor, London. Also *Europa Year Book* (annual editions). Europa Publications, London.

2 Campbell, N.C.G., Graham, J.L., Jolibert, A. and Meissner, H.G. (1988) Marketing negotiations in France, Germany, the United Kingdom, and the United States. *Journal of Marketing*, **52**, 49–62.

3 *Ibid.*

4 Pye, L. (1982) *Chinese Commercial Negotiating Style*. Rand Corporation, Santa Monica, pp. xi–xii.

5 Kennedy, G., Benson, J. and McMillan, J. (1982) *Managing Negotiations*. Prentice-Hall, Englewood Cliffs, NJ.

6 Fisher, R. and Ury, W. (1981) *Getting to Yes*. Houghton Mifflin, Boston.

7 Follet, M.P. (1940) Constructive conflict. In *Dynamic Administration: The Collected Papers of Mary Parker Follett* (eds. H.C. Metcalf and L. Urwick). Harper, New York.

8 Graham, J.L. and Herberger, R.A. (1983) Negotiators abroad — don't shoot from the hip. *Harvard Business Review*, July/August, 160–8.

10
Cross-Cultural Negotiating

10.1 INTRODUCTION

John, a Canadian, had completed a three-year contract in Malaysia and was about to leave. He advertised his old but reliable car for sale. Bala, an Indian, answered, took the car for a test drive and made an offer.

'I suppose you have had many other enquiries?', he asked. 'Yes, but I'll put them off now you've made an offer', said John. Bala nodded, and asked when he could take possession. 'I'm flying out on the seventh of next month, so any day after the fourth', said John — again surrendering important information to no advantage. Bala promised to bring a cheque the following day.

When Bala returned, he said that unfortunately his brother-in-law had advised against the purchase because of the problem of finding spare parts. John suggested that they take the car to be checked by a local garage and obtain information on the availability of parts. Bala agreed. The garage supported John's story. Bala expressed his satisfaction but said that he could not insult his brother-in-law by going against his advice. He would try to convince him that the deal was good.

A few days later, and now only ten days before John's departure, he phoned to say that his brother-in-law was adamant, and had heard that the garage owner might be about to go out of business. However, he (Bala) very much wanted the car and for a price to be decided by a reputable garage that he used, he was prepared to settle the deal.

Bala's garage suggested a reduced price and expressed doubts about the availability of parts. Bala therefore suggested a reduction in the price. Reluctantly, John agreed. Bala said he would need to consult his brother-in-law.

This process of delay continued. John realized that he no longer had time to readvertise the car. This process continued, each time Bala whittling down the price and refusing to commit himself. The day before John's departure Bala handed him a cheque for a price about half that originally agreed and indicated that John could take it or leave it. Having no option, John took it.

What happened? Bala started with relatively little power and finished with a great deal. John threw away his advantage of a large market by accepting Bala's provisional offer at face value and turning away competitors, reducing his market to a single customer. He based his trust upon personal empathy rather than on a realistic assessment of Bala's interests. He failed to anticipate problems and to recognize Bala's capacity to bluff.

John compounded these errors by giving away his departure date and thus placing a time restriction on the sale; he would have done better to bluff by implying a date some time in advance of his actual date. (And he should probably have started negotiating far longer before his departure, and practiced patience.) His bargaining capacity was reduced further by Bala's refusal to accept the opinions of John's garage and instead referring the matter to his relative, whose word could not be challenged for reasons of family honor, and who remained out of the negotiation and inaccessible to John.

This chapter focuses on strategy and tactics within the negotiation. It emphasizes HOW the negotiation is conducted, and shows the importance of effective communication in cross-cultural negotiations.

10.2   NEGOTIATING A RELATIONSHIP

All negotiations pass through identifiable stages, which have varying importance in different cultures. Graham and Herberger distinguish four:[1]

1   Non-task relationship creation.
2   Task-related exchange of information.
3   Persuasion.
4   Concession and agreement.

They suggest that in international negotiations Americans are over-eager to get to what they perceive is the heart of the matter, and rush through to stage 3. In contrast, the Chinese and Brazilians emphasize building rapport and understanding of mutual advantage in doing a deal, and take much longer on the first two stages. In the final stage the Chinese focus on 'hard' issues (price, quantity, specifications, etc.) and this stage may be completed very quickly when bureaucratic clearance has been received.

Hence the Chinese or Brazilian negotiating in the United States finds himself pressured to proceed to the bargaining process more rapidly than he might wish, whereas the American must be prepared to spend more time in developing a shared concept of the mutual advantages of the relationship.

In practice, the Graham and Herberger model is over-systematic. Their stages 3 and 4 cannot usually be distinguished; processes of persuading, and conceding to reach agreement, tend to go together. And even a late point in the negotiation may see new information exchanged (their stage 2). Here we distinguish similar topic areas for reasons of descriptive simplicity, not because they necessarily follow each other sequentially in the negotiation. This section deals with the creation of a good relationship in the opening stage, and the next four sections focus on:

- finding common ground;
- persuasion;
- bargaining and conceding;
- implementation.

10.2.1   Opening Moves: Negotiating Trust

In the first stage of the negotiation, you are trying to establish a good working relationship. Can you communicate effectively with the other side? How far do you trust each other? If others believe that they can rely on your statements and promises they will be influenced by what you say, and hence more willing to do business with you.

You trust the other side when you have reason to believe the following:

(a)   They will not resort to unethical behavior — for instance by staging the negotiation room to your disadvantage, tapping communications with your head office, restricting your food, drink, comfort.
(b)   They will honor any agreement made and do their best to implement it. (This aspect of trust varies between cultures; see section 10.6.)
(c)   They will respect information and opinions made in confidence, and not leak these to your constituents or the media.
(d)   They will do their best to convince their constituents to accept agreements made between you.
(e)   It is in their interests to do business with you.

The last point, which Pye emphasizes in his analysis of negotiations in the People's Republic of China,[2] makes clear that trust must be based on an understanding of the other party's need to conclude the deal. Never depend solely upon personal feelings and empathy as a basis of trust: these personal feelings must be supported by an understanding of the other party's objectives and the alternatives that they have to implementing their agreements. Try to write contingent clauses into the contract that reduce the need to base trust on empathy, however great this may be.

You cannot expect to gain trust by asking for it. Only the naive purchaser buys a used car from the dealer who calls himself Honest Harry and gives more time to insisting that 'you can trust me' than to demonstrating the reliability of his goods.

In Anglo countries, business people are used to dealing with large companies; and an accredited representative of, say IBM or Shell or ICI, is accepted on this impersonal basis. It is taken for granted that the company has too much prestige at stake to trade dishonestly, and any disputes can be quickly sorted out by lawyers. But in cultures which do not have a history of intra-organizational trust and instead emphasize personal contacts, business is still based on relationships with individuals. In these cultures, the cross-cultural manager must be prepared to invest time in building trust in himself or herself as an individual, not merely as the representative of an organization.

Anglos, particularly Americans, are relatively uninhibited about proclaiming their own achievements. This makes sense within a highly individualist and mobile culture, but to other cultures it sounds like boasting. In Russia, bragging about your achievements is perceived as placing yourself above the collective group and is shameful. A Russian immigrant to the United States was frequently reduced to tears by the humiliation of having to extol her own achievements in job interviews.

The Japanese likes hearing his or her success praised as much as does anybody else, but will take care to claim good luck or to accredit the organiztion. So when dealing with a Japanese organization, emulate this modesty. The Anglo might circulate textual evidence of his department's success before the meeting, and in the meeting be content to refer to the text. Further, substitute references to 'I' by 'we'; for instance, 'we increased market share . . .' for 'I increased market share . . .'.

10.2.2 The Benefits of a Long-Term Relationship

You hope that by achieving a relationship of trust in one negotiation, you increase the possibilities of your doing mutually rewarding business together in the future. How far should you explicitly plan for this future? What concessions should you make in order to ensure this? How far can the negotiator afford to moderate demands in a particular negotiation in order to buy some hope of future deals?

Anglo and individual negotiators overwhelmingly focus on short-term issues rather than long-term issues (although research shows that skilled negotiators make twice as many comments on long-term issues than do average negotiators).[3] Other cultures may similarly restrict overt discussion of the long-term, but take account of the implications that a deal has for future dealings when they reach a settlement.

The next highlighted example shows how a deal by two members of a collectivist culture can affect future relationships. We then see the problems that the covert strategy presents to cross-cultural negotiators.

A professor in a Thai university had a car to sell. Her maid suggested that a distant relation, an electrician, might be interested.

The two met and the agreed price was superficially much to the advantage of the electrician.

However, social constraints meant that mutual obligations were created for the future. The electrician was bound to help his family member when he could, and she and the professor were joined in a patron–client relationship. When the professor wanted repairs done to the house, her maid contacted her relation who charged a minimal price; and when the professor's new car broke down, he lent her the old car rent-free until the new car was fixed.

Everyone benefited. The electrician got a good cheap car and a new customer. The maid strengthened her relationship with both parties by acting as agent; with the engineer by procuring car and work, and with her mistress by finding a buyer for the car and a good cheap handyman. Thus she was better placed to call on favors from either side when she needed them. The professor got a purchaser for the car, a rent-free car loan when her new car broke down, and a handyman who was bound by his relationship with the maid to provide reliable service.

In the example, none of the ensuing patterns of obligation and future benefits were proposed at the time of the original sale. The price was negotiated on the basis of a single issue with a minimum of bargaining, and neither side made an explicit attempt to increase the size of the pie. But given the context of existing relationships, the stability of the negotiators' collectivist culture and values attached to giving and reciprocating favors, and the probability that their relationships would extend into the future, the sale created the conditions for future mutual reward. Thus the sale price cannot be taken as a reliable indicator of the success of the negotiation, to either party.

This shows how a small immediate payoff may represent a very satisfactory result when shared cultural values create conditions for an enduring relationship and a stream of mutual benefits. This does not always apply in more mobile and individualist cultures in which perceptions of obligation and reward are different. When less significance is given to creating and maintaining long-term relationships, it makes good sense to invest your energy in baking a bigger pie for immediate consumption.

10.2.3 Betting on a Long-Term Relationship

The cultural outsider cannot guarantee buying into the cultural values associated with negotiating by accepting a small return in the hope of future benefit. In all cultures, the negotiator is looking to maximize his or her total benefits, and has to decide which promises more, the immediate payoff or the undefined long-term payoff. A relationship with a cultural outsider is bound to be less secure over time than with an insider, and the likelihood of future deals is also less. When you cannot realistically expect a long-term relationship to flourish, you might give higher priority to earning as big a profit as you can ethically from the single deal than to investing in the future.

For instance, when negotiating in the People's Republic of China, Pye warns, do not accept at face value rhetoric about future prospects, and do not assume that expressions of trust indicate a willingness to compromise on principles.[4]

How much immediate profit you can afford to invest in the relationship has to be calculated anew with every new deal and every new customer. You have to take into account:

1 His or her personal interests, and yours. For how long can you expect your opposite number to stay in this post, in this company, with this commercial interest? For how long can your opposite number expect *you* to stay in your present post and company, with your present commercial interests? Obviously the shorter the time, the less should be invested in a long-term relationship. The initial stage of the negotiation helps you make this assessment of each other.

2 His or her company interests, and yours. For how long can each of you expect the other's company to continue in this business, at this level of activity? How do predictable changes seem likely to affect your relationship?

3 Your BATNA and the other side's BATNA. What is the alternative to negotiating future deals?

4 The market; this includes looking at sources of demand and supply, your competition and the other side's competition.

5 Cultural priorities. What values does the other side ascribe to long-term business relationships?

10.3   FINDING COMMON GROUND

You hope to build common ground. Your preparation has shown you areas in which it is in your mutual interests to cooperate and you push to the top of the agenda those issues in which you share interests and can solve

A British medical supplies company calculated wrongly when negotiating the sale of training equipment with a Saudi Arabian hospital. Several other firms manufactured very similar products at highly competitive prices. The hospital representative demanded very generous terms. He referred to the advantages of a long-term relationship, but without specifically committing the hospital. The company swallowed the bait, and accepted minimal profit margins in the hope of future advantage.

When the goods were delivered, the hospital representative complained that they failed to meet his needs (while admitting that they met the contracted specifications), and asked for concessions. Still reckoning on the long-term benefits of the relationship and despite incurring losses, the company gave them.

When the agreement expired the consultancy asked to renegotiate a further contract. They were informed that a contract had already been signed with an American company.

The company had wrongly calculated possible long-term benefits as against immediate profits. Because the hospital could choose from a range of suppliers, it had no need to commit itself to this one firm. Given the lack of any real basis for a long-term commitment, the company lost the respect of the other side by making concessions after the deal was signed. Their investment in future prospects was transparent, and their willingness to meet the hospital's demands looked like appeasement. Appeasement always appears weak, and seldom succeeds.

problems most easily. Early conflict sets the conditions for conflict throughout the negotiation, and this you hope to avoid. By avoiding early conflict, you create a sense of trust which will serve you well in the later stages when real differences arise.

References to shared experience and interests help you build this common ground. For instance:

'We both know the problems that can occur in a deal like this.'
'I'm sure you share my sense that we can achieve something useful here.'

Thus you focus on issues and interests rather than on the positions that each takes in regard to these interests.[5] A positional focus implies that there is only one way that your interests can be met, and this limits opportunities for inventing options for mutual gain and enlarging the pie to be shared.

10.3.1   Trading Information

You build common ground by trading information on your principles and perceptions of the issues and interests but without coming to firm agreements about the specifics being negotiated and the precise goals of the negotiation.

You naturally protect information when disclosure seems likely to imperil your chance of achieving an outcome that satisfies your objectives. But the more information you have prepared about your own and the other side, the better able you are to assess the value of the information that you are giving and receiving. If you have prepared well, you can trade information more efficiently in order to further your mutual interests.

If it becomes apparent that you are giving more than you are receiving, then naturally you restrict the flow and make it clear that you expect your generosity to be reciprocated. And decide how you will deal with requests for free technical information in the name of friendship, or on moral grounds in order to assist with the development of a poorer country.

10.3.2   Objective Criteria

How far can you insist on objective criteria in deciding

(a)   what issues should be negotiated?
(b)   what information is relevant to the issues?
(c)   the value of information?
(d)   the reliability of technical information?

Fisher and Ury suggest such criteria as market value, precedent, scientific judgement, professional standards, measures of efficiency, and costs.[6] Suppose that you and a potential purchaser disagree on a price for your car. An agreement to abide by market value and book price for the year and make of the car gives you one measure for reaching a settlement.

In a multi-issue negotiation, agreeing on criteria may not be a simple matter. In a civil law case, attorneys for both sides may bring professional witnesses who offer quite different interpretations of what standards and measures apply in the particular circumstances, and in the event the non-experts (judge or jury) have to decide which criteria can be applied.

McCarthy suggests that emphasizing objectivity too heavily leads us to ignore the use of power.[7] In practice, negotiators do respond to pressure and at the expense of principles, whatever they may say, and negotiators are often far from high-minded in their search for logical solutions. Appeals to objective criteria unsupported by power are meaningless.

It is particularly difficult to establish objective criteria in cross-cultural negotiations, when each side's concept of objectivity is affected by different cultural perceptions. So far as possible, spend time in agreeing upon criteria which are acceptable to both sides, and do not be over hasty in unilaterally forcing your criteria upon the other side.

The introductory case showed members of different cultures failing to agree on objective criteria. The Canadian wished to use the advice of his garage; the Indian depended upon the advice of a family member and then suggested his own garage.

10.3.3   Linking Issues

Research shows that skilled negotiators treat issues independently, and link issues in terms of immediate relevance; but average negotiators are more likely to insist on a strict sequence, settling one issue before moving to the next on the agenda.[8]

Resist pressures to settle issues one after another as though checking a list, and to reach definite agreement on any one issue in advance of others. When an issue is definitely agreed, you can no longer use it in order to squeeze a concession over some other issue. By linking issues you can keep all issues alive in a multi-issue negotiation. For instance:

'We provisionally accept your terms for X, assuming that we can agree on the other issues.'

'We cannot accept your terms for Y because of the expense this causes us. . . . We might be able to get a little closer to your position on Y if we modify the terms for X.'

The speaker is able to use the unsettled decision on X as a means of levering a favorable decision on Y. If X had been agreed definitely, this recourse would not have been available.

If discussion of one issue seems to be leading you into conflict at a point when this has to be avoided, you might do better to leave it aside and move to other areas of discussion. You return to the contentious issue when either it can no longer be avoided or other agreements suggest a solution. For instance:

'Well, it seems that we can't get any further on specifications for the time being. Maybe we should have a look at procedures for quality control and see if that suggests a way to resolve the problem.'

10.3.4   Asking Questions

Your skills in asking questions are important at all stages of the negotiation. Obviously, they are important as a means of defining mutual interests and acquiring information.

The negotiator uses questions to perform a range of functions:

1   Questioning background issues helps you check your understanding of

shared interest. How much common ground do you share, and so how far can you trust the other person?

2 You check your understanding of what has been said; you check whether apparent agreements are provisional or definite — for instance: 'Are you saying that you cannot decide on this point until you have discussed it with your union leaders?' Asking for clarification is particularly important when you are negotiating with members of another culture whose perceptions and priorities vary from yours.

3 You check whether the other person is bluffing.

4 Questions about the other side's needs and problems can be used to build a sense of concern and common interest. You show that you are listening, and develop empathy.

5 You show what points interest you. (Or should you hide your interest by *not* asking about them?)

6 You guide the interaction in the direction you wish it to take, and away from issues that you wish to avoid.

7 A question about a new issue can usefully divert the conversation from conflict — for instance: 'Incidentally, your proposal for a delivery date. If you get the full consignment in one delivery, isn't this going to give you warehousing problems?' is more subtle than 'I think we should talk now about delivery dates', which sounds as though you are forcing your agenda down their throats.

8 Questions asking 'why?' can identify the essential issues, and help weaken premature positions taken on the issues — for instance: 'We can only make deliveries in batches of 25 units.' . . . 'Why?' . . . 'Because our company only ever delivers in batches of 25.' . . . 'Why?' . . . 'Because that is the size of our delivery vans.' . . . 'Then we can help you. We can lease you some of our larger vans.' This persistent use of 'why?' reveals the fundamental problem, and shows new opportunities for cooperation.

 If 'why?' seems too antagonistic, use a softer indirect form: 'I'm interested in how you decide on the figure of 25.'

9 We have seen that in the law court the attorney's rights to ask questions are far less restricted than the accused's rights; the accused is bound to answer the attorney's questions and not vice versa; and the attorney has more power. By asking leading questions like the attorney, you force the other person to defend himself, and throw him on the defensive.

The final function is clearly antagonistic, and should be avoided in the early stages when you are trying to build a relationship of trust in each other's needs to cooperate. At this point your questioning is relatively non-antagonistic.

We have seen that direct questions, which allow for less ambiguity in interpretation and permit a more restricted range of responses, are generally more antagonistic. In the early stages, indirect and open-ended questions express greater courtesy and may elicit unexpected responses which guide your thinking and the negotiation in unexpected and positive new directions.

So 'I'm interested in your ideas on quantity control. Do you expect to be able to use your normal procedures?' is preferable to 'How precisely will you manage quantity control?' And 'I gather that your union is prepared to lift its restrictions on night work' is preferable to 'How can you hope to meet these production schedules when your union is restricting night work?'

If you do not get the answer you want to an indirect question then recycle it, asking for the same information in a different way. Your failure to elicit a response the first time may not be caused merely by the other side's desire to evade. Particularly in a cross-cultural negotiation, the other side may not understand the grammatical and vocabulary forms of your first attempt, or may not understand the rhetorical function of an indirect and ambiguous form.

If further recyclings still fail to get an appropriate answer, then be prepared to recognize this as deliberate evasion, and resort to a more direct and potentially antagonistic form.

10.4 PERSUASION

We deal here with nine tactics used to convince the other side to accept your terms.

10.4.1 Supporting Arguments

The strength of your claim is not dependent upon the number of arguments you provide to support it. One strong argument is sufficient; six weak arguments suggest a lack of focus and give the other side more ammunition with which to attack you. Research shows that skilled researchers provide far fewer arguments to support their claims than do average negotiators.[9]

10.4.2 Counter-Proposals

It is usual for the negotiator to respond to a proposal by putting forward a counter-proposal. However, it may be advantageous to delay a counter-proposal, because this

- gives you time to think;
- keeps the other side guessing about your reactions;

- gives you time to assess all aspects of the proposal and to react in terms of the issues rather than your position.

Research shows that skilled negotiators make immediate counter-proposals far less frequently than do average negotiators.[10]

10.4.3   Silence

Silence is sometimes a strongly persuasive tool in negotiations. A prolonged pause can unnerve the other side when they do not know how to interpret it — as disagreement? displeasure? surprise? thought? Graham notes the success of the Japanese in making much longer pauses than either his American or Brazilian subjects;[11] the American is not accustomed to this behavior and may respond by rushing in to fill it with a new concession. The Brazilian interrupts more than twice as often as the others.

However, do not use silence when this appears to be weakness; for instance, in the face of an attack on your essential interests. A Japanese professor argues[12] that Japanese negotiators surrender about 70 percent of advantageous conditions to foreigners by their failure to project firm opening positions:

'Japanese tend to think that adopting a strong initial position is akin to *yakuza* (gangster) behaviour.
   The Japanese side tends to listen in silence, trying to read the thoughts of the other party. This makes them seem shifty and evasive in Westerners' eyes. . . .
The Soviet style of negotiating is characterized by threatening; in the American and European approach, logic is as important as threats. But Japanese use neither logic nor threats.'

The problem of deciding when to keep silent underlines the importance of developing skills in listening:

(a)   to develop greater understanding of their priorities;
(b)   to consider your own position;
(c)   to tempt them into unconsidered suggestions and comments which you may be able to use against them.

10.4.4   Disagreement

Some disagreement is inevitable; if you neither disagree nor compete, there is no point to the negotiation. But in a cross-cultural setting you cannot always take differences of opinion at face value. They may reflect cultural differences in perception rather than disagreement on substance.

Similarly, you cannot take the absence of disagreement or expressions of agreement at face value. The Japanese avoid saying 'no' whenever possible.

The Briton who starts an utterance by 'I quite agree *but* . . .' or 'That's true up to a point *but* . . .' is actually preparing you for a polite expression of disagreement. Graham notes that his Brazilian subjects used the word 'no' far more often than either Americans or Japanese, but this 'no' preceded a statement of disagreement rather than a negative response to a question.[13]

When you cannot agree with a point and any ambiguity is likely to be damaging, make your disagreement clear and explain why: 'We cannot agree to that. Our government does not permit us to export to those specifications.'

Do not allow disagreement to degenerate into insults and name-calling. This behavior is particularly negative in a culture where face is highly valued and the negotiator is responsible for protecting not only his or her face but also that of the other side.

10.4.5   Threats

Threats are only effective if they can be carried out. For instance, if you threaten to walk out of the negotiation unless a point is agreed by a certain time, be prepared to walk out. If it becomes clear that you are unable to carry out a threat, your bluff is called and you lose credibility.

Retaliating to a threat by issuing a counter-threat is not usually successful in calling the other side's bluff, and probably has a negative impact on the meeting. Examples are:

'If you don't increase the differentials we'll pull out every skilled man in the workshop.'
'If they strike, they're fired.'

This leads to a dogfight, and no one benefits.

The strictures discussed above against taking disagreements at face value in cross-cultural negotiations and forcing the other side to lose face apply here too.

10.4.6   Personal Attacks

Similarly, avoid making personal attacks. If you think your integrity is being attacked, and you cannot explain it in terms of a cultural misunderstanding, try to understand why the attack is being made. Is the other side trying to gain advantage from making you lose your temper? If so, this is all the more reason to keep your temper. Do they wish to break off the negotiations and are trying to push the responsibility on to you? Analyze your own position. If it is in your interests to keep talking, do not make it easy for them to quit, and if necessary practice an avoidance tactic, discussed below.

10.4.7 Avoidance

You may wish to avoid further discussion of an issue because you anticipate that it will generate conflict or will lead you off your agenda. You can avoid a point in various ways:

(a) Introduce a new topic, for instance by asking a question: 'This is by the way, but how will these insurance payments effect your financing?'
(b) Return to a previous stage in the negotiation: 'Sorry, but can I retrack a minute. When you said you couldn't meet this schedule, I think you said something about your labor contract.'
(c) Overtly postpone further discussion: 'Let's pick up on financing in a minute.'
(d) Maintain silence, for instance in response to a threat or some other offensive behavior.
(e) Make a joke: 'That reminds me, did you hear the story about . . .'.

Note, however, that joking is potentially dangerous in a cross-cultural context. A successful joke depends upon shared perceptions of incongruity, and is usually culture-specific. What seems humorous to you may strike members of the other culture as serious, facile, or simply irrelevant. A joke that goes wrong at the wrong moment can have the negative effect of increasing the tension. Stay good humored, but unless you are very knowledgeable of the other culture, avoid using jokes as an avoidance tactic.

10.4.8 Expressing Emotions

Whereas the Japanese tend to hide their emotions, and are not argumentative, Brazilians are emotionally passionate and highly argumentative whether right or wrong. Casse suggests that North Americans lie between these two extremes; they are argumentative whether right or wrong but are impersonal, and less emotional than the Brazilians.[14]

Be careful of using emotional appeals (for instance, to friendship, old time's sake, your personal circumstances, the brotherhood of man) unless you are certain how these will be taken by the other side. This tactic may misfire badly if used with a culture that frowns upon emotion as a negotiating tool.

10.4.9 Your Final Offer

Your making a final offer puts pressure on the other side to meet your terms or break off the negotiation. They cannot be certain that this is not in fact your final offer; but if you are bluffing, and they call it and force you to make further concessions, you lose credibility the next time you declare that 'this is as much as we are prepared to offer.' This tactic is more likely to work in the later stages when both sides are looking for a closure. It is least likely to succeed when made too early, and other issues are still unsettled.

Qualified final offers tell the other side that they must be prepared to make concessions if the negotiation is to continue:

'As things stand, this is our final offer.'
'If you cannot see your way to changing your pricing policy, this has to be as far as we can go.'

10.5   CONCEDING AND BARGAINING

Obviously you are not prepared to concede on your MUST achieve objectives. And you are more prepared to concede on your WOULD LIKE to achieves than on your HOPE to achieves.

You have prepared your confidential list of points on which you are prepared to concede (if necessary). You have selected points which are of little importance to you but should be attractive to the other side. That is, you assess the value of concessions in terms of their needs as much as you do in yours.

For instance, you are negotiating a sale of your food containers with an exporter whose usual supplier has failed him, and who (you guess) needs exceptionally speedy delivery in order to meet a last-minute rush before a holiday season. Making this express delivery will give you only minor problems (your warehouse is well-stocked), but will satisfy one of his MUST achieve objectives. Hence you can make this concession at little cost.

When you agree to the concession, always demand something in return. Never leave a concession in the air, hoping to exploit it at a later time. When your concession is accepted and agreed, it is too late to exploit it. Instead, precede every concession with a conditional IF: '*If* you will accept my X, I will agree to your Y.' And in the case above, assuming that a MUST achieve is to secure specific terms for payment, '*If* you agree to my terms for payment, I'll give you your delivery dates.'

In a multi-issue negotiation, your linking issues gives you greater freedom to demand a concession in return. The more issues that are still provisional, the greater your flexibility. This demonstrates the importance of not reaching premature agreement on points until you have to.

When making a concession, make clear that it is costly to you, and hence should be greatly valued by the other side and demands an equally valuable concession in return. For instance:

'Okay, I'm prepared to look at delivery dates again. [INTRODUCING CONCESSION]. But you realize that this is going to throw out our production schedule and could be very expensive. [REASON FOR OF-FERING A CONCESSION, AND DEMANDING A CONCESSION]. If you give me my terms for payment dates [CONCESSION DEMANDED] I'll give you your delivery dates. [CONCESSION OFFERED].'

At what point in the negotiation are you prepared to agree to concessions? If you make concessions too early, you have nothing left to concede by the final stages when you still need flexibility. If you leave concessions too late, you may have already alienated the other side. In general, make concessions of equivalent steps at a steady rate, matching theirs, and taking into account the time that you expect to devote to the negotiation. But there is no fixed rule, and different cultures follow different styles.

Graham's research suggests that Brazilians tend to demand more; the Japanese ask for higher profits when making the initial offer and are consistent in making small concessions throughout; and Americans are more likely to offer a 'fair' price and make larger initial concessions.[15] Another study shows North Americans making small concessions early in order to build the relationship and usually reciprocating concessions; Arabs making concessions throughout and almost always reciprocating; and Russians making very few and viewing concessions made by the other side as a sign of weakness.[16]

In some cultures, such as Iran, the term 'compromise' has moral connotations and implies a corrupt betrayal of principle. So it has to be kept out of your vocabulary when you describe the bargaining/conceding phase.

10.5.1 Price

How far does the seller's first demand represent the true price at which he or she is prepared to do a deal? One management consultant suggests that there are important differences between cultures. For instance:

'In Thailand, suppose they set you a price. [You should] open at a third, and settle for 50–50%. But in Germany, expect to settle for a difference of 10% on the price. Germans don't negotiate, they start off by finding out precisely what you want then quote the price.'

Graham and Herberger give further examples of cultures where the negotiator sets initial goals on the high side:[17]

'A Chinese or Brazilian bargainer expects to spend time negotiating and expects to make concessions. Americans do not have the same expectations and are often surprised and upset by the other side's "unreasonable" demands. But the demands are unreasonable only from the perspective of the American's slam-bang, "Old West" bargaining style. To the Oriental or Latin American it makes perfect sense to ask for a lot initially.'

Your preparation for dealing with the other culture should tell you what price (including non-financial obligations) you can demand or expect to be demanded of you, and how this relates to the price at which you can expect to settle. The more exaggerated the opening bid, the more time you must expect to invest in bargaining this down to an acceptable settlement figure.

Expect to spend time, and learn to be patient. *The Economist* suggests:[18]

'The non-Western countries seem to understand the immovable nature of many of the world's problems more instinctively than do the countries of the West. It may be time for those entrusted with negotiations involving the destiny of millions to be given a course in the art of patience. America might give a lead. A country which runs courses on the quickest way of getting to "yes" could surely spare some cash to establish a no-less-useful Institute of Patience'.

10.6 IMPLEMENTATION: LEGAL SAFEGUARDS

Negotiators from Anglo cultures tend to assume that, when the contract is signed, their greatest worries are over. A signed agreement is valued as an expression of a genuine will to fulfill its terms. A contract can only be renegotiated if both parties are willing, and the business person who deliberately fails to fulfill a signed contract endangers his or her reputation for fair dealing, and becomes exposed to a legal action.

In other cultures these ethical values associated with a signed contract may not apply, and no clear distinction can be made between negotiating the contract and implementing it. A contract expresses only an honest intention to do business, all other things being equal and in the light of foreseeable events.

For instance, Frankenstein describes the implementation phase as the final stage of a negotiation in the People's Republic of China.[19] He writes:

'Rather than a straightforward realization of the contract, there is a continuing process of adjustment and discussion. Sometimes, the research suggests, the Chinese side tries to expand the scope of the agreement; they refer back to the general principles agreed to at the onset of the talks and base their demands on the requirements of mutual equality and friendship.'

When dealing within his or her culture, a member of a collectivist culture can employ family and social connections as a means of protecting interests and guaranteeing fair play. For instance, if you do not keep to our deal, I inform your other business partners, shame you, and damage your future prospects. In this situation the needs for legal safeguards are fewer. But a member of an individualist culture can rely far less upon social pressure in order to ensure that a settlement is fairly implemented, and has greater need for an efficient and speedy civil legal system.

The Anglo must be particularly prepared to renegotiate during the implementation phase in countries where the law courts do not offer the safeguards to a signed contract that they do at home.

In Japan, parties to a negotiation are expected to resolve disagreements over implementation by reaching consensus; lawyers are only brought in to resolve a conflict as the last resort and the courts may take many years to deliver a judgement. (In 1988, suits arising from the 1968 Minimata mass poisoning case were still dragging through Japanese courts.) Further problems arise in different attitudes towards law designed to protect intellectual property. In 1989 a US Commerce Department official reported to a Senate subcommittee:[20]

'Many practitioners in the United States believe that Japanese courts have been less than friendly in providing a fair measure of protection to patented inventions.'

Similarly in Italy, the courts are overworked and delays are usual. For instance:[21]

'It was really nothing more than a bump on the head, the judge was saying, yet the case has dragged on for nearly a decade.
    He was speaking of an Italian who had the misfortune of having a ladder fall on his head while riding the national railroad. The injury was minor, the judge said, but the passenger sued anyway.
    That was in 1980. The lawsuit did not go to trial until 1983. It took four more years for the case to be thrown out on lack of merit. Three months ago, the passenger filed an appeal, and now this judge has it on his calendar. He figures he may have his ruling ready by 1992.'

You may decide that the costs incurred by the delay in waiting for a legal judgement are prohibitive. When a dispute arises in the implementation phase, you may have to retreat from a principled position of insisting on the letter of the contract, and renegotiate.

This has a number of implications for the Anglo business person:

1 Find out what laws relate to the contract and how they are typically interpreted and implemented.
2 During the initial negotiation, pay careful attention to what the other side says about implementation. Be sympathetic to their expected problems in implementation and look for ways to help them.
3 Look for safeguards which depend upon satisfying their needs and not upon the law courts.

4   Do not be too greedy. If the other side feels at a later stage that they have given too much away, they have little incentive to fulfill the contract. In a developing country which has unstable political institutions, a revolution may throw up a new government which feels free to break one-sided agreements.

5   Immediately after the initial negotiation, fully review your notes of the negotiating process. What problems do you expect the other side to have in implementing their side of the agreement? Start preparing your case for any possible renegotiations.

6   The negotiating team must be involved in the implementation phase and keep abreast of all problems arising. You may soon be back at the negotiating table:

There is an important implication if you come from a culture in which different ethical considerations are associated with a signed contract, the legal system is relatively powerless to enforce it, and renegotiation during the implementation phase is common. When negotiating with a team from a culture in which these conditions do not apply and when the contract is protected by their laws rather than by yours, you must expect them to insist on the negotiated contract being implemented as it stands.

10.7   USING INTERPRETERS

Chapter 11 has more to say about the use of interpreters. Here we focus on their functions in negotiations.

Your ideal interpreter knows enough about the business to translate the technical jargon, and can also translate the informal language you use to establish a personal relationship. The average interpreter may be able to manage one but not both of these skills. The representative of a British confectionery firm doing business in Italy experienced serious difficulties in having her non-technical remarks translated by technically proficient interpreters. Finally, she learnt the language herself in order to master the essential non-technical Italian.

You may sometimes need your interpreter to mediate when cultural misunderstandings occur, but you do not want an interpreter who thinks he or she knows your business better than you do and tries to take over the negotiation. In a Malaysian court I once saw a Chinese–Malay interpreter take several minutes in discussion with two Chinese defendants who had pleaded not guilty, at the end of which they changed their pleas to guilty. In a commercial negotiation, this degree of involvement is excessive.

Even a good interpreter needs to be properly used:

1   Always brief him or her in advance, taking care not to explain your

strategy in detail, particularly if you suspect that the interpreter is a security risk.

2 During the negotiation, speak slowly and carefully.
3 Avoid complex words and phrases where simpler and shorter forms are adequate.
4 Explain complex ideas several times, using a different form each time.
5 Do not speak more than a few sentences without giving time to interpret. Allow him or her to take notes if necessary.
6 Do not interrupt his or her interpretation.
7 Be understanding of mistakes. Do not blame the interpreter in the presence of the other side for mistakes, and do not cause him or her to lose face. An alienated interpreter is more likely to constitute a security risk.

When speaking through an interpreter, keep your eyes on the faces of the other side, not on the interpreter. This helps you assess their feelings, and check from their responses whether the interpretation is accurate.

Unless you know that you speak the other language fluently, use an interpreter. If you are only averagely proficient, your communicative accuracy may break down in a moment of stress. And even when you know the language, using an interpreter gives you two bites of the apple: you have twice the time to consider your responses — once when the other side speaks to the interpreter and once more when the interpreter translates the utterance to you.

10.8 IMPLICATIONS FOR THE MANAGER

- When negotiating, identify how your relationship can affect your mutual interests.

(a) What reasons do *you* have to trust them?
(b) What reasons do *they* have to trust you?
(c) How can your working relationship be improved?
(d) What reasons do you have for supposing that a mutually beneficial settlement can lead to a long-term relationship?
(e) What value do *you* place on a long-term relationship? What can *you* hope to gain from it?
(f) What can *they* hope to gain from it?
(g) What are *you* prepared to concede in order to improve your chance of a long-term relationship?
(h) What do you estimate that *they* are prepared to concede in order to improve their chance of a long-term relationship?

- Estimate the value and price of information.

(a)   What information are *you* prepared to trade, which does not endanger your interests?
(b)   What information should *you* not trade?
(c)   What information do *you* want, that *you* can realistically expect *them* to give?
(d)   What can *you* demand in return for information?
(e)   What are *you* prepared to trade in return for information?
(f)   What objective criteria can be established for assessing the value of information and concessions?

- What persuasive tactics can each side employ?

(a)   What success can *you* expect from threatening, aggressive tactics?
(b)   What success can *you* expect from non-threatening, cooperative tactics?
(c)   Over which issues should *you* be aggressive?
(d)   Over which issues should *you* be cooperative?
(e)   Over which issues do you expect *them* to be aggressive?
(f)   Over which issues do you expect *them* to be cooperative?

- What concessions can each side make?

(a)   What concessions are *you* prepared to make in order to get a satisfactory settlement?
(b)   For each concession offered, what do *you* demand in return?
(c)   What concessions do you expect *them* to offer?
(d)   What are *you* prepared to offer in return for concessions?
(e)   What are *you* prepared to offer in the initial stages?
(f)   What are *you* prepared to accept in the final settlement?
(g)   What can you expect *them* to offer in the initial stages?
(h)   What can you expect *them* to accept in the final settlement?

- What problems can your foresee in implementing a settlement?

(a)   What does the other side mean when *they* make a deal? How far do *they* view a deal as a firm commitment, and how far as a statement of intent only?
(b)   How much do *they* stand to lose by reneging on a deal, measured in terms of *their* reputation for fair dealing and integrity?
(c)   How do legal safeguards protect *your* patent and other intellectual property rights?
(d)   How far can legal safeguards protect *your* interests in the implementation stage?
(e)   What other safeguards can *you* employ to protect *your* interests in the implementation stage?

(f)   What instruments are available to *them* to ensure that *you* implement the settlement?

- What needs do you have for interpretation? In other words, what information do you need to give your interpreter, without endangering your interests?

Developing a Diary: 5

Develop the diary started in Chapters 3, 4, 6 and 7 in order to record your negotiating experiences.

Take notes of the persuasive tactics (giving supporting arguments, making counter-proposals, silence, etc.) you use.

1   How persuasive is each, at that particular stage of the negotiation, and within the cultural context? Rate each on a scale of 1 to 10.
2   What vocabulary and grammatical forms were used to express each?
3   How might each have been more effectively expressed?

Take notes of the forms used by members of the other culture to perform the same tactics. How persuasive are they? How might they improve their use of these tactics?

10.9   SUMMARY

This chapter has shown how to apply your preparation at the negotiation table, and has focused on communication skills. The central sections dealt with five stages in the negotiation. Section 10.2 discussed opening moves and focused on the problems of building a relationship of trust. Section 10.3 dealt with needs to find common ground and link issues, and how trading information and asking different types of questions helps you achieve this. Section 10.4 discussed nine tactics used in persuading the other side. Section 10.5 dealt with techniques for trading and communicating concessions, and section 10.6 with the implementation stage and the extent to which the negotiator can depend upon legal safeguards in different cultures. Section 10.7 suggested how you can get best value from interpreters.

EXERCISES

Exercise 1

This exercise shows how the relationship between the two sides affects the negotiation.

You represent your company which manufactures refrigeration plant. You have arrived in the Republic of Godali to negotiate a large sale to the State Farm Produce Board. At the first meeting, the Minister for Food announces: 'We look for a mutually rewarding relationship, not only now but in the future. We hope that you will take account of this when you submit your terms.'

1   Which factors below cause you
    - to accept the Minister's words at face value, and offer generous 'soft' terms? Why?
    - to hold out for 'hard' terms and a high price? Why?

    (a) Godali is politically very unstable.
    (b) Godali is politically stable.
    (c) You have many competitors.
    (d) You have no major competitors.
    (e) Your company has majority ownership of an important local company.
    (f) Your company has not previously done business in Godali.
    (g) The contract will be guaranteed under your legal system, and Godali has substantial financial holdings in your country.
    (h) The contract will be guaranteed under Godalise law, and the Godalise legal system is notoriously slow.
    (i) Confidential remarks that you made to the Minister's aide at a preparatory meeting were substantially leaked to a Godalise newspaper.
    (j) The Minister has a personal reputation for integrity.

2   What other factors might affect your decision?

Exercise 2

This exercise practices tactics.

Assume that the situation described in Exercise 1 applies. You have decided to hold out for 'hard' terms and a high price, and those factors in (a)–(j) above which caused you to make this decision to demand a high price also apply.

For each situation described below, which response do you choose? Why? What other factors might affect your decision?

1   After much discussion on delivery dates and freight insurance, the leader of the Godalise team suddenly announces: 'We are prepared to meet your terms on delivery dates.'

    (a) Accept the concession and demand that your terms for insurance should also be met.
    (b) Accept the concession and offer a concession on insurance.
    (c) Any other response . . .?

2 After much debate on the price, a junior member of the Godalise team says: 'You do not understand our problems. It seems we overrated your intelligence.'

(a) Walk out.
(b) Demand an apology.
(c) Try to change the topic.
(d) Any other response . . .?

3 But before you have to respond to the situation described in (2), the Godalise team leader himself apologizes for his junior (who is ordered to leave the room) and changes the topic to quality control. He becomes very emotional, reminding you of the values of friendship.

(a) Say nothing, staring at him until he calms down.
(b) Express similar beliefs, reminding him that you also have difficulties.
(c) Suggest an adjournment.
(d) Any other response . . .?

4 Before signing the contract, the Godalise team admit: 'We accept, but we are going to have problems meeting your demand that payment should be made in Japanese yen.'

(a) Express sympathy only.
(b) Suggest an alternative means of payment.
(c) Suggest that the deal cannot be signed.
(d) Any other response . . .?

NOTES

1 Graham, J.L. and Herberger, R.A. (1983) Negotiators abroad — don't shoot from the hip. *Harvard Business Review*, July/August, 160–8 (see 163).
2 Pye, L. (1982) *Chinese Commercial Negotiating Style*. Rand Corporation, Santa Monica.
3 Rackham, N. (1976) The behavior of successful negotiators (Huthwaite Research Group Report). In *International Negotiations: A Training Program for Corporate Executives and Diplomats* (ed. E. Raider). Ellen Raider International, Brooklyn, NY.
4 Pye, L. (1982), *op. cit.*
5 Fisher, R. and Ury, W. (1981) *Getting to Yes*. Houghton Mifflin, Boston.
6 *Ibid.*, p. 89.
7 McCarthy, Lord W. (1985) The rule of power and principle in 'Getting to Yes'. *Negotiation Journal*, January, 59–66.
8 Rackham, N. (1976), *op. cit.*
9 *Ibid.*
10 *Ibid.*
11 Graham, J.L. (1985) The influence of culture on the process of business negotiations: an exploratory study. *Journal of International Business Studies*, Spring, 81–96.
12 Whymant, R. (1988) 'Japanese businessmen are "losers at the negotiation table"'. *Daily Telegraph*, 30 May.
13 Graham, J.L. (1985), *op. cit.*

14 Casse, P. (1981) *Training for the Cross-Cultural Mind* (2nd edn). Society for Intercultural Education, Training & Research, Washington, DC.
15 Graham, J.L. (1985), *op. cit.*
16 Glenn, E.S., Witmeyer, D. and Stevenson, K.A. (1984) Cultural styles of persuasion. *International Journal of Intercultural Relations*, Summer, 11–22.
17 Graham, J.L. and Herberger, R.A. (1983), *op. cit.*, same page.
18 Consider the tortoise. *The Economist*, 28 February 1987.
19 Frankenstein, J. (1986) Trends in Chinese business practice. *California Management Review*, **XXIX**(1), 148–60 (see 149).
20 Hiatt, F. (1989) Frustrated and defeated: a US businessman says farewell to Japan. *International Herald Tribune*, 24–25 June.
21 Haberman, C. (1988) Italian justice: blind, lame and oh so halt. *International Herald Tribune*, 6 December.

11

Using the Other Language

11.1   INTRODUCTION

An Australian in Indonesia negotiates a contract in the medium of English. Fortunately, his counterpart speaks the language fluently. The Australian is confident that his product is the best on the market, and is shocked to discover that the contract has gone instead to a French competitor. The Frenchman has taken the trouble to learn enough Indonesian Malay to greet his host, compliment him on his office, and read a menu.

Using the other person's language is not only a matter of courtesy. It decreases your dependence on him and upon interpreters, and increases your freedom of action and management potential.

Learning a language to the point of fluency is a long and expensive process. This chapter discusses the practical issues involved when the manager embarks upon language training, and considers the alternatives — that other people should learn his or her language, or that communication should be delegated to interpreters and translators.

11.2   LANGUAGE COMPETENCE

The manager who has fluent control over the other culture's language has direct access to members of that culture. Messages intended to convey and enforce decisions, motivate, introduce a new factor into a negotiation, can be communicated directly. At least as significant, feedback from the other person is processed in pure form: the manager communicates and responds to nuances that would be lost in translation.

The expatriate manager who depends entirely upon subordinates speaking his or her language is at a tactical disadvantage when dealing with them and with negotiating partners. The ideal solution is *always* that the manager should be able to use at least some of the other language.

Some multinationals require that local staff above a certain level gain proficiency in the language used in company headquarters and/or English, and this determines promotion prospects. Where control systems are heavily bureaucratic, local managers are more likely to need headquarters language skills, but are less likely to be fully reimbursed for training than when control is enforced by the organizational culture.

In general, and unfortunately, most companies give language acquisition only low priority. No company wants its senior staff investing valuable time in an activity from which the payoff can be only imprecisely calculated.

For the individual manager, learning another language from scratch is a wearisome and demoralizing activity, at least in the early stages. The objective of functional fluency seems a long way off. The manager responsible for deciding million-dollar investments finds it difficult to overcome the psychological barriers against 'going back to school' and embarking on an activity where his initial competence is childlike, and his professional authority counts for nothing.

11.2.1   Reasons for not Learning the Other Language

The following reasons are commonly offered for not learning.

'No time.'
BUT try costing out the potential earnings lost by inefficient communication resulting from not knowing the other language. How does the investment in training compare with other uses of your time?

'Promotion is based on hard figures only.'
BUT you should now be equipped to argue the case for fostering and rewarding behavior that develops good cross-cultural relationships. Knowing something of the other language advances these relationships.

'In my specialist occupation, there is no contact with the locals. Colleagues all speak my language.'
BUT the organization also benefits from your ability to use the language with outsiders, at official functions and social functions. Using at least some of the other person's language helps create a better relationship. Who do you expect to be more effective in France . . . the manager who speaks only English, or the manager who speaks English and French?

'*The overseas assignment is too short.*'
BUT this is an argument for restricting learning rather than for not learning anything.

'*Anything worth writing about this subject is in English.*'
For instance, a journalist comments[1] on the lack of interest most American companies working with Japanese partners show in developing Japanese language skills: 'A common corporate attitude is that if a scientific paper is not published in English it must not be significant.'
BUT this has the disadvantage that the American company has very little access to Japanese-language material other than that supplied (and translated) by its partner. The same article quotes a Japanese professor:

> ' "Patent information is available to all-comers on a nonrestrictive basis, but the text in Japanese is, of course, difficult if not impossible for non-Japanese readers to comprehend." [The article goes on to say that] Japanese information is available. However, time is growing short for Americans who want to find it, for a tougher barrier than mere language is being established. Access to Japan's vast scientific resources — the Japanese assert that in 1982 they held 22% of world-wide scientific and technical information (which has since grown at an average rate of 6% — is rapidly being transferred to the control of the Japanese government.'

'*My language is an international language of business. Let them learn my language rather than me learn theirs.*'
BUT this makes bad business sense. English-speaking companies and managers (for instance) who play down the value of language training should take note of the successes of non-English-speaking multinationals where competence in English and other languages is now perceived to be essential. Increasingly, the manager who refuses to learn and use languages limits his or her chances of advancement. This point is developed below.

11.2.2 English as an International Language

English is the international language of business in two respects, which are not entirely to the advantage of the native English speaker. First, many multinationals use English as their headquarters language even when English is not the language of the country (as in the case of some Scandinavian companies). But this does not help the Anglo manager when dealing with the representative of some other organization or government where this rule is not applied.

Second, English is used as a second language by non-English speakers when it is to their competitive advantage. This means they use it when communicating with a non-English speaker from another country with a different first language and with whom they share only their ability to use English-as-a-second-language, and with a native-English speaker who does not use their language. The non-English-speaking manager learns English in order to deal more effectively with, and compete with, English-speaking counterparts who are not prepared to adapt.

However, in other respects English IS NOT an international language in business. First, business people do not have the same needs for an agreed and restricted code as do air-traffic controllers and pilots, for instance, who are always responsible for human life. Because business people do not have this extreme need, they do not share a consensus on what grammatical and vocabulary items are treated as core. Hence the versions of English dialects used across the business world vary enormously.

Second, the multinational that uses English as its headquarters language and for communicating between head office and branches abroad may also expect these branches to use the local language in their day-to-day affairs. Kuin writes:[2]

> 'Operations usually are, and should be, conducted in the vernacular. The need to learn the local language may vary in importance for managers in different categories (accounting, marketing, production, personnel, and so on), but he who cannot or will not learn languages always remains a stranger in any part of the business but "home". From the viewpoint of job rotation, such a man needs a special tab on his card.'

For instance, one multinational bank operating in Canada has offices in French-speaking Quebec and English-speaking Toronto. Bilingual managers in Quebec are promoted quickly to senior positions in either office. Monolingual English-speaking managers are restricted to Toronto.

Paradoxically, the new need for managers who can speak more than one language springs from the increased internationalism of business. This is illustrated by the top European business schools, which give greater emphasis to teaching international skills and to recruiting an international student body than do their American rivals.[3] They often teach in English, but they

> '. . . favor cosmopolitan candidates with a flair for languages. At INSEAD [in France], all students must speak French and English. More than half are also fluent in German, Spanish or another language.'

11.2.3   Who Cares?

The business people of many countries have known for hundreds of years that they must master other languages in order to survive. This is the case in many small European countries such as the Scandinavian countries,

The Netherlands, and multilingual Switzerland; and in the Eastern Mediterranean a businessman might regularly need at least Arabic, Turkish, French, and English.

Certainly when you work in another country in Europe, its nationals value your speaking and writing their language. One study of the selection criteria desired by representatives of host-country organizations in five European countries discovered that 100 percent (105 respondents) wanted guest managers to have proficiency in the host-country language.[4] French remains the lingua franca of the European Community headquarters in Brussels. In France, it is government policy to resist borrowings from English; the *Dictionary of Official Neologisms* lists 2400 words that bureaucrats should avoid or adopt. 'Jumbo jet' is 'gros porteur', 'one-man show' is 'une spectacle solo', 'boom' is 'boum'.[5]

Until recently, the Anglo countries have been able to depend on internal markets (in the case of the United States) or on traditional Commonwealth markets (in the case of the United Kingdom, Australia, etc.) where English is the language of political power and hence of commerce. Because they have not felt the need, these peoples have a poor record of learning other languages. But these markets have disappeared or changed, and in a new international environment their business people must learn other languages.

Examples of this new awareness are provided in both the United Kingdom and the United States. In the United Kingdom the Pickup Scheme is establishing Language for Export consortia across the country. These teach business people languages and exporting techniques. The Parker Report (1987) discussed the country's diplomatic and business needs for the languages of Africa and Asia. In response the University Grants Committee created 40 new lectureships and doubled the places for students of Chinese, Japanese, and Arabic. And coming reforms to the national schools curriculum are expected to enforce that children will have to learn a foreign language up to the age of sixteen.[6]

In the United States, a newspaper story reports on the increased popularity of foreign language learning in US schools and colleges:[7]

'Foreign economic competition, language experts say, is apparently causing some Americans to finally begin shedding their long-standing indifference to foreign cultures, and the arrogant expectation that others should understand English but Americans need know no language but their own.

. . . According to the Modern Language Association, the number of college and university students studying a language other than English reached 1 003 234 in the autumn of 1986, up 3.9 per cent from 1983, and the first time in 14 years that college foreign-language enrollment topped the million mark. . . . The 12 languages, in order of popularity, are Spanish, French, German, Italian, Russian, Latin, Japanese, Ancient Greek, Chinese, Hebrew, Portuguese and Arabic.'

This re-thinking on the needs of foreign languages for overseas trade has led to the creation of a National Center at Johns Hopkins University to coordinate efforts nationally, to promote research and produce new teaching materials.

11.2.4 Calculating the Value and Expense of Learning

Your need to use the other language and the gravity of communication problems that arise from not having adequate competence can be measured by the probable gains and losses.

The value of acquiring the other language is partly determined by your position and function in the company. For instance, if you are the expatriate chief executive officer of a local branch, you probably spend little time communicating directly with the lower levels, and more time communicating top-level decisions to your senior executives (who may have been promoted because they are proficient in your language) and negotiating with local outsiders, customers, business partners and government representatives. In terms of time invested and opportunity cost, your language training is now correspondingly more expensive than it would be for a subordinate.

If you are unable to use the local language, the losses incurred may also be greater, depending on who else in the organization speaks your language. You will be at a disadvantage in taking and implementing high-level decisions, and in negotiating, unless you can depend on expert interpreters. The direct costs of interpretation costs are probably far less than your learning, but this solution gives you far less hands-on control.

If you are at a second level in the organization, learning the language costs relatively less and strengthens your opportunities for promotion. If your boss does not speak the local language, he is more likely to delegate you to negotiate on his behalf. This gives you a competitive edge over your monolingual peers. In addition, you have a greater capacity to communicate with and control subordinates from the other culture, and this may also give you an edge in a race for promotion.

11.2.5 Fluency and Competence

The organization might ideally wish to staff its operations in the other culture with fluent bilinguals. The newspaper story below, published under the headline 'A Nobel winner's advice to Japan', indicates one definition of fluency:[8]

'TOKYO [AGENCE FRANCE-PRESSE] — Susumu Tonegawa, winner of the 1987 Nobel Prize in Medicine, says his Japanese countrymen should consider trying

Your calculations of the profit from successful language learning and the costs of failure are complicated by a wide range of factors, which include:

1 How significant do you expect your contacts to be with persons who do not speak your language?
2 How much can you afford to pay for communication breakdown? If your relationship with the other party breaks down, how much will it cost you to find alternative employees, business partners, etc.?
3 How much can the other party afford to pay for communication breakdown? If their relationship with you breaks down, how much will it cost them to find alternative employers, business partners, etc.?
4 How important is it to sustain a long-term relationship with the other party?
5 How likely is it that you can sustain a long-term relationship if there are no serious communication problems? Over what time span do you need to communicate?
6 How much importance does the other culture place on your learning the language? That is, how much value do you place on the goodwill that learning the language earns you?
7 How far can you depend on bilingual subordinates?
8 How accessible are reliable interpreting services?

Your calculations lead you to assess the size of the investment you should make in learning the other language.

to "reason in English" to break out of their intellectual conformity and become creative, the Yomiuri newspaper reported Tuesday.

"The consciousness to encourage scientific research is low in Japanese society", said Mr Tonegawa, a professor at the Massachusetts Institute of Technology. "This is one reason why original work is rare in Japan."

"Maybe we should even consider changing our thinking process in the field of science by trying to reason in English", said the geneticist, who has worked for more than 20 years outside Japan. "Research should also be modeled after the West", he added.'

The communicator who reasons in the second language has entirely assimilated the cultural values expressed by that language. Professor Tonegawa is describing the extreme of bilingualism, when the language user is also bicultural and capable of switching between two different sets of values. The company may hope to recruit bilinguals, but cannot normally hope to train a manager with a beginner's command of the other language to this degree of competence. It would make far greater demands on time, energy and expense than the individual manager and the organization can afford. And for most practical purposes this degree of fluency is unnecessary. So the company defines its needs for language competence in terms that can be achieved, and are matched to occupational functions.

At the opposite extreme, suppose that you are in Poland for a couple of hours only to sign a pre-negotiated deal. You disembark at Warsaw airport and greet your hosts in Polish. You can learn these few phrases on the flight over, and even these are adequate to project goodwill and demonstrate an eagerness to reach a mutually satisfactory agreement. Learn the absolute minimum of

- expressions to greet;
- expressions to apologize;
- 'please';
- 'thank you'.

Learn the cultural conventions that decide when these expressions are used. Because most cultures are proud of their cuisines, and you can expect to be entertained, learn the names of the more famous dishes. At dinner you may be toasted, and will show empathy with the other culture by responding appropriately. Here are a few from around the world:

French: A votre santé!
German: Prosit!
Scandinavian: Skoal!
Spanish: Salud!
British English: Your very good health! (formal) or Cheers! (less formal)
Mandarin Chinese: [KAM-pay]!
Cantonese Chinese: [YUM-sing]!
Japanese: [KAM-pai]!
Korean: [KON-be]!
Thai: [Chai-yo]!

Competence has to be defined in terms of what you wish to do with the language, which means defining needs. The Japanese scientist who wishes to reason in English is less than competent if (much) less than bilingual. The manager who needs only to make polite greetings at the airport develops his competence from a tourists' phrase book. Most managers need to communicate a range of functions somewhere between these two extremes, and hence need a level of competence between the two which can be achieved with correspondingly intermediate resources.

The communicative functions that a manager performs in his or her own language and may need to perform in the other includes the following:[9]

(a) exerting direct control over day-to-day activities;
(b) taking, communicating and implementing decisions;
(c) developing and exercising authority and status;

(d) communicating with superiors, peers, subordinates;
(e) communicating and negotiating with business partners;
(f) communicating with government officials;
(g) creating trust and goodwill, making contacts;
(h) interpreting political, economic, cultural trends;
(i) reading reports, memos, letters, etc.;
(j) writing reports, etc.;
(k) communicating in formal and informal meetings;
(l) making formal and informal presentations;
(m) making telephone calls.

These functions can be prioritized, in terms of your needs for language competence in specific activities. Which functions must you perform yourself in the other language? Which can you perform in your own language, expecting the receiver to use it with you? Which should you perform through the medium of interpretation? The next chapter goes into greater detail to show how needs analysis prioritizes language learning needs. Here we are concerned with the general issue of using the other language as against the alternatives.

11.3   YOUR USING THEIR LANGUAGE, AND THE ALTERNATIVES

The alternatives to the manager achieving full competence are that he or she should achieve competence in some functions, and otherwise depend upon one of the following:

• Members of the other culture using the manager's language. In practice, this means hiring local managers who already speak the expatriate manager's language as a second language or can be trained to speak it.
• Delegating communication to interpreters of spoken language and translators of written text. (These functions are often undertaken by the same person. For the sake of convenience, we henceforth refer only to interpreters except in instances when the distinction is important.)
• A combination of these solutions.

When the manager cannot devote the resources to developing a fluent command of the other language, these alternatives provide the only practical solutions to the communication problem. Here we look at the various factors that guide the manager in deciding which solution to adopt. Each solution to the lack of a common working language has disadvantages as well as advantages.

11.3.1   The Manager Learns the Other Language

THE ADVANTAGES

We have already seen the general reasons why it might be in the company's interests that the expatriate manager learns some of the other language. There are other gains:

1   Increased control; independence from interpreters and local managers, and a greater ability to check on their work.
2   Increased prestige and authority, both within the organization and in dealing with local outsiders.
3   Increased capacity to negotiate.
4   Increased value to the organization. Language skills give the manager added value.
5   Increased opportunities for job mobility.
6   Access to the other culture and an understanding of how its members perceive reality.

THE DISADVANTAGES

1   Cost, measured in terms of training, time, energy, etc.
2   A little learning is a dangerous thing. The organization and the manager needs to be realistic about his or her actual competence in the other language.
3   Some cultures are deeply suspicious of foreigners (in particular of foreigners who are competent in their language) and may prefer to supply interpreters and translators. For instance, a Briton who had learned Arabic in Egypt and spoke it with an Egyptian accent was posted to Benghazi in Eastern Libya, where Egyptians are often the object of deep suspicion. He overcame the problem of being mistaken for an Egyptian by first speaking in English, and establishing his cultural identity; then he asked permission to switch languages, and if the other person was willing, used Arabic.
4   The manager may only wish to spend a short time in the culture, and fears that if he speaks the language competently the organization may keep him posted there indefinitely. The organization needs to guarantee the maximum duration of the assignment.
5   Organizational fears that a manager who speaks the language competently will 'go native' and tend to represent local interests against home interests. A company with this attitude will maintain a policy of frequently circulating its managers and/or keeping them socially and professionally isolated from local contacts.
6   From the organization's point of view, a bilingual manager commands higher market value and is better equipped to switch to a competitor. For

instance, an American company exporting to Japan has to calculate the advantages of employing an English–Japanese bilingual against the potential damage of his suddenly quitting for a competitor. This has implications for the company's salary costs; the value placed on language competence always has to be reflected in rewards.

11.3.2 Local Managers Learn the Manager's Language

THE ADVANTAGES

The advantages to the expatriate manager and the organization when the local managers learn his or her language are:

1 The local managers develop a new skill, can communicate more widely with other branches of the organization, other individuals within it, and other organizations and individuals.
2 The local managers are qualified to attend professional skills training when training is given in the expatriate manager's language.

The advantages enjoyed by the local managers who learn the expatriate manager's language are perhaps greater. They

1 Create dependency relationships and become indispensable in dealings between the expatriate manager and the local workforce, and with other organizations and individuals.
2 Develop a new skill, hence are of greater value to the company, and have greater access to the job market.
3 Are qualified for other professional skills training when this is given in the other language.

THE DISADVANTAGES

1 The expatriate manager is dependent on the local managers.
2 The local managers now command higher market value and are better equipped to switch to a competitor. Malaysia provides an example. By law, all organizations above a certain size are obliged to hire a quota of at least 30 percent Malays at all levels. The shortage of educated English-speaking Malays (as opposed to Chinese and Indians, who together comprise about 50 percent of the population) means that those who meet these requirements are in very high demand, command very high salaries and switch jobs frequently. But note that in many European countries the managerial class is largely bilingual from schooling; hence skills in the second language command less on the market.

11.3.3   The Communications Job is Delegated to Interpreters

THE ADVANTAGES

1   The organization avoids the expense of training.
2   The organization avoids the disadvantages of training either expatriate or local managers to a point at which they command higher prices on the job market than the organization can pay. There is less chance of losing skilled managers to competitors.
3   Time invested in training start-up is minimalized (the interpreter may need some technical training) and results are immediate.
4   The organization has some guarantee of communicative efficiency.

THE DISADVANTAGES

1   Interpretation removes direct control from the manager. Unless the manager has some of the other language, he or she has no means of directly checking on reliability.
2   The manager is dependent on a person who may have inadequate technical or professional experience of the operation, and has no formal responsibility for outcomes.
3   In some cases, delegating communication responsibilities can endanger security.
4   It solves none of the morale problems associated with the manager's exclusion from the host culture. The manager does not enjoy direct access to the culture, and has no means of assessing how far he or she is being fed 'official' values and how far the interpreter is reliably reporting actual values.
5   The manager learns no new skills and his or her value to the organization is not enhanced.
6   Communications are restricted by the interpreter's schedule.
7   The manager's capacity to form direct personal relationships with negotiating partners etc. is reduced, and these have to be mediated through a third person.
8   Reliability can never be absolutely guaranteed or checked, particularly when the interpreter is asked to interpret idioms and metaphors which have no precise equivalents in the other language. For example, at a US–Soviet conference, 'out of sight, out of mind' was translated into Russian and back into English as 'invisible lunatic'. And in China, 'Come alive with Pepsi' was rendered as equivalent to 'Pepsi brings your ancestors back from the dead'. (In China the tradition of paying respect to the family's ancestors still has cultural significance.)

11.3.4 A Combination of the Above Solutions

A manager operating in another culture may plan a combination of learning the language him or herself, having other people learn his or her language, and using interpreters, that best exploits the advantages associated with each of the alternatives listed above, and reduces the disadvantages.

This solution is most practicable when the manager can invest only very limited resources to language learning. The section above on functions suggested how a combination of using the language oneself and using interpreters can be most effectively used in a negotiation. At certain points you may choose to take on responsibilities for communication yourself and use local managers and/or interpreters to monitor your performance, and at other points pass the responsibility over to them and monitor theirs to the extent that your competence allows.

This underlines the need to prioritize your communication needs to perform different functions. Your needs for technical precision, relationship creation, formality and informality determines how the alternative solutions are applied, and hence how resources are invested in developing them.

11.4 TRAINING A NON-MANAGERIAL WORKFORCE IN THE MANAGER'S LANGUAGE

The cross-cultural manager may also have to decide whether to train the non-managerial workforce to use a language. This situation occurs commonly when the workforce is immigrant. In some instances a national government requires the company to train expatriate workers. The Swedish government rules that foreign workers hired after 1973 should receive 240 hours of language instruction on company time.

In other cases, needs to increase production and enforce internal economies force the organization to arrange language training. Several years ago this was the experience of the General Foam Division of Tenneco Inc., USA.[10] At least 75 percent of the employees were Spanish-speaking. At the time that top management decided to train the Spanish workforce in English and the English-speaking supervisors in Spanish, the turnover rate averaged between 30 and 40 percent. The classes had an immediate effect. The company had fewer accidents, fewer union grievances, better production:

'Analyzing reasons for the success, General Foam officials feel that more than language interaction was involved. Formerly, problems stemmed not just from workers' failure to grasp supervisors' instructions, but even more from a refusal to admit it. Latin pride forbade it. . . . When learning a new language became an official value (for supervisors as well as for employees), the same workers went out of their way to add to their vocabularies, to make sure they understood exactly what the supervisor meant when he gave instructions.'

This implies that the value of language training for an immigrant workforce is enhanced when local supervisors also receive some training in the immigrants' language.

The language problems became more complex when the workforce represents a number of national cultures, who perhaps hold highly negative stereotypes of each other. Ford's workforce at Cologne in Germany consists of only about 50 percent native German speakers; the rest include both Greeks and Turks, who have a long history of conflict. In such a context training in the organization's working language not only has the normal advantages associated with language training (which General Foam discovered), but also allows these different groups a medium by which to communicate on 'neutral' ground. This can alleviate the dangers of cultural and racial tensions spilling over into the workplace.

The communication needs of the workforce and their immediate supervisors are prioritized in terms of *who* they need to communicate with and *why*. The Thai assembly plant of an American computer company employed four English-speaking expatriates in top management and a Thai workforce comprising approximately twelve second-level managers and a workforce of a hundred. The Thai managers needed English to speak with their superiors (three of whom had some Thai), write telexes, reports and letters, and Thai with their subordinates. The workforce spoke only Thai and had little direct contact with top-line management, but needed some English to read operating instructions on the imported equipment and materials. Their needs were sharply delineated compared with those of the General Foam immigrant Spanish speakers.

In the General Foam case:[11]

> 'The classes were not designed to enable students to read Shakespeare and Cervantes in the original or to equip tourists to describe the glories of an unfamiliar landscape — they concentrated instead on shopfloor necessities.'

They learned to speak and understand terms related to the industrial process, and to read signs such as 'No Smoking' and phrases in the union contract. They learned to communicate with their supervisors, who were trained in the Spanish for operating and safety instructions.

11.4.1   Non-Instrumental Needs of the Workforce

Employees who cannot interact with the host culture either inside or outside the workplace are demoralized, insecure, and at risk of misunderstanding important messages in the native language. A newspaper story tells of a Pakistani immigrant to the United Kingdom found guilty of making false claims for housing benefits.[12] The judge ordered that he learn English as part of a probation order, and commented:

> 'He says he is British. . . . A person who lives here has a *duty* to understand the language so he can give truthful information.' (Emphasis added.)

The immigrant employee's alienation has serious implications for job efficiency and turnover. The General Foam language classes brought to light problems that were essentially cultural.[13] For instance, management had failed to understand the resentment at the standard 15-minute lunch break. They had not realized that, unlike the American worker, who is willing to make do with a sandwich, Latins treat lunch as the main meal of the day, and the Spanish workforce was bringing in prepared dishes of rice, beans and port to heat on any hot surfaces they could find — including machinery — but the 15 minutes were usually over before the food was ready. Once management understood the reason for the resentment, they installed ovens to heat the food in advance.

> 'We have regular human relations sessions, and the workers could have explained the situation at any of those. . . . But they never did. Probably they felt touchy about talking about an alien custom. They stopped feeling alien after the classes started. In fact, our human relations sessions became 100% more productive.'

This case shows how language training enabled the firm to identify and meet both the work-related and non-instrumental needs of their workforce. Workers previously inhibited from communicating their cultural problems were motivated to greater involvement in the host culture by their mastery of linguistic functions that were not always directly related to operations.

In general, learners who achieve sufficient linguistic competence to succeed in one area of activity — the workplace — are motivated to expand their competence into other areas of activity. An immigrant workforce that can speak the local language is able to read newspapers, understand media, make friends, and visit public places including restaurants and bars. The better the immigrant workforce is able to use the local language the better it can adjust to its environment, and the higher its morale and productivity.

11.4.2   Advantages and Disadvantages of Training the Workforce

THE ADVANTAGES

The advantages of a workforce that can comprehend spoken and written instructions, communicate with supervisors, and (in the case of an immigrant workforce) communicate with the host culture have been shown. In addition:

1   The workforce are more adaptable and can be moved to other tasks.
2   They have higher morale, and this has implications for preventing and resolving conflicts, productivity, turnover, etc.
3   Where the workforce consists of a number of ethnic and cultural groups, a lingua franca helps lessen the danger of conflict between the groups.

THE DISADVANTAGES

1   The costs of training and time off the job.
2   From the organization's point of view, a better trained workforce have increased job mobility and it may be necessary to increase remuneration in order to keep them. This can be partly offset by limiting the syllabus to language items that are highly specific to the job and cannot be applied in other enterprises. In the case of an immigrant workforce, a highly restricted syllabus does not directly help them to adjust to the cultural environment, although it might motivate them to do so.
3   Local historical and political events may motivate locals *not* to learn and use your language. (This may apply at all local levels of the organization.) For instance, in Iran before the fall of the Shah, and in the Philippines before the collapse of Marcos, the climate of nationalism and revulsion against American involvement in supporting these unpopular regimes meant that many people made a conscious effort to use their own language whenever possible and not to use English, which was associated with foreign influence. In such situations, demanding that local employees use your language can have negative effects on morale and relationships. The expatriate manager will achieve far more by making the effort to learn at least some of the local language and to meet his or her local managers half way.

11.5   IMPLICATIONS FOR THE MANAGER

These questions help you weigh the alternatives; that is, whether (i) you learn the other language, (ii) managers in the other culture learn your language, (iii) the communications job is delegated to interpreters, or (iv) a combination of these solutions is applied.

- How important is it that you should be able to communicate directly with members of the other culture? (Take into account the significance of your contacts, the value of successful relationships, costs of unsuccessful relationships, market conditions, the importance the other culture places on you learning its language.)

1(a) very important;
1(b) moderately important;
1(c) not important.

- For what length of time do you expect to be committed to working with the other culture?

2(a) long term;
2(b) intermediate term;
2(c) short term.

- How much training will you need to satisfy your communication needs, taking into account your needs and existing competence?

3(a) a great deal of training;
3(b) a moderate amount of training;
3(c) not much training.

- How expensive is it to your organization that you train in the other language to a competence adequate to meet your needs? Estimate direct training costs, costs of time and replacements, opportunity costs. Cost out the training and estimate expense in terms of the expected returns.

4(a) very expensive;
4(b) moderately expensive;
4(c) not very expensive.

- How useful to you personally is it to train in the other language? Take into account your enhanced market value.

5(a) very useful;
5(b) moderately useful;
5(c) not very useful;

- How competent are members of the other culture in your language?

6(a) very competent;
6(b) moderately competent;
6(c) not very competent.

- How easily can you arrange for members of the other culture to train in your language?

7(a) easily;
7(b) moderately easily;
7(c) not easily.

- How expensive is it to your organization that members of the other culture train in your language up to an adequate competence? Cost out the training and estimate expense in terms of the expected returns. Estimate direct training costs, costs of time and replacements, opportunity costs, likelihood and cost of losing trained staff, etc.

8(a) very expensive;
8(b) moderately expensive;
8(c) not expensive.

- How available and efficient are interpretation services? Take into account your needs for technical interpretation.

9(a) very available and/or competent;
9(b) moderately available and/or competent;
9(c) not very available and/or competent.

- How secure are interpretation services? Take into account your needs for security.

10(a) very secure;
10(b) moderately secure;
10(c) not at all secure.

If you score 1(a) (very important), 2(a) (long term), 3(c) (not much training), 4(c) (not very expensive), 5(a) (very useful), 6(c) (not very competent), 7(c) (not easily), 8(a) (very expensive), 9(c) (not very available and/or competent), 10(c) (not at all secure) — then consider investing in your training.

If you score 1(c), 2(c), 3(a), 4(a), 5(c), 6(a), 7(a), 8(c), 9(c), 10(c) — then you might decide to shift responsibilities for using a second language and where necessary learning your language to managers in the other culture.

If you score 1(c), 2(c), 3(a), 4(a), 5(c), 6(a), 7(a/b/c), 8(a/b/c), 9(a), 10(a)

— then you might decide to delegate the communications job to interpreters.

If you score across these standards, then consider the advantages and costs of combining these solutions; for instance, training yourself up to a lower than desired level of competence, or limiting your training to specific communication skills, and relying otherwise on members of the other culture to use your language and on interpreters.

Even if you decide to make managers in the other culture responsible for learning your language, and/or to delegate the communications job to interpreters, STILL learn the necessary minimum (see section 11.2.5).

11.6 SUMMARY

This chapter has considered the value of fluency in the other language. Section 11.2 discussed the reasons why companies are interested in training their managers in second languages and cultures, and why governments support this trend. Section 11.3 discussed the value of your using the language, and the alternatives. Section 11.4 dealt with the needs to train a non-managerial workforce in the manager's language.

EXERCISES

Exercise 1

This exercise shows factors involved in deciding how to overcome communication problems.

A multinational computer company headquartered in the USA has branches throughout South East Asia. These are responsible for assembly, sales, and some production. The Indonesian branch has approximately 200 employees. It is managed by an expatriate American (who speaks only English) and all other employees are Indonesians. Twelve of the local Indonesian managers have responsibilities for ordering supplies from the company's US supplies depot in New Hampshire. Unfortunately they have a history of writing poor and sometimes ambiguous Fax messages. The resulting errors are causing considerable inconvenience and cost.

Finally the New Hampshire supplies manager has warned that unless some solution is found, he and his staff will no longer respond to orders from Indonesia.

The company has long-term plans for this otherwise very successful branch and over the next ten years hopes to develop and expand its assembly and production capacities.

How should the company respond to this problem? Evaluate the solutions below. What factors influence your answer?

(a) All Fax messages to the USA should be checked by the manager.

(b) All orders should be telephoned.
(c) The Indonesian managers should be taught general English skills.
(d) The Indonesian managers should be taught English writing skills.
(e) The New Hampshire supplies staff should be taught Malay reading skills, and all Fax messages should be sent in Malay both ways.
(f) The Indonesian managers should be let go, and replaced by expatriate Americans.
(g) The Indonesian managers should be let go, and replaced by Indonesians with better English language skills.
(h) A bilingual Indonesian should be added to the local staff with responsibilities only for writing English.
(i) An English–Malay interpreter should be hired to assist the New Hampshire staff.
(j) The New Hampshire supplies manager should be replaced.
(k) Any other solution . . .?

Now suppose that only two Indonesians have this responsibility. How does this affect your answer?

If instead 25 Indonesians have this responsibility. How does this affect your answer?

Finally, suppose that the company expects to withdraw its Indonesian operation within the next three years. How does this affect your answer?

Exercise 2

This exercise examines how the acquisition of a second language can affect power relationships within an organization.

The Darana Trading Company (DTC) is headquartered in the Kingdom of Darana. It sets up an overseas branch in the Republic of Godali. The peoples of the two countries speak different languages, Daranese and Godalese. In each country, very few speak the other's language. Daranese culture is highly individualist, and Godalese culture highly collectivist.

The chart in Figure 11.1 shows how this overseas branch (DTCG) is staffed. The brackets show first the nationality of each member of staff (D or G), and then the language(s) he speaks (D or G; D + G; or G + D). For instance, manager B is a Daranese national and speaks both Daranese and Godalese.

When the General Manager needs to negotiate with representatives of the Godalese government, whom he knows speak only a little Daranese, which of these is he most likely to do:

(a) Go alone?
(b) Take manager A with him?
(c) Take manager B with him?

Manager A returns to work at the Darana headquarters, and the company considers promoting assistant manager D. Why might this be in the company's interests? Why might it be in the company's interests to leave him in his present job?

The company promotes D, then looks for a Godalese to fill the vacancy at assistant manager level. Supervisor G is promoted. How does this affect the two managers? How does it affect the other three assistant managers?

Then supervisor H decides to invest his own time and resources in learning

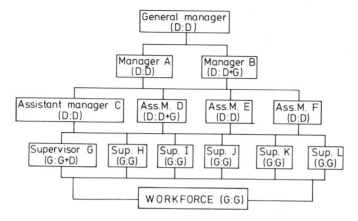

Figure 11.1

Daranese. The company rewards his initiative by promoting him up to the level of assistant manager. This causes G to wonder: supposing the company invested in language training for all other supervisors and 50 percent of the workforce? Whom in the company can he expect to support this proposal? Whom can he expect to oppose it? Why? And is this mass training in his own interests?

Finally, suppose that the cultural norms are not as described above (Daranese culture highly individualist, Godalese culture highly collectivist). How are all your earlier answers affected when the following conditions apply?

(a) Daranese culture is highly collectivist and Godalese culture highly individualist.
(b) Both cultures are highly collectivist.
(c) Both cultures are highly individualist.

NOTES

1   Kotler, M.L. (1987) Japan speaks a different language on business. *Asia Wall Street Journal*, 3 December.
2   Kuin, P. (1972) The magic of multinational management. *Harvard Business Review*, November/December, 89–97 (see 92).
3   Tully, S. (1988) Europe's best business schools. *Fortune*, 23 May, 106–10.
4   Zeira, Y. and Banai, M. (1985) Selection of expatriate managers in MNCs: 'the host-environment point of view. *International Studies of Management and Organization*, **XV**(1), 33–51.
5   Markham, J.M. (1989) Pardon my English, but did someone say 1992? *New York Times*, 21 May.
6   Ethnic children may face classroom ban on native languages. *The Times* (London), 16 August, 1989.
7   Mitgang, L. [AP] (1987) Foreign language study is surging in popularity in US. *Bangkok Post*, 24 November.
8   *International Herald Tribune*, 14 October 1987.

9   Yates, StJ.C. (1982) Defining and assessing levels of job-related performance. In *English for International Communication* (ed. C.J. Brumfit). Pergamon, Oxford, pp. 92–122.

Yates provides a list of skills derived from analysis of Swedish employees' communicative needs. The following fragment lists the Listening and Speaking Skills:

Face-to-face dealings with customers/suppliers/agents, etc.
Dealing with visitors
Attending conferences/seminars
Verbally relaying information
Training
Internal business meetings
External business meetings and negotiations
Making public statements
Use of the telephone
Ancillary and office services (typing/translating/interpreting)
Entertainment and other social purposes

Similar lists detail reading and writing skills.

10   When language is a barrier. *Business Week*, 28 February 1970.
11   *Ibid.*
12   'Learn English' order to Asian. *Daily Telegraph* (London), 6 May 1988.
13   When language is a barrier. *Business Week*, 28 February 1970.

12
Implementing a Language Policy

12.1 INTRODUCTION

A multinational set up a project in South China. After two years a new manager was sent out with responsibilities for getting operations into full swing. He had been trained in Mandarin Chinese before the assignment since it was assumed that he would need to communicate regularly with central government officials. In fact, official communications were relatively few and were handled by interpreters. He used Mandarin to express courtesies at official receptions but otherwise had much greater needs for Cantonese, in practice a different language, to communicate with the local workforce.

This demonstrates the importance of precise needs analysis. The decision that he should be taught Mandarin, not Cantonese, was based on experiences in the first two start-up years of the project when the need to communicate with officials was greater than the need to interact with a workforce. Insufficient attention had been paid to the actual demands of his job.

The chapter shows how to translate the discussion in the previous chapter into practical terms and to implement a language policy for your organization. Specifically:

- It shows how to conduct needs analysis and to apply it, for instance in a language training program.
- It explains the occupational concerns of the applied linguist and their relevance to the cross-cultural manager who needs to buy language training skills, either for himself or herself or for other people.

- It deals with the problems of organizing and contracting language training.
- It discusses feasible objectives, shows how to go about buying professional services, and warns against the pitfalls.

12.2   DECIDING ON LANGUAGE TRAINING

Managers often experience great difficulty when they come to contract language training programs. Vast resources are devoted to badly thought out programs on the basis of marketing materials that the manager would dismiss out of hand if they were directed to selling a service that came within his or her area of expertise. Part of the difficulty lies in identifying the nature of the service that is required.

The manager's difficulties are understandable. The processes involved in teaching and learning languages are mysterious and intangible. The manager is conditioned by training and professional experience to look for the formulae by which the uncertainties can be controlled, and the value of an investment calculated; language learning and use does not lend itself to precise formulation.

It is still impossible to predict accurately who will and who will not be able to learn a particular language and specify the conditions for learning, and assess competence in communicative skills in different situations. (Don't believe anyone who tells you that these problems have been overcome and that they have the answer — they don't.) But you can narrow the odds against success. The risks can be reduced to the level of those associated with buying any other skill and should not prevent you buying the best help available. This means applying realistic criteria in assessing your training needs and in negotiating a workable contract with professional teachers and applied linguists able to provide the training services needed.

As a manager, it is not your responsibility to design a training program yourself, but you do have the job of managing and monitoring whoever is appointed for this task. Assuming that your training department does not have an applied linguist on its staff, you need to contract an outsider.

12.2.1   Hiring a Specialist

You need a specialist who can take responsibility for:

- conducting a needs analysis;
- implementing the needs analysis;
- conducting aptitude and other testing, where appropriate;
- designing the language training program;
- advising on or organizing the language teaching.

You may decide to hire an individual or an institution, and are most likely to choose a reputable university language department or language school. Before making your choice, take advice from a university, your embassy if you are based abroad or the embassy of the country you are going to, business acquaintances, international aid and appropriate education organizations such as the British Council, United States Information Service, the Alliance Francaise, the Goethe Institut, etc. (These institutions may themselves be able to offer the services you need, but before signing them still take advice from neutral parties.)

The activities for which the specialist is responsible are discussed below.

12.3   IDENTIFYING AND MEETING NEEDS

Obviously you want the trainee to achieve competence in the other language, but as we saw in the previous chapter this begs the question: competent to do what?

The answer to this question can only be provided by an appropriate needs analysis. Analyzing the learner's needs is an essential stage in preparing a language training program and cannot be based on guesswork. Many good language programs have had no useful effect because needs have not been analyzed adequately, and thus the programs are aimed at achieving inappropriate goals. The introductory story gives an example.

12.3.1   Needs Analysis

Needs analysis serves several functions;

1 It identifies the *area* of competence; that is, language skills and functions which the trainee requires.
2 It identifies the *degree* of competence; that is, the standard of proficiency required.
3 By specifying required competences, an appropriate implementation of the analysis ensures that training is directed, and up to an appropriate level. This represents a financial saving for the organization. Overtraining wastes resources as much as under-training, and an organization no more wishes to over-train its members than to over-order raw materials. Similarly, misdirected training is as wasteful as using the wrong teaching materials.
4 By specifying required competencies, an appropriate implementation of the analysis ensures that the relevance of the training is apparent. Relevance in training is motivating whereas a lack of obvious relevance is

Relationship	Who needs to communicate, and with whom?
	superiors/peers/subordinates
	insiders/outsiders (customers, negotiating partners, government representatives, etc)
	Formal relationships (strangers)/informal (colleagues)
	Antagonistic/neutral/supportive
	Knowledgeable/ignorant
	Their expectations and needs
Topic	Occupational and non-occupational activities for which the other language is needed (how are these prioritized?)
	technical/general business/formal/informal (etc.) topics
Message structure skills	Channels in which productive skills (speaking/writing) and receptive skills (listening/reading) are needed (how are these prioritized?
	Modes (how are these prioritized?)
	Skills target level needed (elementary/intermediate/advanced)
	Skills level on entry to the program
Situation	Office/shop-floor/meetings/domestic/formal/informal/etc. (Where is the other language used in preference to the manager's first language?)
Time	Length of time of interactions. (When is the other language used in preference to the manager's first language?)
Purpose	General-purpose/special-purpose (occupational/academic; defined by other parameters)
	Language functions (see the suggestions in the previous chapter.)
Expense	Costs of training, including opportunity costs
	Cost advantages over other forms of language acquisition (training the other party/interpretation)

demotivating, and the morale of the trainees suffers. This also impinges on the value of the financial investment made in training.

12.3.2   The Parameters of Needs Analysis

A simple analytical instrument is usually quite sufficient. The MODE ANALY-SIS MODEL developed in Chapter 5 is applied here to serve this, its fourth function. The basic parameters are glossed to account for needs.

Two immediate problems arise, which we see below are interrelated:

- How much of the other language does the trainee need to learn?
- What skills and functions does the trainee need to perform?

12.3.3   How Much Training is Needed?

This question asks about the level of language skills that the trainee needs to acquire. That is, how much does the employer need to invest in training, and what is it worth to the employer to invest in training above this point? The interaction below illustrates the problem.

The scene is the 'economy' section of an aircraft. The passenger is European and the stewardess comes from the Indian sub-continent; neither speaks English as a first language.

Passenger:	'I wonder if you would be so good as to confirm whether whisky is sold in the transit lounge at Dubai?'
Stewardess:	'We touch down at Dubai in fifteen minutes, sir.'
Passenger:	'No no, can one obtain whisky there?'
Stewardess:	'Sorry sir, the bar is closed until touchdown.'
Passenger:	(LOUDER) 'No no, Dubai — whisky — yes — no?'
Stewardess:	(FLUSTERED) 'I ask.' (GOES TO THE GALLEY, AND DOES NOT REAPPEAR)

The stewardess has been trained to produce formulaic utterances and to understand the usual questions put to her. Her restricted competence is sufficient in most communicative situations, but not in all. She cannot cope with questions slightly outside the norm, particularly when asked in an elaborated grammatical style (the first question). Her first two answers show that she latches on to the last significant vocabulary item heard in the questions (Dubai, whisky) and produces formulaic answers that relate to them. But in this context, her utterances are inappropriate.

In his third attempt, the passenger makes the common mistake of reducing his request to a form that is supposed to be simple, but is instead meaningless. He makes things worse by shouting, which adds to the stewardess's confusion.

How much is it worth to the airline to invest in training her to a higher level, at which she can cope both with the few non-formulaic questions that she might be asked, and with questions asked in a non-standard style (over-elaborated, over-simplified, socially inappropriate, or just ungrammatical)?

The costs of advanced training, and her added value on the job market, have to be measured against the intangible value of enhanced customer relations.

12.3.4   What Skills and Functions are Needed?

Two cases will show the difficulty of pinpointing the language functions that the trainee needs to acquire.

A company based in Malaysia decided to provide English language training for its legal staff who dealt with foreign customers. The managing director explained what he thought was needed, and the resulting program focused on the forensic skills used in the courtroom. The program was well designed but irrelevant, and so had little effect; the lawyers needed to negotiate, not examine witnesses. The managing director should have had less confidence in his own judgement and instead trusted in the expert applied linguist.

In the second instance, a British language school was contracted to plan and teach a program of medical English for physicians. The inadequacies of the program quickly became apparent. The school had written a program of academic medical English which heavily emphasized medical terminology, whereas the physicians, already in practice, needed the skills to communicate with patients who used informal words to describe their symptoms.

The needs analysis supported (but not supplanted) by experience and intuition determines the following features of the language training program:

- content;
- methodology (classroom teaching, distance teaching, one-to-one tuition, more or less behavioral, more or less communicative, etc.);
- standards at entry and exit;
- methodology for trainee assessment at entry and exit;
- methodology for program evaluation;
- teaching skills required.

Content can range from GENERAL (for application to an indefinite range of communication needs) to SPECIAL-PURPOSE (for application to restricted and tightly specified needs).

12.3.5   General Language Programs

These programs presuppose that the trainees' needs cannot be satisfied by learning a restricted language code. Content is selected and graded according to linguistic criteria. For instance, elementary classes teach:

(a) Most frequently used grammatical and vocabulary items.
(b) Items that have most 'coverage' and can be applied most widely.

(c) Items that are least complex and easiest to learn (in practice, this often means items that are easiest to teach).
(d) Items that have most direct equivalence to corresponding items in the learner's native language.
(e) Items upon which more advanced learning is dependent. To take a very simple example from English teaching, it is usually thought necessary to teach pronouns (I, you, he, she, etc.) before verbs. This does not necessarily apply in teaching languages where pronoun use is optional.

Progressively more advanced classes teach items that are less frequently used, have less coverage, etc.

12.3.6   Special-Purpose Programs

These programs select and grade content in terms of a particular activity. For instance:

(a) *Occupational purposes*: programs teach the vocabulary and grammatical forms most frequently used in practicing a specific occupation (there are programs for conducting international business, for doctors, for hotel staff, for airline crews, etc.).
(b) *Academic purposes*: to study a specific discipline (the language of economics, of mathematics, of biology, etc.).
(c) *Particular skills*: to practice language skills such as writing or speaking, and sub-skills such as telex-writing or letter-writing.
(d) *Combinations of these purposes*: for instance, skills to read academic science text, to write business letters, to negotiate legal contracts.

At the extreme of special-purpose programs are those specific to the occupation and the organization, using in-house terminology that cannot be understood by outsiders. This strategy of teaching a highly restricted and artificial code offers the following ADVANTAGES:

1 There is security.
2 There is ease and cheapness of training and learning.
3 All language learnt is precisely related to task requirements.
4 The disadvantages normally associated with language training (and discussed in the preceding chapter, section 11.3) apply minimally. For instance, trainees are not provided with general skills that enhance their value on the job market and thus make them more likely to quit their jobs with you.

The strategy also presents DISADVANTAGES:

1 The code cannot be applied to non-routine tasks, particularly when these

involve interactants who are not members of the organization and do not use the code.

2   The advantages normally associated with language training (also discussed in section 11.3 of the preceding chapter) apply minimally. For instance, trainees have very limited means to communicate outside precisely defined roles and functions.

The less restricted and specific the code taught, the less these advantages and disadvantages apply. For instance, training an engineer to use a 200-word lexicon of in-house terminology is relatively cheap and limits his skills to performing a narrow range of specific tasks within the company. Expanding that lexicon to 500 words makes him more adaptable to other activities, but costs more and enhances his value in the labor market.

The commercial language-for-specific-purposes textbook market is dominated by English-teaching texts. But the same principles can be applied as readily in designing programs that teach other languages.

The manager does not normally wish to invest in training the learner (him/herself or others) to communicate for purposes which have no functional value to the organization; General Foam (see Chapter 11) rightly perceived that equipping their Spanish employees to read Shakespeare would have been wasteful of resources and demotivating. Some special-purpose focus is almost always necessary.

12.3.7   Balancing General and Special Needs

The issue then arises: how much general language does the learner need to acquire, and how much language specific to the occupation and job?

In general, the employee can make do with highly specialized language skills when the occupation is repetitive and the communication is restricted in terms of the number of interactants, the range of functions, and the terminology. For instance, the factory worker might need only to read operating instructions on imported machinery, and a language program designed to cater for these needs will be highly focused and give far greater emphasis to terminology than to wide general skills. He will need to recognize imperative and conditional grammatical forms associated with the function of instruction:

'This way up.'
'First, free the motor of its protective packaging.'
'Don't open the valve unless/until/when the light shows.'
'If the light shows, turn off the motor.'

The employee who has contact only with his supervisor needs a restricted range of spoken productive skills and a range of aural receptive skills limited to comprehending what the supervisor says. This includes the grammatical forms and vocabulary used in performing and responding to supervisory functions of giving instructions, feedback, etc. This range is taught to both employee and supervisor in their respective other-language.

When the employee needs to communicate with outsiders whose priorities cannot be so closely predicted and cannot be coached, needs for receptive skills are much greater.

Two examples will illustrate special-purpose language programs designed to meet the needs of different occupational groups.

Caterpillar Tractor realized that severe communication problems occurring between English-speaking managers and supervisors and non-English-speaking members of the workforce were harming production. The company developed a one-way (reading) system of printed communication called Caterpillar Fundamental English (CFE). This condensed and simplified standard English, and consisted of 800 words, made up of 70 verbs, 450 nouns, 100 prepositions, and 180 adjectives, adverbs, and pronouns. The program is taught to the workforce over 30 lessons by instructors who must know English and the trainees' language.

The second illustration comes from Thailand. A number of large corporations had become very conscious of their problems in negotiating contracts with foreign organizations in the medium of English. The cause of the problem seemed to be that corporation lawyers lacked expertise in translating Thai legal terminology and concepts into English, were unable to interpret and write English-language contracts, and could not properly advise their non-legal colleagues on the legal implications of English-medium contracts. The corporations negotiated with a local business school to develop the following program suited to the needs of their legal staff who could pass an entry test in intermediate level general English skills:

- a legal English comprehension module, which taught skills in understanding contracts written in English;
- a legal English writing module, which taught skills in writing simple contracts in English, using English equivalents of Thai legal terminology, and advising non-specialist translators in writing more complex contracts;
- a legal English negotiation module, which taught spoken and aural comprehension skills needed in taking part in negotiations and advising management negotiation colleagues.

Both the Caterpillar program and the Thai legal programs were highly specialized and designed for employees whose needs could be tightly identified. Beyond that they have little in common, and the type of solution applied to either one was inappropriate to the other. The first assumes no prior knowledge of the language, and teaches a highly restricted 'artificial' code to low-level employees, for reading purposes only, designed to facilitate simple assembly operations. The second teaches high-level professionals those communication skills appropriate to a range of different negotiating situations. These skills are not used routinely, and are not limited to the workplace. The trainee must have intermediate general reading, writing, speaking and listening English skills that have to be acquired *before* admission to the program and which are then practiced and refined within a skills-focused syllabus.

Hence the balance between general skills, that can be applied across a range of activities, and specific skills, that have far more limited range, varies very widely and in any particular instance can only be identified by research into the individual's needs. Give more emphasis to teaching general skills, or require competence in these for entry to a specialized program when:

1 The organization needs to invest in the trainee's long-term development into new spheres of activity. This is more likely to apply to the new manager who can expect to work in a range of functional areas in his career, than to the assembly-line worker.
2 Training costs are acceptable.
3 The investment loss incurred if the trainee quits and sells his new language skills on the market is acceptable; or can be minimized, for instance by some form of bonding.
4 A wide range of oral and literate skills are required and the terminology cannot be tightly specified. Needs analysis gives you the answer to this question.

12.3.8   Conducting the Needs Analysis

How your specialist identifies the trainees' needs and designs a program to meet them depends on

- how many trainees are involved;
- the language to be learnt;
- whether training is to take place within the home culture or the local culture.

No training situation precisely replicates another, and hence analytical strategies appropriate to one have to be modified to suit another. Here is one example of how a specialist might go about analyzing needs.

Assume that you already have a competent model user of the other language in post, performing a relatively routine task; that you need to train other managers to perform the same spoken functions; and that the research is conducted in post. The first stage of needs analysis is conducted by simple questionnaires and interviews, based again on application of the MODE ANALYSIS MODEL. These questions are put to your models and to the persons with whom they need to communicate — their superiors, peers, and if possible, to their subordinates. These people may give very different answers, and this shows the need for investigation.

The specialist shadows the models in their professional activities for at least a day when these are routine, and longer in other cases, observing the full range of their communicative interactions within the organization. And the discrepancy between how they describe their language needs and how they actually communicate may again surprise you. The discrepancy is more likely to stem from their difficulties in objectifying and describing their personal experiences than from duplicity. The interactions that one remembers as most important may not necessarily be those in which you spoke most or that the other interactant(s) remember as significant. (You can test this by recording an informal discussion between friends, then ask each to recall what he or she said, and check the descriptions against the actual data.)

This observation goes beyond checking the questionnaire and interview findings. It includes noting all text that has to be read or written in the other language (notices, memos, instructions) and recording samples of spoken communication. (Video recordings are often essential in sophisticated linguistic analysis; but to collect the data needed in designing a language program they are more trouble than they are worth. Audio is sufficient.)

The collection of recorded data need not be extensive, and even a little gives the researcher an invaluable bank of authentic material that can be used in designing the program. It will include authentic sample utterances that can be applied in writing materials.

The specialist notes the interactants and tries to estimate the importance of the different communications. This tells him when formal grammatical accuracy is important (for instance, when giving new safety instructions) and when the communicator needs only get across the general drift of an idea (for instance, when conveying routine instructions). He might decide that the teaching material should reflect the frequency of which particular functions and grammatical and vocabulary items are expressed, and alternately might give greater priority to teaching important items, even when these occur relatively infrequently.

If the specialist cannot collect authentic communications — perhaps for reasons of security or inconvenience — he may stage simulations of the target activities record and exploit these.

This research plan has to be modified if the company does not have a model who already uses the other language appropriately. If this is your situation, then collect the same information when the native language is used and decide which interactions and messages would be more effective in the other language. And if you or some other manager is being posted out to another culture which you cannot reliably approximate in your home culture, then ask the assistance of your other-culture partners in giving you the information you need. It is, after all, in their interests as much as yours that communication problems should be reduced to a minimum and that language training should be appropriate.

12.4   ORGANIZING AND IMPLEMENTING THE PROGRAM

We are concerned here with the other activities conducted by the specialist, and which you will need to monitor.

12.4.1   Testing

The specialist may also decide to predict the trainees' learning behavior by means of a LANGUAGE LEARNING APTITUDE TEST. This gives some idea of expected rates of achievement and hence of the desired complexity of the teaching materials, and helps weed out those trainees on whom the training investment is likely to be wasted. Use this test when you can afford to choose between employees, all of whom are otherwise qualified for posting to the other culture.

When the trainees already have some knowledge of the other language, use a PROFICIENCY TEST, and/or a DIAGNOSTIC TEST, as a means of testing their present performance levels against those which you expect them to acquire, and of diagnosing their problems.

Tests also have to be prepared to assess the trainees on exit from the program; this is dealt with in section 12.4.5.

12.4.2   Selecting the Training Materials

It should not take more than a few weeks to collect the essential data and make a preliminary analysis. Your specialist is now in a position to check this output against the corpus of extant published and unpublished materials and decide if any of this is appropriate. A good applied linguist should know what the market has to offer in the general area of your needs. You will be faced with one of three alternatives:

1   The market offers appropriate material. In this case, use it; it will save you the costs involved in implementing either of the other two alternatives.

2 The market offers some appropriate material, which has to be augmented by additional material tailor-made to your specific requirements.
3 The market offers no appropriate material, in which case you need to contract a full tailor-made program that fits your requirements.

It is not your job to know how a language syllabus is designed and materials written. But here are some points that you will need to take into account as the manager responsible for deciding whether to use published material or to contract.

Materials writing is extremely expensive, labour intensive, and takes time. One university program in Malaysia required about nine man-years to construct 120 hours of special-purpose material, most of which was rejected after one piloting. If time is short or the target learners consist of only one group or even one individual, do not bother contracting. Use published materials (which you can be sure have already been piloted, tried and tested and thus carry a guarantee of quality), even if these are not precisely appropriate. On the other hand, if you expect to have to arrange language programs for a number of groups over a number of years, contracting tailor-made materials or a full program and investing in the time of writing and piloting may be a good investment.

The commercial market offers material aimed at different levels of competence and at different age groups. If your trainees are at an elementary stage, make sure they are given *adult* elementary material. Almost nothing is more likely to kill their motivation than elementary material prepared for children.

12.4.3 Organizing the Training Program

When selecting the training materials your specialist should also be planning how to implement the program. Check that you agree on the following points:

1 The timetable for program planning; training dates, times and venues (assuming that the program is to be classroom taught rather than self-access); homework assignments.
2 The syllabus of training materials. In normal circumstances, materials should be issued to trainees and yourself well in advance of when they are to be taught.
3 Numbers of participants.
4 Entry levels of competence. Trainees at very different entry levels need to be catered for by different programs.
5 Exit levels of competence — what the trainee should know on coming out of the program.
6 Valid testing instruments to assess trainee levels at entry and exit.

7   Qualifications and responsibilities of classroom trainers (or tutors, when the program is self-access).

8   Program evaluation instruments, preferably conducted by some neutral party. You need to know whether the program has met its objectives and you are getting value for money. If it has not, how does this effect your contractual obligations?

12.4.4   Hiring Trainers

The language teaching business is a semi-profession in the sense that entry is unrestricted. Every country operates laws restricting medical practice to qualified persons, and these give some guarantee of quality; but this is not the case in the language teaching business. Some institutions are by any standards highly professional in the qualifications and experience they demand from their members, and in the services they offer. But the bottom levels of the business are packed with unqualified and inexperienced persons. However naturally gifted, they cannot usually be expected to deliver professional services at the level you expect.

As a very general rule, do *not* hire an individual or institution who comes unrecommended, or anyone unqualified, again unless they come very highly recommended. A warm personality is not sufficient. Conducting a needs analysis and writing a program require specialist skills. Do not assume that a skilled primary school teacher is equally well qualified to teach at an occupational/professional level; different teaching skills are required.

Do *not* be taken in by the argument that any native speaker can teach their language; your driving skills do not make you an expert car mechanic.

Finally, do *not* hire anyone who offers to teach you the language 'painlessly' or 'the natural way, the way a child learns its native language'. While you do want to learn to communicate naturally and effortlessly, this does *not* make the learning process equally natural and effortless. Obviously you hope it will be fun and interesting, but do not expect to accomplish much without hard work. Do not expect to learn vocabulary by osmosis. Unless you are a very highly gifted learner, sooner or later you will need to sit down and learn lists of words by heart.

As for learning some other language 'the way a child learns', try watching a child learn. For perhaps an average of ten hours a day it listens, mimics, constructs generalizations, practices to itself and with other people, revises its generalizations, tries again — a process that has taken over 20 000 hours by its fourth birthday. No organization can afford to invest that time in training an employee. It is precisely because this 'natural' process of language learning is so uneconomical and inefficient that experts have constructed grammars and structured teaching materials.

In short, be as tough-minded in hiring language training services as you are when hiring any other training service. Insist on a professional service. By demanding quality you meet your own needs and contribute to the professionalization of the language training business overall, and that is to the advantage of everyone but the charlatans.

12.4.5   Other Conditions for Success

A number of other conditions must be met if the program is to succeed:

1   Classes should be held on company time. When the organization pays for the time it demonstrates the importance it places on acquisition of the language. If it is to the company's advantage that the individual learns this new skill, he should not be expected to acquire it in his own time as a 'hobby'. This includes time spent out of class on homework; which should be remunerated as equivalent to overtime. Costs incurred in traveling to and from classes when these are held off the organization's premises should be reimbursed.

2   Trainees should be suitably motivated to learn the language. Trainees at all levels should be guaranteed that acquisition of the new skills at the desired level of competence will be rewarded, for instance by raises and promotion.

3   Among managers, language skills should be treated as management skills, equivalent to skills in accounting or human resources management.

4   The relevance of the syllabus to needs must be explicit. A superficially irrelevant syllabus is demotivating and worse than useless.

5   Trainees should use the language in real communicative situations (that is, not just classroom practice) as soon as possible after the learning process. This demonstrates the value of learning, and their success in using the language in real situations motivates further learning.

6   Classes should be held regularly — ideally several times a week, for at least four or five hours a week. The more intensive the program the better. A hundred hours spread over a month is invariably more effective than the same time spread over a year. Hence the actual costs in raising the trainee to the desired standard are less.

7   If possible, classes should be held on the organization's premises; this demonstrates the organization's commitment. In this case classes are given precedence over other activities and are not disturbed by colleagues, telephones, or secretaries. Try to have a room reserved for classes where teaching materials can be permanently stored, and where tables and chairs do not have to be rearranged from some function before every class begins. When these conditions cannot be guaranteed, and classes are held off the premises, if necessary transport should be arranged.

12.5   FEEDBACK

You need to obtain feedback on the program while it is in progress, on termination, and some time after termination when the trainees are at post using the skills they have learned. Feedback should answer several questions:

1   Does the program meet its declared objectives?
2   Is the content of the materials appropriate? Does it teach in the appropriate area of competence and at the appropriate level of competence?
3   Are the declared objectives appropriate? Should they be modified to meet the needs of any future groups of trainees?
4   Are the specialist and trainers/tutors performing adequately?

The functions of feedback are:

- to tell you whether you are getting value for money;
- to tell you what improvements can be made should you need to mount the program again;
- to check on your needs analysis (which can give you feedback on the job specification);
- to motivate the specialist, trainers (or tutors) and trainees.

All groups will benefit and perform better if they know that you and the organization are committed to the program's success, and will be more willing to make positive suggestions for improvement. Do not let them think that you have lost interest as soon as the program has got under way.

Obtain feedback from:

- the specialist;
- the trainers (or tutors);
- the trainees;
- other persons responsible for administering the program;
- managers responsible for vetting the professional activities of the trainees when they are at post, using their new skills within the local culture.

Obtain feedback by means of:

- program evaluation instruments;
- questionnaires;
- interviews and informal discussions.

5　Are the training materials adequate? How can they be improved?

6　Are the trainees motivated? Are they working adequately? Do they perceive the relevance of the training? How can motivation be improved?

7　Are assessment procedures appropriate?

8　Is the timetabling appropriate?

9　Is the venue (and where this applies, transportation) appropriate?

10　What suggestions do the specialist, trainers (or tutors), and trainees have to improve the program and its administration?

12.6　IMPLICATIONS FOR THE MANAGER

Assume that you have to organize training for a group of your junior managers in language X. The questions below develop some of the issues raised by the application of the MODE ANALYSIS MODEL in section 12.3.

You will not be able to answer all these questions accurately because you are not qualified to estimate how many hours instruction are needed to teach particular skills. Nevertheless, they illustrate the issues that you will need to agree with your contracted specialist.

1　List the occupational activities that the job entails. In which of these do they need the other language?

2　With whom do they need to communicate in these activities?

3　(a) What productive language functions (speaking and writing) MUST they perform in language X (for instance, greetings, giving orders, writing memos)?

(b) What productive language functions would you PREFER them to perform in language X?

(c) What other productive language functions MIGHT they need to perform in language X?

4　(a) With whom must they communicate the essential functions you listed in response to 3(a) above?

(b) With whom will they communicate the non-essential but preferred functions you listed in response to 3(b) above?

(c) With whom will they communicate the non-essential functions you listed in response to 3(c) above?

5　Your answers to question 4 indicate the numbers of persons involved and their status and power. It may lead you to revise the priorities you listed in answer to question 3.

6 (a) What receptive language functions (listening, reading) MUST they perform in language X (for instance, understanding spoken reports, reading letters)?
   (b) What receptive functions would you PREFER them to perform in language X?
   (c) What other receptive language functions MIGHT they need to perform in language X?

7 (a) With whom must they communicate the essential functions you listed in response to 6(a) above?
   (b) With whom will they communicate the non-essential but preferred functions you listed in response to 6(b) above?
   (c) With whom will they communicate the non-essential functions you listed in response to 6(c) above?

8 Your answers to question 7 indicate the numbers of persons involved and their status and power. It may lead you to revise the priorities you listed in answer to question 6.

This next stage demonstrates the calculations necessary in costing out the program.

9   How many managers do you plan to train?
10 Estimate the earnings to the company accruing from their mastering the skills listed in answer to questions 3 and 6 above. Take into account any expected losses from their failing to master these skills.
   (a) Estimate for the 'MUST have' skills (3(a) and 6(a)) only.
   (b) Estimate for the 'MUST have' and the 'PREFER to have' skills (3(a), 3(b), and 6(a), 6(b)).
   (c) Estimate for the 'MUST have', 'PREFER to have', and 'MIGHT have' skills (3(a), 3(b), 3(c), and 6(a), 6(b), 6(c)).

11 Now assume that the 'MUST have' skills require 40 hours of tuition, the 'PREFER to have' skills a further 40 hours, and the 'MIGHT have' skills a further 40 hours. Of how many hours tuition should the program consist?

12 Cost out the program including:
   (a) the following fixed costs:
      • specialist's fee ($3000)
      • administration (including 12 hours of your time; secretarial, janitorial and catering staff)
      • installation (including power)
      • trainee assessment and program evaluation costs (allow $1000)
      • other fixed incidentals.

(b) the following variable costs:
  - training costs at $30 per trainee per hour; in total not less than $90 and not more than $450 the group per hour
  - trainees' time off the job.
  - textbooks and secretarial expenses at $50 per trainee.
  - other variable incidentals.

13 Will the program show a profit? Do you now wish to change your answer to question 11? If necessary, recalculate your answers to questions 11 and 12.

This questionnaire is oversimplified at a number of points. For instance, it ignores levels of competence required, and entry and exit levels of competence. The hours needed to master skills at 'MUST have', 'PREFER to have' and 'MIGHT have' priorities have been calculated arbitrarily and differ according to the industry, occupation of the trainees, language to be learnt, area of competence required, and entry and exit levels of competence required. Costs of specialist consultancy and tuition differ between and within different countries. It has been assumed that the program exploits published texts, and that there is no call to contract tailor-made (and much more expensive) original material.

Nevertheless, even this simplification indicates the range of decisions that have to be taken when buying a language training program.

12.7. SUMMARY

The previous chapter dealt with the advantages and disadvantages of using the other language as against alternative means of communicating with members of the other culture. This chapter has gone one step further. It assumes a decision has been taken to use the other language and the need to organize and buy training in it.

Section 12.2 indicated the conditions under which language training is most effective. Section 12.3 illustrated needs analysis with the mode analysis model, and discussed problems of calculating how much to invest in language training and what general and special skills to invest in. Sections 12.4 and 12.5 discussed further issues that the manager needs to take into account when briefing a consultant specialist.

EXERCISES

These exercises give practice in needs analysis.

Exercise 1

Assume that a member of another culture, speaking a different first language, has been indefinitely posted to your organization with responsibilities that duplicate your own. This person speaks and writes your language at a general elementary level.

Design a model for analyzing his or her needs, indicating what levels and areas of competence are needed in order to perform the job appropriately.

Use the mode analysis model as in section 12.3.3 and the questions in section 12.6. Add any further categories you think necessary in order to pinpoint the individual's needs as precisely as possible and to specify a teaching program.

Exercise 2

Assume that the colleague whose needs analysis you prepared above is accompanied by a dependent spouse. This spouse speaks and writes your language at a similar elementary level and needs to develop his or her skills in order to perform such activities as

- participating in social and cultural life with members of your organization and host community;
- communicating with trades people, school teachers, domestic servants, etc.;
- reading newspapers, signs, cooking instructions, etc.

Design a model for analyzing his or her needs, indicating what levels and areas of competence are needed.

Compare this needs analysis with the one in Exercise 1. Where do levels and areas of competence correspond and fail to correspond? (For instance, you may decide that the dependent spouse has greater needs for a higher general level of competence than does your new colleague.)

13
A Cross-Cultural Management Communications Audit

The cross-cultural management communications audit serves a range of functions.

1 It is a descriptive instrument for modeling the communications patterns in your place of work and with outsiders. It enables you to identify significant differences between the typical communications patterns of your home culture and the other culture.
2 It is a diagnostic instrument. It shows why communication problems arise, and indicates appropriate action-plans for resolving the problems.
3 It is an instrument for predicting the affects of cross-cultural differences and for planning appropriate communication systems.
4 It is a check on your understanding of the main points covered in this book, and summarized in the IMPLICATIONS FOR THE MANAGER sections in Chapters 2–12.

The audit is most effective when it is conducted:[1]

PERIODICALLY. A periodic assessment of the situation gives you comparisons on a longitudinal basis. It shows how far the situation has improved or worsened. How can changes be explained? These factors may be significant:

(a) factors in the macro environment, including political, economic, social, cultural changes; market fluctuations;
(b) factors within the organization, including policy changes, recruitment and promotion practices, business success or failure, the introduction of technology.

INDEPENDENTLY. A self-audit is bound to reflect the subjective feelings of the auditor. An audit made by an outsider, such as a consultant, always has the virtues of greater objectivity.

COMPREHENSIVELY. An effective communications audit covers all aspects of how members of the organization communicate between themselves and with outsiders. It shows both strengths and weaknesses.

SYSTEMATICALLY. The parameters provide an orderly sequence of steps for analyzing communications conducted by the organization. These parameters are interrelated.

The cross-cultural management communications audit consists of five parameters, which are described below.

1. EXTRA-ORGANIZATIONAL COMMUNICATIONS ENVIRONMENT PARAMETER

(A)   How do you rate the local culture along these dimensions?
    (a) low power distances — 6:5:4:3:2:1 — high power distances
    (b) highly individualist — 6:5:4:3:3:1 — highly collectivist
    (c) high uncertainty avoidance — 6:5:4:3:2:1 — low avoidance
    (d) highly feminine — 6:5:4:3:2:1 — highly masculine

(B)   How does the rating on each of these dimensions affect relationships and communications between the organization and the following entities?
    (a) competitors within the culture group
    (b) customers within the culture group
    (c) suppliers within the culture group
    (d) joint-venture partners, subsidiaries, parents, licensors, licensees, etc., within the culture group
    (e) government and other official bodies within the culture group
    (f) trades unions
    (g) professional and trade associations
    (h) entities (a)–(g) above within another culture group
(C)   How are relationships and communications between the organization and its external environment affected by changes in the following environments?
    (a) the economic environment
    (b) the market environment
    (c) the technological environment; technological innovation
    (d) the political environment; the affects of new laws.

2. INTER-ORGANIZATIONAL COMMUNICATIONS ENVIRONMENT PARAMETER

(A)   How does the rating on each of the dimensions listed in 1(A) affect FORMAL relationships and official communications between the following entities, when all members belong to the SAME CULTURE GROUP?
(a)   various levels of management
(b)   various levels of management and the workforce
(c)   divisions, departments
(d   functional groupings
(e)   other groups within the organization

(B)   How does the rating on each of the dimensions listed in 1(A) affect FORMAL relationships and official communications between the entities above, when members belong to DIFFERENT CULTURE GROUPS?

(C)   How does the rating on each of the dimensions listed in 1(A) affect INFORMAL relationships and unofficial communications between the entities above, when all members belong to the SAME CULTURE GROUP?

(D)   How does the rating on each of the dimensions listed in 1(A) affect INFORMAL relationships and unofficial communications between the entities above, when members belong to SOME OTHER CULTURE GROUP?

If necessary, specify the parameters of the other culture group, identify significant differences, and predict areas of misunderstanding and disagreement.

3. COMMUNICATIONS STRATEGY PARAMETER

(A)   Assess the communicative strategies adopted by the organization (and/or groups within the organization)
• when dealing with some OTHER ORGANIZATION/GROUP
• when this other party belongs to the SAME CULTURE in these situations:
i   in conflict with a more powerful organization/group
ii   in conflict with a less powerful organization/group
iii   in conflict with an equally powerful organization/group
iv   selling to a more powerful organization/group
v   selling to a less powerful organization/group
vi   selling to an equally powerful organization/group
vii   buying from a more powerful organization/group

  viii buying from a less powerful organization/group
  ix buying from an equally powerful organization/group
  x doing a deal to mutual advantage with a more powerful organization/group
  xi doing a deal to mutual advantage with a less powerful organization/group
  xii doing a deal to mutual advantage with an equally powerful organization/group
  xiii obtaining information/advice/other help from a more powerful organization/group
  xiv obtaining information/advice/other help from a less powerful organization/group
  xv obtaining information/advice/other help from an equally powerful organization/group
  xvi persuading/influencing a more powerful organization/group
  xvii persuading/influencing a less powerful organization/group
  xviii persuading/influencing an equally powerful organization/group
  xix others

(B) For each situation, which strategies is the organization likely to adopt (assuming personal relationship between individuals to be neutral)?

STRATEGIES:

(a) negotiate:	6	5	4	3	2	1
(b) attempt to persuade:	6	5	4	3	2	1
(c) invite participation:	6	5	4	3	2	1
(d) enter overt conflict:	6	5	4	3	2	1
(e) achieve mutual interest:	6	5	4	3	2	1
(f) impose terms:	6	5	4	3	2	1
(g) influence through third parties:	6	5	4	3	2	1
(h) create obligation:	6	5	4	3	2	1
(i) create dependency relationships:	6	5	4	3	2	1
(j) exercise formal power attributes:	6	5	4	3	2	1
(k) limit the basis of discussion:	6	5	4	3	2	1
(l) play for time:	6	5	4	3	2	1
(m) respond immediately:	6	5	4	3	2	1
(n) others:	6	5	4	3	2	1

(C) Assess the communicative strategies adopted by the organization (and/or groups within the organization)
  • when dealing with some OTHER ORGANIZATION/GROUP
  • when this other party belongs to SOME OTHER CULTURE.

Use the SITUATIONS and STRATEGIES listed in 3(A) and 3(B) above.

If necessary, specify the parameters of the other culture group, identify significant differences, and predict areas of misunderstanding and disagreement.

(D) Assess the communicative strategies adopted by INDIVIDUAL MEMBERS of the organization.
- when dealing with some other individual WITHIN THE ORGANIZATION
- when this other individual belongs to the SAME CULTURE.

Use the STRATEGIES listed in 3(B) and the SITUATIONS listed below.

i   in conflict with a more powerful individual within the same group (e.g. the same division, department, functional area)

ii   in conflict with a less powerful individual within the same group

iii   in conflict with an equally powerful individual within the same group

iv   in conflict with a more powerful individual from some other group

v   in conflict with a less powerful individual from some other group

vi   in conflict with an equally powerful individual from some other group

vii   controlling a less powerful individual within the same group

viii   controlling an equally powerful individual within the same group

ix   controlling a less powerful individual from some other group

x   controlling an equally powerful individual from some other group

xi   taking directions from a more powerful individual within the same group

xii   taking directions from an equally powerful individual within the same group

xiii   taking directions from a more powerful individual from some other group

xiv   taking directions from an equally powerful individual from some other group

xv   doing a deal to mutual advantage with a more powerful individual within the same group

xvi   doing a deal to mutual advantage with a less powerful individual within the same group

xvii   doing a deal to mutual advantage with an equally powerful individual within the same group

xviii   doing a deal to mutual advantage with a more powerful individual from some other group

xix   doing a deal to mutual advantage with a less powerful individual from some other group

xx   doing a deal to mutual advantage with an equally powerful individual from some other group

xxi   obtaining information/advice/other help from a more powerful individual within the same group

xxii   obtaining information/advice/other help from a less powerful individual within the same group

xxiii   obtaining information/advice/other help from an equally powerful individual within the same group

xxiv   obtaining information/advice/other help from a more powerful individual from some other group

xxv   obtaining information/advice/other help from a less powerful individual from some other group

xxvi   obtaining information/advice/other help from an equally powerful individual from some other group

xxvii   persuading/influencing a more powerful individual within the same group

xxviii   persuading/influencing a less powerful individual within the same group

xxix   persuading/influencing an equally powerful individual within the same group

xxx   persuading/influencing a more powerful individual from some other group

xxxi   persuading/influencing a less powerful individual from some other group

xxxii   persuading/influencing an equally powerful individual from some other group

xxxiii   others

(E)   Assess the communicative strategies adopted by the individual
- when dealing with an INDIVIDUAL WITHIN THE SAME GROUP
- when this other individual belongs to SOME OTHER CULTURE
- when dealing with an INDIVIDUAL FROM SOME OTHER GROUP
- when this other individual belongs to SOME OTHER CULTURE.

Use the SITUATIONS listed in 3(D) and the STRATEGIES listed in 3(B) above.

If necessary, specify the parameters of the other culture group, identify significant differences, and predict areas of misunderstanding.

4. COMMUNICATIONS MODE PARAMETER

(A) Assess the communicative modes adopted within the organization. Assume relationships between individuals to be neutral, and apply
    (a) the SITUATIONS listed in 3(A)
    (b) the STRATEGIES listed in 3(B)

(B) List the modes associated with each SITUATION and STRATEGY
- when dealing with some OTHER ORGANIZATION/GROUP
- when this other party belongs to the SAME CULTURE

Apply
    (a) the SITUATIONS listed in 3(A)
    (b) the STRATEGIES listed in 3(B)

(C) List the modes associated with each SITUATION and STRATEGY
- dealing with a group within the SAME ORGANIZATION
- this other group belongs to the SAME CULTURE

(D) List the modes associated with each SITUATION and STRATEGY
- dealing with an individual within the SAME ORGANIZATION
- this other individual belongs to the SAME CULTURE

(E) List the modes associated with each SITUATION and STRATEGY
- when dealing with some OTHER ORGANIZATION/GROUP
- when this other party belongs to SOME OTHER CULTURE

(F) List the modes associated with each SITUATION and STRATEGY
- dealing with a group within the SAME ORGANIZATION
- this other group belongs to SOME OTHER CULTURE

(G) List the modes associated with each SITUATION and STRATEGY
- dealing with an individual within the SAME ORGANIZATION
- this other individual belongs to SOME OTHER CULTURE.

5. COMMUNICATIONS STYLE PARAMETER

(A) Assess the communicative styles adopted by the organization (and/or groups within the organization)
- when dealing with some OTHER ORGANIZATION/GROUP
- when this other party belongs to the SAME CULTURE.

Apply
    (a) the SITUATIONS listed in 3(A)

    (b) the STRATEGIES listed in 3(B)
    (c) the MODES listed in 4

(B)   For each SITUATION, STRATEGY and MODE, what communicative styles are typically applied (assuming relationships between individuals to be neutral)?
    (a) formal — 6:5:4:3:2:1 — informal
    (b) ambiguous/indirect — 6:5:4:3:2:1 — unambiguous
    (c) consensual — 6:5:4:3:2:1 — antagonistic
    (d) logical — 6:5:4:3:2:1 — analogical
    (e) discursive — 6:5:4:3:2:1 — brief
    (f) other — 6:5:4:3:2:1 — . . .

NOTE

1 Kotler describes these essential characteristics of a marketing audit in Kotler, P. (1988 edition) *Marketing Management*. Prentice Hall International Editions, Englewood Cliffs, NJ, pp. 746–52.

Bibliography

Almaney, A.J. (1981) Cultural traits of the arabs: growing interest for international management. *International Management Review*, **21**(3), 10–18.

Argyle, M. and Dean, J. (1965) Eye contact, distance and affiliation. *Sociometry*, **28**, 289–304.

Benedict, R. (1946, 1974) *The Chrysanthemum and the Sword: Patterns of Japanese Culture*. New American Library, New York.

Brown, R. and Gilman, A. (1960) The pronouns of power and solidarity. In *Style in Language* (ed. T.A. Seboek). MIT Press, Boston, Mass. pp. 253–76.

Brumfit, C.J. (1982) *English for International Communication*. Pergamon, Oxford.

Campbell, N.C.G., Graham, J.L., Jolibert, A. and Meissner, H.G. (1988) Marketing negotiations in France, Germany, the United Kingdom, and the United States. *Journal of Marketing*, **52**, 49–62.

Casse, P. (1981) *Training for the Cross-Cultural Mind* (2nd edition). Sietar, Washington, DC/Intercultural Press, Chicago.

Chilcott, J.G. (1968) Some perspectives for teaching first generation Mexican Americans. In *Readings in the Socio-Cultural Foundations of Education* (eds J. G. Chilcott *et al*.). Wadsworth, Belmost, Mass., pp. 358–68.

Chilcott, J.G. *et al*. (eds) (1968) *Readings in the Socio-Cultural Foundations of Education*. Wadsworth, Belmost, Mass.

Eisenberg, E.M. (1984) Ambiguity as strategy in organizational communication. *Communication Monographs*, **51**, 227–42.

Eisenberg, E.M. and Witten, M.G. (1987) Reconsidering openness in organizational communication. *Academy of Management Review*, **12**(3), 418–26.

Europa Year Book (annual editions). Europa Publications, London.

Fisher, R. and Ury, W. (1981) *Getting to Yes*. Houghton Mifflin, Boston, Mass.

Follet, M.P. (1940) Constructive conflict. In *Dynamic Administration: The Collected Papers of Mary Parker Follett* (eds H.C. Metcalf and L. Urwick). Harper, New York.

Frankenstein, J. (1986) Trends in Chinese business practice. *California Management Review*, **XXIX**(1), 148–60.

Glenn, E.S., Witmeyer, D. and Stevenson, K.A. (1984) Cultural styles of persuasion. *International Journal of Intercultural Relations*, Summer, 11–22.

Graham, J.L. (1985) The influence of culture on the process of business negotiations: an exploratory study. *Journal of International Business Studies*, Spring, 81–96.

Graham, J.L. and Herberger, R.A. (1983) Negotiators abroad — don't shoot from the hip. *Harvard Business Review*, July/August, 160–8.

Graves, D. (1979) The impact of culture upon managerial attitudes, beliefs and behaviour in England and France. In *Managerial Communication* (ed. T. D.
Weinshall). Academic Press, London, pp. 250–3.

Greenbaum, S., Leech, G. and Svartvik, J. (1980) (eds) *Studies in English Linguistics for
Randolph Quirk*. Longman, London.

Hall, E.T. (1955) The anthropology of manners. *Scientific American*, **192**, 84–90.

Hall, E.T. (1960) The silent language in overseas business. *Harvard Business Review*,
May/June, 87–96.

Hall, E.T. (1972) Silent assumptions in social communication. In *Communication in
Face to Face Interaction* (eds J. Laver and S. Hutcheson). Penguin, Harmondsworth,
UK, pp. 274–88.

Hall, E.T. and Whyte, W.F. (1961) Intercultural communication: a guide to men of
action. *Human Organization* **19**(1), 5–12.

Harris, P.R. and Moran, R.T. (1979, 1987) *Managing Cultural Differences*. Gulf,
Houston, Tx.

Hearn, L. (1894) The Japanese smile. In *Glimpses of Unfamiliar Japan*. New York.

Hewitt, J.P. and Stokes, R. (1975) Disclaimers. *American Sociological Review*, **40**, 1–11.

Hiroki Kato (1988) From FOBs to SOBs: Japanese vary too. *Newsaction*, **3**(1). Northwestern University, Evanston, Ill.

Hofstede, G. (1980) Motivation, leadership, and organization: do American theories
apply abroad? *Organizational Dynamics*, Summer, 42–63.

Hofstede, G. (1983a) The cultural relativity of organizational practices and theories.
Journal of International Business Studies, Fall, 75–89.

Hofstede, G. (1983b) National cultures in four dimensions. *International Studies of
Management and Organization*, **XIII**(1–2), 46–74.

Hofstede, G. (1984a) Cultural dimensions in management and planning. *Asia Pacific
Journal of Management*, January, 81–99.

Hofstede, G. (1984b) *Culture's Consequences*. Sage, Beverly Hills.

Hunt, J.G. and Blair, J.D. (1986) (eds) *1986 Yearly Review of Management* of the *Journal
of Management*, 1(12)2.

International Marketing Data and Statistics (annual editions). Euromonitor, London.

Jaeger, A.M. (1986) Organizational development and national culture: where's the
fit?' *Academy of Management Review*, **11**(1), 178–90.

Jefferson, G. (1972) Side sequences. In *Studies in Social Interaction* (ed. D. Sudnow).
Free Press/Macmillan, pp. 294–338.

Kennedy, G., Benson, J. and McMillan, J. (1982) *Managing Negotiations*. Prentice Hall,
Englewood Cliffs, NJ.

Klineberg, O. (1935) *Race Differences*. New York.

Kotler, P. (1988 edition) *Marketing Management*. Prentice Hall International Editions,
Englewood Cliffs, NJ.

Kuin, P. (1972) The magic of multinational management. *Harvard Business Review*,
November/December, 89–97.

La Barre, W. (1947) The cultural basis of emotions and gestures. *Journal of Personality*,
16, 49–68.

Langer, E.J., Blank, A. and Chanowitz, B. (1978) The mindlessness of ostensibly
thoughtful action. *Journal of Personality and Social Psychology*, **36**, 635–42.

Laurent, A. (1983) The cultural diversity of Western conceptions of management.
International Studies of Management and Organization, **XIII**(1–2), Spring/Summer,
75–96.

Laver, J. and Hutcheson, S. (1972) (eds) *Communication in Face to Face Interaction*.
Penguin, Harmondsworth, UK.

Lee, J.A. (1966) Cultural analysis in overseas operations. In *Harvard Business Review*, March/April, 106–14.

Masaaki Imai (1975) *Never Take Yes For An Answer*. Simul, Tokyo.

McCarthy, Lord W. (1985) The rule of power and principle in 'Getting to Yes'. *Negotiation Journal*, January, 59–66.

Mendenhall, M. and Oddou, G. (1985) The dimensions of expatriate acculturation: a review. *Academy of Management Review*, **10**(1), 39–47.

Micheli, L. McJ., Cespedes, F.V., Byker, D. and Raymond, T.J.C. (1984) *Managerial Communication*. Scott, Foresman, Glenview, Ill.

Mintzberg, H. (1975) The manager's job: folklore and fact. *Harvard Business Review*, July/August, 4–16.

Neghandi, A.R. and Prasad, S.B. (1971) *Comparative Management*. Appleton-Century-Crofts, New York.

Pascale, R.T. (1978) Communication and decision making across cultures: Japanese and American comparisons. *Administrative Science Quarterly*, **23**, 91–110.

Pascale, R.T. and Athos, A.G. (1981) *The Art of Japanese Management*. Warner, New York.

Pye, L. (1982) *Chinese Commercial Negotiating Style*. Rand, Santa Monica, Ca.

Rackham, N. (1982) The behavior of successful negotiators (Huthwaite Research Group Report, 1976). In *International Negotiations: A Training Program for Corporate Executives and Diplomats* (ed. E. Raider). Ellen Raider, Brooklyn, NY.

Raider, E. (1982) *International Negotiations: A Training Program for Corporate Executives and Diplomats*. Ellen Raider, Brooklyn, NY.

Roberts, G. (ed.) (1985) *Guide to World Commodity Markets*. Economist Books, Kogan Page, London/Nichols Publishing, New York.

Ross, H., Bouwmeesters, J. and other Institute staff (1972) *Management in the Developing Countries*. UN Research Institute for Social Development, Geneva.

Seboek, T.A. (1960) (ed.) *Style in Language*. MIT Press, Boston, Mass.

Sinclair, J.McH. (1980) Discourse in relation to language structure and semiotics. In *Studies in English Linguistics for Randolph Quirk* (eds S. Greenbaum, G. Leech, and J. Svartvik). Longman, London, pp. 110–24.

Sommer, R. (1959) Studies in personal space. *Sociometry*, **22**, 247–60.

Stewart, R. (1979) Diary keeping. In *Managerial Communication* (ed. T.D. Weinshall). Academic Press, London, pp. 33–54.

Sudnow, D. (1972) (ed.) *Studies in Social Interaction*. Free Press/Macmillan, New York.

Tannen, D. (1985) Cross-cultural communication. In *Handbook of Discourse Analysis* (ed. T. Van Dijk), Vol. 4. Academic Press, London, pp. 203–15.

Timm, P.R. (1980) *Managerial Communication: A Finger on the Pulse*. Prentice Hall, Englewood Cliffs, NJ.

Torbiörn, I. (1982) *Living Abroad*. Wiley, New York.

Tygier, C. (1983) *Basic Handbook of Foreign Exchange*. Euromoney Publications, London.

Van Dijk, T. (1985) (ed.) *Handbook of Discourse Analysis*. Vol. 4. Academic Press, London.

Weick, K.E. and Browning, L.D. (1986) Argument and narration in organizational communication. In *1986 Yearly Review of Management* of the *Journal of Management* (eds J.G. Hunt and J.D. Blair), **12**(2), 243–59.

Weinshall, T.D. (1979) (ed.) *Managerial Communication*. Academic Press, London.

Westwood, R.G. and Everett, J.E. (1987) Culture's consequences: a methodology for comparative management studies in Southeast Asia. *Asia Pacific Journal of Management* (Singapore), **4**(3), 187–202.

Woodworth, W. and Nelson, R. (1980) Information in Latin American organizations: some cautions. *Management International Review*, **20**(2), 61–9.

Yates, StJ.C. (1982) Defining and assessing levels of job-related performance. In *English for International Communication* (ed. C.J. Brumfit). Pergamon, Oxford, pp. 92–122.

Zeira, Y. and Banai, M. (1985) Selection of expatriate managers in MNCs: the host-environment point of view. *International Studies of Management and Organization*, **XV**(1), 33–51.

Newspapers and General-Interest/Non-Academic Journals

Asia Wall Street Journal
Asiaweek
Bangkok Post
Business Week
Chicago Tribune
Daily Telegraph (London)
Economist
International Herald Tribune

Nation (Bangkok)
New York Times
New York Times Magazine
Newsweek
The Times (London)
Wall Street Journal
World Executive Digest

Index

COUNTRIES, CULTURES, LANGUAGES, PEOPLES

NAME INDEX

GENERAL INDEX